ST. CHARLES COUNTY COMMUNITY COLLEGE
3 9835 00046620
S0-BBR-013

Tramping With Tramps

PATTERSON SMITH REPRINT SERIES IN
CRIMINOLOGY, LAW ENFORCEMENT, AND SOCIAL PROBLEMS

A listing of publications in the SERIES *will be found at rear of volume*

Josiah Flynt. St. Petersburg, Russia
August 8th, 1897.

PUBLICATION NO. 140: PATTERSON SMITH REPRINT SERIES IN CRIMINOLOGY, LAW ENFORCEMENT, AND SOCIAL PROBLEMS

Tramping With Tramps

STUDIES AND SKETCHES OF VAGABOND LIFE

Josiah Flynt

[Josiah Flint Willard]

With Prefatory Note by
Hon. Andrew D. White

REPRINTED WITH
INDEX ADDED

MONTCLAIR, NEW JERSEY
PATTERSON SMITH
1972

Originally published 1899 by The Century Co.
Reprinted 1972 by
Patterson Smith Publishing Corporation
Montclair, New Jersey 07042

Library of Congress Cataloging in Publication Data

Willard, Josiah Flynt, 1869—1907.
Tramping with tramps.

(Patterson Smith reprint series in criminology, law enforcement, and social problems. Publication no. 140)

Reprint of the 1899 ed. with index added.

1. Tramps. I. Title.

HV4488.W6 1972 301.44'94 72-129317

ISBN 0-87585-140-1

This book is printed on
three-hundred-year acid-free paper.

TO

MY MOTHER

EMBASSY OF THE UNITED STATES OF AMERICA,
BERLIN, April 19, 1899.

DEAR MR. FLYNT:

Your letter of March 27 and accompanying articles have greatly interested me.

As you know, I consider the problems furnished by crime in the United States as of the most pressing importance. We are allowing a great and powerful criminal class to be developed, and while crime is held carefully in check in most European countries, and in them is steadily decreasing, with us it is more and more flourishing, increases from year to year, and in various ways asserts its power in society.

So well is this coming to be known by the criminal classes of Europe that it is perfectly well understood here that they look upon the United States as a "happy hunting-ground," and more and more seek it, to the detriment of our country and of all that we hold most dear in it.

It seems to me that the publication of these articles in book form will be of great value, as well as of fascinating interest to very many people.

Yours faithfully,

ANDREW D. WHITE.

MR. JOSIAH FLYNT.

AUTHOR'S NOTE

DURING my university studies in Berlin I saw my fellow-students working in scientific laboratories to discover the minutest parasitic forms of life, and later publishing their discoveries in book form as valuable contributions to knowledge. In writing on what I have learned concerning human parasites by an experience that may be called scientific in so far as it deals with the subject on its own ground and in its peculiar conditions and environment, I seem to myself to be doing similar work with a like purpose. This is my apology, if apology be necessary, for a book which attempts to give a picture of the tramp world, with incidental reference to causes and occasional suggestion of remedies.

Thanks are due to Houghton, Mifflin & Co. for permission to reprint the papers, "The Children of the Road" and "Old Boston Mary," published in the "Atlantic Monthly"; to Harper & Brothers for similar permission in regard to the papers entitled "Jamie the Kid" and "Club Life among Outcasts," published in "Harper's Monthly Magazine," and "What the Tramp Eats and Wears" and "One Night on the 'Q,'" which appeared in "Harper's Weekly." To the Forum Publishing Company I am also indebted for permission to reprint from the "Forum" the paper called "The Criminal in the Open."

JOSIAH FLYNT.

CONTENTS

PART I — STUDIES

PART II — TRAVELS

PART III — SKETCHES

PART IV — THE TRAMP'S JARGON

INDEX

LIST OF ILLUSTRATIONS

PART I

STUDIES

PART I

STUDIES

Tramping with Tramps

PART I—STUDIES

I

THE CRIMINAL IN THE OPEN

UP to the present time the criminal has been studied exclusively behind prison-bars, after he has been caught, tried, and convicted. Out of durance he is his own master, and is naturally averse to being measured and experimented upon by scientists; hence the criminologist has been forced to await the almost certain vicissitudes which bring him once more inside a prison-cell. Here he has been subjected to the most minute examinations; and there exists a bulky literature on the results which these examinations have brought to light. We have volumes, for instance, about the criminal's body, skull, and face, his whimsical and obscene writings on prison-walls, the effect of various kinds of diet on his deportment, the workings of delicate instruments, placed on his wrists, to test the beat of his pulse under various conditions, the stories he has been persuaded to tell about his life, his maunderings when under the influence of hypnotism, and numerous things, anthropological and psychological, which have been noted down, compared, and classified.

Out of this mass of information, gathered in great part by prison doctors and other prison officials, the conclusion has been drawn that the criminal is a more or less degenerate human being. There are differences of opinion in regard to the degree of his degeneracy; but all investigators agree upon the main fact, while some go so far as to claim that he is abnormally deficient in mental and moral aptitudes, and, in a large number of instances, should be in an insane asylum rather than in a penitentiary. Human justice recoils from a severe treatment of the man who, though an outbreaking sinner, bears evidence of being sinned against as well as sinning; and yet, before we can safely fall in with this view, we must carefully consider the theory on which it is based, and its claims to a scientific foundation.

The first question with which to begin a scientific investigation of this sort is, it seems to me, this: "Where may we hope to find the criminal in his most natural state of body and mind—in confinement, a balked and disappointed man, or in the open, faring forth on his plundering errands, seeking whom and what he may devour?" That he should be studied when undergoing punishment goes without saying; but I claim that imprisonment should be considered rather as an incident in his existence than its normal sphere, and that, because it has not been so regarded, we have to-day a distorted view of the criminal and an illogical tendency in penology.

It is now more than a decade since I became acquainted with tramps. My purpose in seeking them out was to learn about their life; and I soon saw that, to know it well, I must become joined to it and be part and parcel of its various manifestations. At different times during this period,—some of them lengthening out into months,—I have lived intimately with the vagabonds of both England and the United States. In the tramp class, or so near it that the separation is almost imperceptible, are to be found any number of criminals associating freely, either for purposes of business or sociability, with their less ambitious brethren. In nearly every large city of the two countries mentioned I know something about them, and in not a few instances I have succeeded in becoming well acquainted with notorious members of their class. My desire is to tell of the impression they make on one who studies them in their own habitat, that I may be able to show how different is the outdoor criminal from his convicted brother shut in behind prison-bars.

I

I MUST first note the species of criminal that I have met in the open. Lombroso and other investigators classify the cases they have studied as political, instinctive, occasional, habitual, and professional; but, so far as my finding is concerned, only one class is of any great importance—the professional. That there are also instinctive criminals, as well as occasional, I am well aware; but they form a very small part of that outcast world that I know best, and cannot be taken as definitely representative of it. It is the man who wilfully and knowingly makes a business of crime or is experimenting with it from commercial motives that I have found in largest numbers "on the road"; and it is he, I believe, who appears oftenest in our criminal courts. To be sure, he tries to make out that he is not a wilful offender, and often succeeds in convincing a jury that he is not; but this is due to his cleverness and trained abilities.

Contrary to a more or less popular opinion, I must also say that the criminals I am acquainted with are not such because they are unable to keep body and soul together in any other way. The people who go into crime for this reason are far less numerous than is generally supposed. It is true that they come, as a rule, from the poverty-stricken districts of our large cities, and that the standard of life in these districts, particularly for families, is pitifully low; but a single person can live in them far more easily than the philanthropists think. The necessaries of life, for instance, can be had by simply begging; and this is the way they are found by the majority of people who are not willing to work for them. The criminal, however, wants the luxuries of life as well; he seeks gold and the most expensive pleasures that gold can buy; and to get them he preys upon those who have it. He thinks that if all goes well he may become an aristocrat; and having so little to lose and so much to gain, he deliberately takes his chances.

I must say furthermore that those criminals who are known to me are not, as is also popularly supposed, the scum of their environment. On the contrary, they are above their environment, and are often gifted with talents which would enable them to do well in any class, could they only be brought to realize its responsibilities and to take advantage of its opportunities. The notion that the criminal is the lowest type of his class in society arises from a false conception of that class and of the people who compose it. According to my experience, they are mainly paupers; and they have been such so long, and are so obtuse and unaccustomed to anything better, even in the United States, that they seldom make any serious effort to get out of their low condition. Indeed, I think it can be said that the majority of them are practically as happy and contented in their squalor and poverty as is the aristocrat in his palace. In Whitechapel as well as in the worst parts of New York, for example, I have met entire families who could not be persuaded to exchange places with the rich, provided the exchange carried with it the duties and manners which wealth presupposes; they even pity the rich, and express wonder at their contentment "in such a strait-jacket life."

In this same class, however, there are some who are born with ambitions, and who have energy enough to try to fulfil them. These break away from class conditions; but, unfortunately, the ladder of respectable business has no foothold in their environment. No one of their acquaintance has gone springing up its rounds in tempting promotions; and although the city missionary tells them that there are those who thus succeed, they will not believe him—or, rather, they prefer to believe the, to them, far more probable stories of success which they read in the "Police Gazette" and the "Criminal Calendar." Most of them know perfectly well that the success thus portrayed is the result of law-breaking, and that they will be punished if caught trying to achieve it; but it is a choice between the miserable slum, which they hate, and possible wealth, which they covet, and they determine to run the risk.

Not all of these ambitious ones are endowed with an equal amount of energy. Some are capable only of tramp life, which, despite its many trials and vicissitudes, is more attractive than the life they seek to escape. Those with greater energy go into crime proper; and they may be called, mentally as well as physically, the aristocracy of their class. This is my analysis of the majority of the criminal men and women I have encountered in the open, and I believe it will hold good throughout their entire class.

Concerning their nationalities, I must say that most of them are indigenous to the countries in which they live. In this country it is often said that foreigners are the main offenders, and a great deal has been written about the dumping of European criminals on American shores; but the main offenders, in the open at least, are natives, and are generally of Irish-American parentage. In England, unmixed blood is a little more noticeable. Ireland is said to be the least criminal land in all Europe, and this may be the case so far as local crime is concerned; but more criminals trace their ancestry back to that country than to any other where English is spoken. Indeed, in America it is considered something quite out of the ordinary if the criminal cannot attach himself somehow or other to the "Emerald Isle"; and nothing has hindered me more in my intercourse with him than the fact that my own connection with it is very slight.

In regard to the ages of the criminals I have met, it is difficult to write definitely; but the average, I think, is between twenty-five and thirty years. The sex is predominantly masculine. For every female criminal I have found twenty males; and the proportion in the United States is even higher. It cannot, however, be inferred that the women of the same original environment are less ambitious than the men; but they take to the street, instead of to crime, to satisfy their love of high living, and they hope to find there the same prizes that their brothers are seeking by plunder. It is a mistake to say that all these women are driven to the street by the pangs of hunger. A great many are no doubt thus impelled; but I believe there are multitudes who are there merely to satisfy their ambitious and luxurious tastes.

As the degeneration of the criminal is said by the criminologists to be physical, mental, and moral, I shall take up the subject, as it pertains to the criminals I have studied, from these different points of view.

II

It has of course been impossible for me, a fellow-traveler with tramps and but a casual observer of criminals, to conduct my investigations as scientific observers of prison specimens have done. I have not been permitted, for instance, to measure their skulls; neither have I been able to weigh them, to inspect their teeth and palates, nor even to test their pulse under excitement. It has been possible for me, however, to study their countenances, to get acquainted with their type, as it is called, and to compare it, as I have seen it in the open day, with its pictorial representation in books and pamphlets. As a rule, these pictures are very different from the type that I know. Only in a few cases have they ever approximated to the truth; and why artists have given us such as their models is more than I can understand. In New York I once showed a criminal one of these caricatures and asked what he thought of it. He replied, "Why, I would n't be found dead lookin' like that!" —a sentiment which I consider both justified and representative. The trouble is that writers about crime have usually picked out as illustrations for their books the very worst specimens possible; and the public has been led to consider these as true representatives of the entire class. A retreating forehead, for example, and the most depraved expressions of the eyes and mouth are to-day considered typical stigmata of the criminal's face. The majority of those that I am acquainted with, particularly those under thirty years of age, if well dressed, could pass muster in almost any class of society; and I doubt very much whether an uninitiated observer would be able to pick them out for what they are. After thirty years of age, and sometimes even younger, they do acquire a peculiar look; but, instead of calling it a criminal look, in the sense that the instinctive offender is criminal, I should describe it as that of a long resident in a penitentiary. Prison life, if taken in large doses and often enough, will give the most moral men in the world prison features; and it is no wonder that men who make a business of crime and are so much in prison possess them. Even men who are busied in the detection of crime have more or less similar facial characteristics. I have never met a detective who had been long in the service that did not have some features or habits common to the criminals he was engaged in hunting down; and I know several detectives who have been taken for criminals by criminals, simply because of their looks.

In regard to other abnormalities, such as absence of hair on the face, remarkable eyesight, length of certain fingers, insensibility to pain, unusual development of the lower jaw, high cheek-bones, fixed eyes, projecting ears, and stooping shoulders, which are said to differentiate the criminal from the ordinary human being, I can only report that I have not found them to be any more noticeable in the criminal class than among normal people. In the majority of cases the criminal can grow a beard, and is glad that he can do so. Without this ability to change his looks he would be greatly handicapped in his business; and, as I know him, he usually has a beard once in two years. It has been said that his habit of tattooing is evidence of his obtuseness to pain; but it is not easy to see why. At the worst, it is not a trying ordeal; and the little suffering that it does occasion is as much felt by the criminal as by any one else. Moreover, those that I know are not so prone to be tattooed as is reported. Indeed, it is considered a mistake to have marks on the body, for they naturally aid detection.

On all these questions of the senses, criminologists have relied altogether on what the criminal himself has told them. They give him something to taste or smell, or prick him with a needle, and his reply is noted down as scientific evidence. How do they know that he has not some object in view in telling them what he does? He may want to appear degenerated or queer, or is perhaps simply mischievous and says the first thing that comes into his head. Until instruments have been invented which can discover the truth quite independently of the criminal's personal testimony, nothing really positive can be known concerning whatever freaks of the senses may have been wrought in the criminal's organization.

The general health of the criminal is good. Up to twenty-five years of age he is as hardy and vigorous as the average person. Although he comes from the slums, he gets somehow a very fair constitution; and if he would only take care of it, he might live to a good old age. When he nears his thirtieth year, however, his strength and vigor begin to fail him. By that time he has served a number of terms in prison, and it is this existence that drags him down. In the open he seems able to endure a great deal and still keep his health; but behind the bars, care for him as the penologists will, he weakens and withers away. This side of his life has scarcely received the attention it deserves from investigators who find the criminal diseased. That he becomes diseased must be readily admitted; but, as a rule, it is only after society has shut him up in its penal institutions. Stand, for instance, at the doors of one of these institutions when a ten-year convict is released, and see how he looks. I once did this; and a worse wreck of a formerly strong man I have never encountered—a being ruined in both body and mind, a victim of passions which in the open he would have abhorred.

There is no better proof that it is the prison, and not his life and business, that makes the criminal diseased than that furnished by tramps. These men live almost entirely in the open, and, as a general rule, have a harder life than a criminal; yet they are about the healthiest people in the world. In the United States it is one of their superstitions that they simply cannot die, like other men, of disease, but have to be killed. This is what happens to a great many of them. They fall from freight-trains at night, or are found starved to death, locked fast in a box-car on some distant side-track.

III

FINDING the criminal diseased and abnormal physically, it is only natural that investigators should have found him equally abnormal in mind; but this, too, I have not discovered.

Lack of will-power, for example, is one of the first delinquencies noted in criminology; and yet out of prison and in the open, the will is one of the criminal's strongest points. Most of them have enough of it, at least while they are young, to satisfy any one; and could they but be brought to use it in honest industry, they might become the most successful people in the world. The trouble is that they will do the things which society considers and punishes as crime. They think that they can " get on " faster in their profession than in any other; and they bend every energy to achieve their ambition. Because this ambition is so flatly contradictory to what is upright and honest, it is common, not only among criminologists, but with the general public as well, to speak of the criminal as one weak of will. I think this is one of the greatest mistakes in psychology. Napoleon I, for instance, was instrumental, directly or indirectly, in the deaths of nearly two million people, and was one of the most unscrupulously ambitious human beings that have ever lived; yet his passes for one of the strongest wills the world has known. The unimperial criminal, on the other hand, if he be unsuccessful, is catalogued by prison psychologists as a pathological specimen simply because he wills to do wrong.

This strange classification is doubtless to be accounted for on the ground that the criminal in prison has been taken to be the natural criminal. Behind the bars he does indeed become somewhat volatile, and finds it hard to concentrate his mind; but this is due to imprisonment and its harassing trials rather than to innate deficiency. The strongest of wills would deteriorate under such conditions, and perhaps even more rapidly than that of the criminal who, from the very nature of his trade, expects and plans for a certain amount of exile.

The charge of impatience, which is so often brought against him, may be explained in the same way; and the tramps are again good illustrations. As a class they are the most patient people imaginable, and are able to endure pleasantly any amount of ruffling circumstances. Where, for example, is there a calmer and more stoical human being than the American "hobo," waiting through rain or shine at the railway watering-tank for the freight-train that shall carry him farther on the road? He will stay there for days, if necessary, rather than pay the regular fare on the passenger-trains; and nothing arouses his scorn more than the dilettante, or "gay-cat," as he calls him, who gives up waiting and buys a regulation ticket. The criminal, after a certain age, often lacks this ability to hang on; but his nerves and general equipoise have been disturbed by imprisonment. Even the tramp is a less patient person in county jails than he is in the open; but his stay there is so short, and the confinement, compared with that in convict prisons, is so much easier to bear, that he soon recuperates. I can write from personal experience on this point; for, as an American tramp, I have had to take my share of jail life, and I have never been so nervous and impatient as when undergoing it. In the open, on the other hand, I have never been so healthy and under control. If a few days' confinement can have such an effect upon an absolutely voluntary prisoner, what must be the effect of years of this sort of life upon the man who hates prison as he does poison, and is not sure that when he is released an officer may not be waiting to read him a warrant for another arrest? Criminologists who believe in the innate nervous weakness of the criminal would do well to test their own nerves during even voluntary residence in prison-cells in order to estimate their power to disturb a natural equilibrium.

It is also said that the criminal is more or less an epileptic. Lombroso makes a great deal of this supposition; and there are other students of the subject who go quite as far as he does. I have never met a pure epileptic criminal on the road, and I cannot recall having heard the subject discussed by tramps or criminals in any way that would lead me to believe the disorder at all common among them. Among tramps a favorite trick is to feign epilepsy; and I have seen it done with a fidelity to the "real thing" that was remarkable. Whether or not criminals also feign in prison, I am not prepared to say; but if they are as clever as tramps at it, I can well believe that they might deceive even the very elect among specialists.

I have also failed to find insanity common among criminals. Among those under twenty-five years of age, I have never known one clear case; and the few cases that I have known after that period have been men who have had long sentences in prison, and whose confinement, I have no doubt, has had much to do with their mental derangement.

There is no better evidence of the criminal's ability to reason than the fact that, the minute he is convinced that crime does not pay, he gives it up. Even at the start he is not sure that it will pay; but, as I have said, having so little to lose and so much to gain, he takes his chances. After a time, long or short according to his success, he generally comes to the conclu-

DISCOURAGED CRIMINALS.

sion that it does not pay, or at least that he lacks the wit to make it successful; and he drops it, becoming what I call a discouraged criminal. There is a difference of opinion among criminals as to how much imprisonment is necessary to convince a man that he is not getting his fair share of the prizes of his profession; but, so far as I have been able to make inquiries, I should say that between ten and fifteen years are enough to frighten the average man out of the business. Some stick to it with even twenty years spent behind the bars; but they are generally those who have been uncommonly successful in making large catches, and have risked "just one more job" in order to win the "great stake" that is to make them rich.

The main reason why the criminal is afraid to go beyond the fifteen-year limit is that, after that time, unless he be an uncommonly clever man, he is likely to get what is called "the shivers"—one of the weirdest disorders to which the human body ever yields. Men describe it differently; but, by all accounts, the victim is possessed by such a terror of capture that each member of his body is in a constant tremor. Instances have been known where, owing to a sudden attack of this shivering palsy, he has had to quit a "job" that was almost finished. If these fits once become customary the man is unqualified for any kind of work ever after, and usually ends his life in the lowest class of the outcasts' world—the "tomato-can tramp class."

It is interesting to note where criminals draw the dividing-line between success and failure. Generally speaking, they consider a man fairly successful if between imprisonments he gets a "vacation," as they call it, of eight or ten months, and is lucky enough during this period to make sufficient "hauls" to compensate him for the almost inevitable punishment that follows. The understanding, of course, in all this is that he gets the benefit, either in carousals or more practical investments, of the money he has been lucky enough to win. As a rule, however, the plunder usually goes in debauches, and very quickly, too; but the criminal always hopes to recoup himself by a great stake which is to be put away in safety. If he be a man of average criminal wit and experience, particularly the latter, he can frequently secure the vacation of eight months for a number of years. But the more confinement he suffers the more reckless he becomes, and the less able to think carefully; and there are a great many men who soon find that even six months is the most that they can count on. This time, however, is not enough, as a rule, for the hauls necessary to offset the expected term in prison; and the criminal is usually clever enough to get out of the business. He then bids good-by to his more tenacious brethren and joins the tramp class, where he is made welcome by others who have joined it before him. He becomes a tramp because it is the career that comes nearest to the one he hoped to do well in. Besides affording considerable amusement, it also permits the discouraged man to keep track of the comrades whom he used to know in the higher walks of outlawry; and this is an attraction not to be overlooked.

It is usual to classify the criminal according to the crimes he commits. One classification, for example, makes murderers the least intelligent; vagabonds, sexual offenders, and highwaymen a little more so; while the fraudulent class, pickpockets and burglars, are accounted the most gifted of all. I think this a fair division and one that will generally hold good; but I have found that criminals who commit crimes against property, or the fraudulent class, are far and away in the majority. Their native intelligence will compare favorably with that of the average run of people; and I have been unable to discover any mental defects until they have been a long time in prison. Nearly all of them can read and write very well indeed; and there are many who have read far more than the ordinary business man. I have met men, very low-born men too, who, while in prison, have read through more volumes of philosophy and history than even the usual college student can boast in his reading; and they have been able to converse very wisely on these subjects. These same men have acquired the rudiments of their studies in reformatory and industrial institutions, and have succeeded in continuing them in the libraries of penitentiaries. I know one criminal who in his prison-cell informed himself about a branch of chemistry simply for purposes of business: he was thought at the time to be more or less crazy.

Prison officials are often deceived by criminals in regard to their acquirements in learning. In many prisons, diligence and progress in study earn as much promotion as general good conduct does; and as the average prisoner has every reason to desire the benefits which promotions bring with them, he tries after a fashion to progress. But what is this fashion? Very frequently this: On his arrival at the prison, instead of telling the truth to the officials who quiz him about his abilities, he says that he does not even know the alphabet, and is consequently given very light mental work. He is thus able to advance rapidly, and his teachers pride themselves on his quickness to learn and their ability to teach. Ere long he gets into a better class, and so on until he has enjoyed all the benefits which precocity can earn. There are other men who profess ignorance in order to appear simple and unknowing, and thus create the impression that they are not so guilty as they are taken to be. Many times and in many cases the criminal is a little cleverer than the people who are examining him; and one cannot set a high value on statistics concerning his intelligence. If the student of criminology could and would eavesdrop for a while at some "hang-out" in the open, and hear the criminal's own account of the way he is investigated, he might learn "foxier" methods of dealing with his subject.

One other fact belongs properly to this division: The professional criminal is not, in his own class, the revolutionary creature that he seems when preying upon the classes above him. His attitude toward society in general is without doubt disrespectful and anarchistic, and it is usually immaterial to him what happens to society as such, so long as he can make a "stake"; but in his own environment he is one of the most conservative of human beings. There is no class, for instance, where old age and mature opinion receive more respect and carry more weight; and, as a general thing, the young men in it—the radical element—are expected to take a back seat. At a hang-out gathering they must always show deference to the older men, and nothing is so severely judged as "freshness" on their part.

I think this is a characteristic of the criminal that might be turned to good account if he should ever be won over to respectable living: in affairs of the State, provided he had a fair share of this world's goods, he would be found invariably on the conservative rather than on the radical side.

IV

I COME now to the question of the criminal's moral responsibility. Can he be held definitely answerable for his evil-doing, or is he morally insane and unable to distinguish between right and wrong? The instinctive criminal must be irresponsible, and his treatment should be such as we give to insane people. As I know him, he cannot help his criminal actions; it is in him to do them; and the only merciful thing is to put him where he at least cannot continue his depredations on society, and where, if cure be possible, he may be in the hands of specialists best fitted to help him. But, as I said at the outset, he is not the sort of criminal that I have found in largest numbers in the open. It is the commercial criminal that predominates there; and, as a rule, he can be held responsible for his evil-doing.

It is often said that his lack of remorse for his crimes proves him to be morally incompetent; but this opinion is founded on insufficient knowledge of his life. He has two systems of morality: one for his business, and the other for the hang-out. The first is this: "Society admits that the quarrel with me is over after I have served out my sentence; and I, naturally enough, take the same view of the matter. It is simply one of take and pay. I take something from society and give in exchange so many years of my life. If I come out ahead, so much the better for me; if society comes out ahead, so much the worse for me, and there is no use in whimpering over the transaction." So long as he remains in the business he thinks it only fair to "stick up for it"; and he dislikes and will not associate with men who denounce it in public.

This is his attitude toward the world at large. He puts on a bold front, and, as he himself says, "nerves" the thing through. In the bosom of his hang-out, however,—and this is where we ought to study his ethics,—he is a very different man. His code of morals there will compare favorably with that of any class of society; and there is no class in which fair dealing is more seriously preached, and unfair dealing more severely condemned. The average criminal will stand by a fellow-craftsman through thick and thin; and the only human being he will not tolerate is the one who turns traitor. The remorse of this traitor when brought to bay by his former brethren I have never seen exceeded anywhere. It was my fate some years ago, while living with tramps, to be lodged in a jail where one of the prisoners was a "State's evidence" witness. He had been released from prison by promising to tell tales on an old man,—

who was supposed to be the main culprit in the crime in question,—and was lodging in the jail until the trial was over. Unfortunately for him, some of the prisoners had known him prior to this episode in his career; and they sent him to Coventry so completely that his life in the jail became unbearable, and he almost died ere he could give his testimony. At night we could hear him groaning in his sleep as if he were undergoing the most fearful torture, and in the daytime he slunk around the corridors like a whipped dog. He lived to give his evidence in the trial, and was released from durance; but a few days later he was found dead by his own hand. When the inmates of the jail heard of his fate they relented a little in their hatred of him; but the final opinion was that suicide was the best solution of the problem.

It is thought by criminologists that the good fellowship of the criminal is due to self-preservation and the fear that each man will hang separately if all do not hang together. They maintain that his good feeling is not genuine and spontaneous emotion, and that it is immaterial what happens to a "pal" so long as he himself succeeds. This is not my experience in his company. He has never had the slightest intimation that I would return favors that he did me; and in the majority of instances he has had every reason to know that it was not in my power to show him the friendliness he wanted. Yet he has treated me with an altruism that even a Tolstoi might admire. At the hang-out I have been hospitably entertained on all occasions; and I have never met a criminal there who would not have given me money or seen me through a squabble, had I needed his assistance and he was able to give it. This same comradeship is noticeable in all his relations with men who are in the least connected with his life and business; and it is a notorious fact that he will "divvy" his last meal with a pal. To have to refuse the request of one of his fellows, or to do him an unkindness, is as much regretted by the criminal as by any one else; and I have never known him to tell me a lie or to cheat me or to make fun of me behind my back.

There are also some things in his relations with the outside world which, in his heart of hearts, he regrets and repents of as much as he does the misdeeds in his own world. He always feels bad, for instance, when he takes money from the poor. It sometimes happens in his raids that he makes mistakes and gets into the wrong house, or has been deceived about the wealth of his victims; and if he discovers that he has robbed a poor man, or one who cannot conveniently bear the loss, he is ashamed and never enjoys the plunder thus won. He is too near the poor, in both birth and sentiment, not to feel remorse for such an action; and I have known him to send back money after he has discovered that the person from whom he took it needed it more than he.

The taking of life is another deed that he regrets far more than he has been given credit for. One thinks of the criminal as the man who has no respect for life, as one who takes it without any twitchings of conscience; but this is not the general rule. The business criminal never takes a life, if he can help it; and when he does, he expects, in court, to receive the death-penalty. Indeed, he believes, as a rule, that murder deserves capital punishment; and I have often heard him express wonder at the lightness of the penalties which murderers receive.

At the hang-out a favorite topic of discussion is, which penalty is preferable—life-imprisonment or death. The consensus of opinion has generally run in favor of life-imprisonment, even with no hope of pardon; but I have never heard a whimper against the justice of the death-sentence.

It is also true that the majority of criminals regret finding a man in their class who has once belonged to a better one. They are invariably sorry that he has lost caste, no matter what the circumstances have been that have brought him low, and are more likely to help him back to decent society, providing he shows repentance and willingness to do better, than they are to help themselves.

Philanthropists might learn a great deal of charity from the criminal. His idea is that it is better to keep a member of a respectable class of society from falling than it is to raise some one in a lower class to a higher one—a philosophy which I think very sound.

One more regret which nearly all criminals of the class I am considering have experienced at one time or another in their lives, is that circumstances have led them into a criminal career. Their remorse may be only for a moment, and an exaggerated indifference often follows it; but while it lasts it is genuine and sincere. I have never known a criminal well who has not confessed to me something of this sort; and he has often capped it with a further confidence—his sorrow that it was now too late to try anything else.

V

SUCH, in hurried and transitory outline, is the impression the criminal has made upon me in the open day. The mistakes which criminologists have made in regard to his case seem to me to be these: They have failed to take note of the fearful effects of confinement upon his health; they have allowed themselves to be deceived by him in regard to his intelligence; and they have judged of his moral status simply from his "faked" attitude toward the world at large, failing to take into account his ethics among his fellows. I believe, too, that they are on the wrong track in their studies of the criminal's skull. They have examined it in all manner of ways with an ever-varying result; for each investigator comes to a different conclusion. Far better for criminology to study the criminal's *milieu;* and until this is done thoroughly and conscientiously, he cannot be reasonably apprehended and scientifically treated.

So far as our present knowledge of his case can help us, he himself teaches what ought to be done with him. I have written of the discouraged criminal—the man who has given up crime because he has discovered that it was not worth the pains it cost him. Punishment, or expiatory discipline, if you please, has brought him to this conclusion. Here is good penology for us. If a man does wrong, wilfully and knowingly, he must be disciplined till he learns that society will not tolerate such conduct. The discouraged criminal is one who has been thus instructed. Now that he is a tramp, the same principle must be applied to him again: make him a discouraged vagabond. Such is the treatment which society must bring to bear on the deliberate law-breaker.

If I have studied the criminal to any purpose, it is with the resulting conviction that he is physically, mentally, and morally responsible; and that, though unhappy in his birth and environment, the very energy which has enabled him to get away from his poverty is the "promise and potency" of a better life. And human hope looks forward to a day when, in the regeneration of his class, he shall be born into better things than crime.

II

THE CHILDREN OF THE ROAD

I

THE real "road" is variously named and variously described. By the "ambulanter" it is called Gipsyland, by the tramp Hoboland; the fållen woman thinks it is the street, the thief, that it means stealing and the penitentiary; even the little boy who reads dime novels and fights hitching-posts for desperados believes momentarily that he too is on the real road. All these are indeed branches of the main line. The road proper, or "the turf," as the people who toil along its stretches sometimes prefer to call it, is low life in general. It winds its way through dark alleys and courts to dives and slums, and wherever criminals, hoboes, outcast women, stray and truant children congregate; but it never leads to the smiling windows and doorways of a happy home, except for plunder and crime. There is not a town in the land that it does not touch, and there are but few hamlets that have not sent out at least one adventurer to explore its twists and turnings.

The travelers, as I have said, are of all kinds, conditions, and ages: some old and crippled, some still in their prime, and others just beginning life. To watch in thought the long and motley procession marching along is to see a panorama of all the sins, sorrows, and accidents known to human experience. Year after year they trudge on and on, and always on, seeking a goal which they never seem to find. Occasionally they halt for a while at some half-way house, where they have heard that there is a resting-place of their desire; but it invariably proves disappointing, and the tramp, tramp, tramp begins afresh. Young and old, man and woman, boy and girl, all go on together; and as one dies or wearies of the march, another steps into his heel-tracks, and the ranks close up as solidly as ever.

The children of the road have always been to me its most pitiful investiture, and I have more than once had dreams and plans that looked to the rescue of these prematurely outcast beings. It needs skilled philanthropists and penologists, however, for such a work, and I must content myself with contributing experiences and facts which may perhaps aid in the formation of theory, and thus throw light upon the practical social tasks that are before us.

There are four distinct ways by which boys and girls get upon the road: some are born there, some are driven there, others are enticed there, and still others go there voluntarily.

Of those who are born on the road, perhaps the least known are the children of the ambulanters. The name is a tramp invention, and not popular among the ambulanters themselves. They prefer to be called gipsies, and try at times, especially when compelled by law to give some account of themselves, to trace their origin to Egypt; but the most of them, I fear, are degenerated Americans. How they have become so is a question which permits of much conjecture, and in giving my own explanation I do not want it to be taken as applicable to the entire class. I know only about fifty families, and not more than half of these at all familiarly; but those whom I do know seem to me to be the victims of a pure and simple laziness handed down from generation to generation until it has become a chronic family disease. From what they have told me confidentially about their natural history, I picture their forefathers as harmless village "do-nothings," who lounged in corner groceries, hung about taverns, and followed the fire-engine and the circus. The second generation was probably too numerous for the home parish, and, inheriting the talent for loafing, started out to find roomier lounges. It must have wandered far and long, for upon the third generation, the one that I know, the love of roaming descended to such a degree that all North America is none too large for it. Go where one will, in the most dismal woods, the darkest lanes, or on the widest prairies, there the ambulanter may be found tenting with his large and unkempt family. He comes and goes as his restless spirit dictates, and the horse and wagon carry him from State to State.

It is in Illinois that I know his family best. Cavalier John, as he proudly called himself, I remember particularly. He gave me shelter one night in his wagon, as I was toiling along the highway south of

Ottawa, and we became such good friends that I traveled with his caravan for three days. And what a caravan it was! A negro wife, five little mulattoes, a deformed white girl, three starved dogs, a sore-eyed cat, a blasphemous parrot, a squeaking squirrel, a bony horse, and a canvas-topped wagon, and all were headed "Texas way." John came from Maine originally, but he had picked up his wife in the West, and it was through their united efforts in trickery and clever trading that they had acquired their outfit. So far as I could learn, neither of them had ever done an honest stroke of business. The children ranged from three years to fourteen, and the deformed girl was nearly twenty. John found her among some other ambulanters in Ohio, and, thinking that he might make money out of her physical monstrosities as "side-shows," cruelly traded off an old fox for her. She ought to have been in an insane asylum, and I hope John has put her there long ago. The other "kidlets," as they were nicknamed, were as deformed morally as was the adopted girl physically. They had to beg in every town and village they came to, and at night their father took the two oldest with him in his raids on the hen-roosts. It was at town and county fairs, however, that they were the most profitable. Three knew how to pick pockets, and the two youngest gave acrobatic exhibitions. None of them had ever been in school, none could read or write, and the only language they spoke was the one of their class. I have never been able to learn it well, but it is a mixture of Rom and tramp dialects with a dash of English slang.

On the journey we met another caravan, bound West by way of Chicago. There were two families, and the children numbered sixteen; the oldest ranging from fifteen to twenty, and the youngest had just appeared. We camped together in a wood for a night and a day, and seldom have I sojourned in such company. John had given me a place with him in the wagon, but now the woman with the babe was given the wagon, and John and I slept, or tried to, "in the open." In the other wagon, both sexes, young and old, were crowded into a space not much larger than the ordinary omnibus, and the vermin would have made sleep impossible to any other order of beings. The next day, being Sunday, was given over to play and revel, and the poor horses had a respite from their sorrows. The children invented a queer sort of game, something like "shinny," and used a dried-up cat's head as block. They kicked, pounded, scratched, and cursed one another; but when the play was over all was well again, and the block was tucked away in the wagon for further use. Late at night the journeys were taken up once more, one caravan moving on toward Dakota, and the other toward the Gulf.

"Salawakkee!"[1] cried John, as he drove away; and the strangers cried back, "Chalamu!"[2]

I wonder what has become of that little baby for whom I sat the night out? It is over ten years ago now, and he has probably long since been compelled to play his part in crime, and scratch and fight as his older brothers and sisters did on that autumn Sunday morning. Certainly there is nowhere in the world a

[1] So long. [2] Live well.

more ferocious set of children than these of the ambulanters. From morning till night it is one continual snap and bite, and the depraved fathers and mothers look on and grin. They have not the faintest ideal of home, and their only outlook in life is some day to have a "rig" of their own and prowl throughout the land, seeking whom they may devour. To tame them is a task requiring almost divine patience. I should not know how to get at them. They laugh at tenderness, never say "Thank you," and obey their parents only when driven with boot and whip. I wish that I could suggest some gentle method by which they could be rescued from the road and made good men and women. It always seems harsh to apply strict law to delinquents so young and practically innocent, but it is the only remedy I can offer. They must be put under stiff rule and order, and trained strictly and long. Although lacking gipsy blood, they have acquired gipsy character, and it will take generations to get it out of them. Just how many children are born on the road is a question which even the ambulanter would find difficult to answer. They are scattered so widely and in such out-of-the-way places that a census is almost impossible. In the families that I have met there have never been less than four children. Gipsy Sam once told me that he believed there were at least two hundred ambulanter families in the United States, but this will strike every one as a low estimate; however, if this is true, and each family has as many boys and girls as those that I have met, then there must be at least a thousand of their kind.

Another kind of ragamuffin, also born on the road,

and in many ways akin to the ambulanter, although wanting such classification, is the one found so often in those families which every community supports, but relegates to its uttermost boundary-lines. They are known as "the McCarthys," "the Night-Hawks," or "the Holy Frights," as the case may be. I have found no town in the United States of twenty thousand inhabitants without some such little Whitechapel in its vicinity, and, like the famous original, it is often considered dangerous to enter unarmed. Speaking generally, there is a great deal of fiction afloat concerning these tabooed families, a number of them being simply poor or lazy people whom the boys of the vicinity have exaggerated into gangs of desperados. There are, however, some that are really very bad, and I have found them even in new little villages. They are not exactly out-and-out criminals whom the police can get hold of, but moral lepers who by public consent have been sentenced to live without the pale of civilization.

Some years ago I had occasion to visit one of these miniature Whitechapels. It was situated in a piece of woods not far from St. Paul, Minnesota, and belonged by right of appropriation to three families who were called "the Stansons." A tramp friend of mine had been taken sick in their camp, and I was in duty bound to go out to see him. I managed to find the settlement all right, but was stopped about a hundred yards from the log shanties by a bushy-bearded man, barefooted and clad only in trousers, who asked my errand. My story evidently satisfied him, for he led the way to the largest of the shanties, where I found

THE MODE OF TRAVEL THAT ATTRACTS BOYS.

my friend. He was lying in the middle of the floor on some straw, the only furniture in the room being a shaky table and a three-legged chair. All about him, some even lying in the straw beside him, were half-clothed children of both sexes, playing "craps" and eating hunks of bread well daubed with molasses. I counted nine in that shanty alone, and about as many again in the other two. They belonged severally to six women who were apportioned after Mormon custom to three men. The tramp told me in his dialect that they really were Mormons and came from Utah. He was passing by their "hang-out," as he called it, when taken ill, and they hospitably lodged him. He said they had not been there long, having come up the river from Des Moines, Iowa, where they had also had a camp; but long enough, I discovered on my return to St. Paul, to acquire a reputation among the city lads for all kinds of "toughness." I suppose they were "tough" when considered from certain view-points, but, as the tramp said, it was the silliest kind he had known. They were not thieves, and only luke-warm beggars, but they did seem to love their outlandish existence. The children interested me especially, for they all spoke a queer jargon which they themselves had invented. It was something like the well-known "pig Latin" that all sorts of children like to play with, but much more complicated and difficult to understand. And, except the very youngest, who naturally cried a little, they were the jolliest children I have ever seen in such terrible circumstances. The mothers were the main breadwinners, and while I was there one of them started off to town on a begging trip, with a batch of children as "guy." The men sat around, smoked, and talked about the woods. The tramp told me later, however, that they occasionally raided a hen-roost. Since my visit to the Stansons I have seen three of the children in different places: one, a cripple, was begging at the World's Fair; another was knocking about the Bowery; and the third, a girl, was traveling with an ambulanter in the Mohawk valley.

Not all of these families are like the Stansons. A number are simply rough-and-tumble people who haunt the outskirts of provincial towns, and live partly by pilfering and partly from the municipal fund for the poor. Somehow or other the children always dodge the school commissioners, and grow up, I am sorry to say, very much like their usually unmarried parents. On the other hand, there are several well-known organized bands, and they thrive mainly, I think, in the South and West. Near New Orleans there used to be, and for aught I know they are still there, "the Jim Jams" and "the Rincheros"; near Cairo, Illinois, "the River Rats"; near Chicago, "the Dippers"; and not far from New York, in the Ramapo Mountains, I knew of "the Sliders," but they have since moved on to new fields. Each of these families, or collection of families, had its full quota of children. Very often the public becomes so enraged at their petty thefts that an investigation is ordered, and then there is a sudden packing of traps and quick departure to a different neighborhood, where a new name is invented. But the family itself never dies out entirely.

There are a few children who are born in Hoboland.

Now and then, as one travels along the railway lines, he will come to a hastily improvised camp, where a pale, haggard woman is lying, and beside her a puny infant, scarcely clothed, blinking with eyes of wonder upon the new world about him. I know of no sadder sight than this in all trampdom. Not even the accident of motherhood can make the woman anything but unhuman, and the child, if he lives, grows up in a world which I believe is unequaled for certain forms of wickedness. Fortunately, his little body usually tires of the life ere he comes to realize what it is, and his soul wanders back to regions of innocence, unsoiled and unscarred.

I wonder whether there are still men in Hoboland who remember that interesting little fellow called "the Cheyenne Baby"? Surely there are some who have not forgotten his grotesque vocabulary, and his utterly overpowering way of using it. There are different stories concerning his origin, and they vary in truthfulness, I have heard, as one travels southward from the Northern Pacific to Santa Fé. I give the one told in Colorado. It may be only a "ghost-story," and it may be true; all that I know is that it is not impossible. According to its teaching, his mother was once respectable and belonged to the politest society in the Indian Territory. When quite a young girl she carelessly fell in love with a handsome Indian chief, and, much to the disgust of her friends, married him and went away into his camp. It must have been a wild life that she led there, for within a year she was separated from him and living with another Indian. It is the same pitiful story for the next five years;

she was knocked about from tent to tent and camp to camp. Her enemies say that she liked that kind of life, but her friends know better, and claim that she was ashamed to go home. However it was, she went over to the cow-boys after a while, and it was then that the baby was born, and she met the man, whoever he was, that introduced her into Hoboland. She appeared one night at a hang-out near Denver, and there was something so peculiarly forlorn about her that the men took pity on her and pressed her to stay. This she did, and for some time traveled with the hoboes throughout the districts lying between Cheyenne and Santa Fé. The boy became a sort of "mascot," and was probably the only child in Hoboland who was ever taught to be really good. The mother had stipulated with the men that they should never teach him anything bad, and the idea struck them as so comical that they fell in with it. Though they swore continually in his presence, they invariably gave him some respectable version of the conversation; and while about the only words he knew were curses, he was made to believe they signified the nicest things in the world. He died just as unknowing as he had lived, but it was a cruel death. He and his mother, together with some companions, were caught one night in a wreck on the Union Pacific, and all that the survivors could find of him to bury was his right arm. But that was bravely honored, and, unless the coyotes have torn down the wooden slab, the grave can still be found on the prairies.

I cannot leave this division of my theme without saying something about that large army of unfathered children who, to my mind, are just as much born on the road as the less known types. True, many of them are handed over at birth to some family to support, but the great majority of these families are not one whit better than the ambulanters. They train the orphans put into their care, in sin and crime, quite as carefully as the hobo does his beggar boy. These are the children who make up the main body of the class I have been considering, and it seems to me that they increase from year to year. At present the only legitimate career for them is that of the outcast, and into it they go. Few, indeed, succeed in gaining a foothold in polite society. Their little lives form the border-land of my second class, the children driven to the road.

II

Concerning the children who are forced upon the road there is a great deal to be said, but much of this talk should be directed against the popular belief that their number is legion. Socialists particularly think that hundreds upon hundreds of boys and girls are compelled by hunger to beg and steal for a living. In England I once heard a labor agitator declare that there are a million of these juvenile "victims of capital" in the United States alone. I do not know where the man got his information, but if my finding counts for anything it is deplorably unsound. I cannot claim to have studied the subject as carefully as is necessary to know it absolutely, but in most of our large cities I have given it close attention, and never have I found anything like the state of affairs which even the general public believes to exist. For every child forced by starvation to resort to the road I have met ten who were born there, and nearly the same number who were enticed there. In saying this, however, I do not want to draw emphasis or sympathy away from that certainly existing class of children who really have been driven into outlawry. But it is an injustice to our sober poor to say that they exist in those large numbers that are so often quoted. Not long ago I made it my special business for a while to look into the condition of some of these compulsory little vagabonds in New York city. I picked out those children whom one sees so often pilfering slyly from the groceryman's sidewalk display. It is an old, old trick. The youngsters divide themselves into "watchers" and "snatchers"; the former keeping an eye on the police as well as the owners of the things coveted, and the latter grabbing when the wink is given. The crime itself is not a heavy one according to the calendar, but it is only a step from this to picking pockets, and only a half-step farther to highway robbery. I chose this particular class because I had often noticed the members of it in my walks through the city, and it had seemed to me the least necessary of all. Then, too, there was something in the pinched faces that made me anxious to know the children personally on grounds of charity. The great majority of youthful travelers on the road are comparatively well fed, to say the least, and, much as one pities their fate, he will seldom have cause to weep over their starved condition. But here was something different, and I fancied that I was to get a glimpse into the life of those people to whom the socialist points when asked for living examples of human woe caused by inhuman capitalists.

It was not hard to "get in" with the children. Finding that I was willing to play with them at their games in the alleys and on top of their rickety tenement-houses, they edged up to me rather cordially, and we were soon "pals." There was nothing very new in their life, but I was struck with the great interest they took in their petty thefts. In the midst of the most boisterous play they would gladly stop if some one suggested a clever plan by which even a can of preserves could be "swiped," as they called it, and the next instant they were trying to carry it to a finish. They were not what I could call instinctive criminals —far from it; but a long intimacy with the practices of outlawry, though small in their way, had so deadened their moral sense that sneak-thieving came to them almost as naturally as it does to the kleptomaniac. Even in their games they cheated whenever it was possible, and it seemed to me that the main fun was seeing how cleverly and yet boldly they could do so without being detected. I recall distinctly one afternoon when we were playing "Hi spy." A little fellow called Jamie took me aside, and in the most friendly way advised me not to be so "goody-goody." I had been very unlucky in getting caught, and he said that it was because I gave in too quickly.

"When ye hear yer name," he continued, "jus' lie low, 'cause like as not the catcher ain't seen ye, 'n' if he has he can't prove it; so ye 'r' all right anyhow. Ye 'll always be 'It' if ye don't do something like that;

'n' there ain't no fun in that, is there?" he added, winking his left eye in a truly professional manner.

So much for their native endowment. Their accomplishment in thieving, I have no doubt, kept them often from going hungry, notwithstanding the fact that there was honest industry at home, generally that of the mother, while the father's earnings went almost bodily into the publican's till.

I found it much more difficult to make friends with the parents, but succeeded in several cases—that is, with the mother; the father I usually found drunk at the saloon. I shall not try to give an account of the squalor and sorrow that I encountered; this has been done in other places by far more able pens than mine; but I cannot forbear making a note of one little woman whom I saw sewing her very life away, and thinking all the while that she was really supporting her hungry children. I shall never forget the picture she made as she sat there by the alley window, driving the needle with lightning-like rapidity through the cloth—a veritable Madonna of the Needle. Her good cheer was something stupendous. Not once did she murmur, and when her brute of a husband returned, insanely intoxicated, she took care of him as if he were the best man in the world. I was careful that she did not hear from me about the tricks of her wayward children. Some day, however, I fear that one of them will be missing, and when she goes to the police station to make inquiries I should rather not confront her. The main reason why hungry boys and girls are found upon the road is drunken fathers.

There are also children who, instead of being forced

to steal, are sent out into the streets by their parents to beg. From morning till night they trudge along the busy thoroughfares, dodging with cat-like agility the lumbering wagons that bear down upon them, and accosting every person whom their trained eyes find at all likely to listen to their appeals. Late at night, if perchance they have had the necessary luck during the day, they crawl back to their hovels and hand over the winnings to their heavy-eyed fathers. Or, as often happens, if the day has been unsuccessful and the pennies are not numerous enough to satisfy their cruel masters, they take refuge in some box or barrel, and pray to the beggar's Providence that the next day will go better.

They come, as a rule, from our foreign population. I have never found one with American-born parents, and in many instances the children themselves have emigrated from Europe, usually from Italy. There is no doubt that they have to beg to live; but when one looks a little further into their cases, a lazy or dissipated parent is usually the one to blame. Then, too, mendicancy is not considered disgraceful among many of our immigrants, and they send their children into the streets of our cities quite as freely as they do at home. They also are mainly at fault for that awful institution which some of our large towns support, where babies are rented to grown-up beggars to excite the sympathy of the passers-by. I looked into one of these places in San Francisco, while traveling with the hoboes, and it was the very counterpart of an African slave-market. A French-Canadian woman, old enough to be the great-grandmother of all her wares, kept it.

She rented the babies from poverty-stricken mothers, and re-rented them at a profit to the begging women of the town. There were two customers in the place when I entered, and the old wretch was trying in true peddler style to bring out the good points of four little bits of humanity cuddled together on a plank bed.

"Oh, he 's just the kind you want," she said to one of the women; "never cries, and"—leaning over, she whispered in a Shylock voice—"he don't eat hardly anything; *half a bottle o' milk does him the whole day.*"

The woman was satisfied, and, paying her deposit of two dollars, took the sickly thing in her arms and went out into the town. The other could find nothing that suited her, but promised to return the next day, when a "new batch" was expected.

Such are the main avenues by which boys and girls are driven to the road in the United States. Hunger, I candidly admit, is the whip in many instances, but the wielder of it is more often than not the drunken father or mother. It is the hunger that comes of selfish indulgence, and not of ill adjusted labor conditions.

III

Of my third class, those who are enticed to the road,—and their number is legion,—I have been able to discover three different types. The old roadster knows them all. Wherever he goes they cross his path, and beg him to stop awhile and tell them of his travels. They seem to realize that they have been swindled—that the road is, after all, only a tantalizing delusion; but they cannot understand why it appeals to so many of their elders, and it is in the hope that these will in the end put them on the right track for the fun they are seeking that they hail them, and cry, "What cheer?" It is a pitiful call, this, and even the "old stager" winces at times on hearing it; but he cannot bring himself to go back on "the profession," and quickly conquering his emotion, he gives the tiny traveler fresh directions. The boy starts out anew, hoping against experience that he is at last on the right route, and plods on eagerly until stopped again at some troublesome cross-road where he does not know which turn to take. Once more he asks for directions, once more receives them, and so the ceaseless trudge goes on. It is mainly at the cross-roads that I have learned to know these children. Notwithstanding my alien position, they have hailed me too, and inquired for sign-posts. I have seldom been able to help them, even in the way that I most desired, but surely there are others who can.

The children of this third class that one meets oftenest are what the older travelers call "worshipers of the tough." They have somehow got the idea that cow-boy swagger and the criminal's lingo are the main features of a manly man, and having an abnormal desire to realize their ideal as quickly as possible, they go forth to acquire them. The hunt soon lures them to the road, and up and down its length they scamper, with faces so eager and intent that one is seldom at a loss to know what they are seeking. There are different explanations of the charm that this wild life has for them. A great many people believe that it is purely and simply the work of the devil on their evil-bent natures; others, that it is the result of bad training; and still others, that it is one form of the mimicry with which every child is endowed in larger or smaller degree. I favor the last opinion. In the bottom of their hearts they are no worse than the average boy and girl, but they have been unfortunate enough to see a picture or hear a story of some famous rascal, and it has lodged in their brains, until the temptation to "go and do likewise" has come upon them with such overwhelming force that they simply cannot resist. Each one has some particular pattern continually before his eyes, and only as he approaches it does he feel that he is becoming tough. Now it is "Blinkey Morgan" that fascinates him, and, despite his terrible end, he strives to be like him; then it is "Wild Bill," whoever he may be; and not unfrequently it is a character that has existed only in dime novels, or not even so substantially as that.

I remember well a little fellow, about thirteen years old, who appeared in Indian-scout attire one night at a hang-out near McCook, Nebraska. He dropped in while the tramps were cooking their coffee, and seldom has there been such a laugh on the "Q" railroad as they gave on seeing him. It was impolite, and they begged his pardon later, but even his guardian angel would have smiled. He was dressed from head to foot in leather clothes each piece made by himself, he said, and at his belt hung an enormous revolver, which some one had been careful enough to make useless by taking out an important screw. It was in the hope of finding one at the camp that he visited it, but the men made so much of him that he remained until his story was told. It was not remarkably new, for all that he wanted was a chance to shoot Indians, but his hero was a little unusual,—Kalamazoo Chickamauga, he called him. When asked who he was and where he had lived, all that the youngster could say was that he had dreamed about him! I saw him again a week or so later, not far from Denver, tramping along over the railroad-ties with long strides far beyond his measure, and he hoped to be at "Deadtown," as he miscalled Deadwood, in a few days. He had not yet found a screw for his "gun," but he was sure that "Buffalo Charley" would give him one.

Of course this is a unique case, in a way, for one does not meet many lads in such an outfit, but there are scores of others just as sincere and fully as innocent. If one could only get hold of them ere they reach the road, nearly all could be brought to reason. They are the most impressionable children in the world, and there must be a way by which this very quality may be turned to their advantage. What this way shall be can be determined only by those who know well the needs of each child, but there is one suggestion I cannot forbear making. Let everything possible be done to keep these sensitive boys and girls, but particularly the former, from familiarity with crime. Do not thrust desperadoism upon them from the shop-windows through the picture-covered dime novels and the flaring faces of the "Police Gazette." It is just such teaching by suggestion that starts many an honest but romantic boy off to the road, when a little cautious legislation might save him years of foolish wandering, and the State the expense of housing him in its reformatories later on. I write with feeling at this point, for I know from personal experience what tantalizing thoughts a dime novel will awaken in such a boy's mind. One of these thoughts will play more havoc with his youth than can be made good in his manhood, and lucky is he whom it does not lure on and on until the return path is forever lost.

Something like these children in temperament, but totally different in most other respects, are those lads that one meets so often on our railroads, drifting about for a month or so from town to town, seldom stopping in any of them over a day, and then suddenly disappearing, no one knows where, to appear again, later, on another railroad, frequently enough a thousand miles distant. Occasionally they are missed from the road for over a year, and there is absolutely no news of their whereabouts; but just as they are almost forgotten they come forward once more, make a few journeys on the freight-trains, and vanish again. There are cases on record where they have kept this up for years, some of them coming and going with such regularity that their appearances may be calculated exactly. Out West, not very long ago, there was a little chap who "showed up" in this way, to use the expression that the brakemen applied to him, every six weeks for three years, but this was all that was known concerning him. When asked who he was and where he belonged, he gave such evasive answers that it was impossible to come to any trustworthy conclusion about him. He would have nothing to do with the people he met, and I have heard that he always

YOUTHFUL TRESPASSERS.

rode alone in the box-cars. In this last respect he was a notable exception, for, as a rule, these little nomads take great pleasure in talking with strangers, but they are careful not to say too much about themselves. They ask questions principally, and skip from one subject to another with a butterfly rapidity, but manage to pick up a great deal of knowledge of the road.

The tramps' theory of them is that they are possessed of the "railroad fever," and I am inclined to agree with them, but I accept the expression in its broader sense of *Wanderlust.* They want to get out into the world, and at stated periods the desire is so strong and the road so handy that they simply cannot resist the temptation to explore it. A few weeks usually suffice to cool their ardor, and then they run home quite as summarily as they left, but they stay only until the next runaway mood seizes them. I have been successful in getting really well acquainted with several of these interesting wanderers, and in each case this has been the situation. They do not want to be tough, and many of them could not be if they tried; but they have a passion for seeing things on their own hook, and if the mood for a "trip" comes, it seems to them the most natural thing in the world to indulge it. If they had the means they would ride on Pullman cars and imagine themselves princes, but lacking the wherewithal, they take to the road.

I knew in New York State a boy of this sort who had as comfortable a home as a child could wish, but he was cursed with this strange *Wanderlust*, and throughout his boyhood there was hardly a month that he did not run away. The queerest things enticed him to go. Sometimes the whistle of a railway-engine was enough to make him wild with unrest, and again the sight of the tame but to him fascinating village street was sufficient to set him planning his route of travel. In every escapade it was his imagination that stampeded him. Many a time, when he was in the most docile of moods, some fanciful thought of the world at large, and what it held in waiting for him, would dance across his brain, and before he could analyze it, or detect the swindle, he was scampering off for the railroad station. Now it was a wish to go West and play trapper and scout, and then it was the dream of American boyhood,—a life cramped but struggling, and emerging in glorious success as candidate for the Presidency. Garfield's biography, I remember, once started him on such a journey, and it took years to get the notion out of his head that simply living and striving as Garfield did was sure to bring the same results. Frequently his wanderings ended several hundred miles from home, but much oftener in some distracting vagabond's hang-out in a neighboring city. Fortunately the fever burned itself out ere he had learned to like the road for its own sake, and he lived to wonder how he had harbored or indulged such insane impulses. A large number of these truants, however, have no good homes and indulgent parents to return to, and after a while the repeated punishment seems to them so unjust and cruel that there comes a trip which never ends. The *Wanderlust* becomes chronic, and mainly because it was not treated properly in its intermittent stage. There is no use in whipping these children; they are not to blame; all that one can do is to busy their imaginations in wholesome ways, watch them carefully, and, if they must wander, direct their wanderings. In many cases this is possible, for the fever breaks out among children of the best birth as well as among those of the lowest; and in these instances, at least, the parents have much to answer for if the children reach the road. I look upon this fever as quite as much of a disease as the craze to steal which is found now and then in some child's character, and it deserves the same careful treatment. Punishment only aggravates it, and develops in the boy a feeling of hatred for all about him. I firmly believe that some day this trouble in so many boys' lives will be pathologically treated by medical men, and the sooner that day comes the better will it be for many unfortunate children.

It is a different story that I have to tell of the children decoyed into Hoboland. True, they also are, in a measure, seized with this same *Wanderlust*, and without this it would be impossible for the tramp to influence them as he does; but, on the other hand, without him to excite and direct this passion, very few of them would ever reach trampdom. He happens along at their very weakest moments, and, perceiving his advantage, cruelly fires their imagination with tales of adventure and travel, and before they discover their danger he has them in his clutches. It is really one of the wonders of the world, the power that this ugly, dissipated, tattered man has over the children he meets. In no other country that I have visited is there anything like it. He stops at a town for a few hours, collects the likely boys about him at his hang-out, picks out the one that he thinks will serve him best, and then begins systematically to fascinate him. If he understands the art well (and it is a carefully studied art), he can almost always get the one he wants. Often enough his choice is some well-bred child, unaccustomed, outside his dreams, to any such life, but the man knows so perfectly how to piece out those dreams and make them seducingly real that in a moment of enthusiasm the youngster gives himself up to the bewitching influence and allows the wretch to lead him away. As a rule, however, his victims are the children of the poor, for they are the easiest to approach. A few hours of careful tactics, provided they are in the mood, and he has one of them riding away with him, not merely in the box-car of a freight-train, but on the through train to Hoboland.

Watch him at his preliminary work. He is seated on the top of an ash-barrel in a filthy back alley. A crowd of gamins gaze up at him with admiring eyes. When he tells his ghost-stories, each one thinks that he is being talked to just as much as the rest, and yet somehow, little by little, there is a favorite who is getting more and more than his share of the winks and smiles; soon the most exciting parts of the stories are gradually devoted to him alone, but in such an artful way that he himself fails to notice it at first. It is not long, however, before he feels his importance. He begins to wink, too, but just as slyly as his charmer, and his little mouth curls into a return smile when the others are not looking. "I 'm his favorite, I am," he thinks. "He 'll take me with him, he will, and show me things."

He is what the hobo calls "peetrified," which means, as much as anything else, hypnotized. The stories that he has heard amount to very little in themselves, but the way they are told, the happy-go-lucky manner, the subtle partiality, the winning voice, and the sensitiveness of the boy's nature to things of wonder, all combine to turn his head. Then his own parents cannot control him as can this slouching wizard.

In Hoboland the boy's life may be likened to that of a voluntary slave. He is forced to do exactly what his "jocker" commands, and disobedience, wilful or innocent, brings down upon him a most cruel wrath. Besides being kicked, slapped, and generally maltreated, he is also loaned, traded, and even sold, if his master sees money in the bargain. There are, of course, exceptions, for I have myself known some jockers to be almost as kind as fathers to their boys, but they are such rarities that one can never count upon them. When a lad enters trampdom he must be prepared for all kinds of brutal treatment, and the sooner he forgets home gentleness the better will it be for him. In payment for all this suffering and rough handling, he is told throughout his apprenticeship that some day he too will be able to "snare" a boy, and make him beg and slave for him as he has slaved for others. This is the one reward that tramps hold out to their "prushuns," and the little fellows cherish it so long that, when their emancipation finally comes, nearly all start off to do the very same thing that was done to them when they were children.

West of the Mississippi River there is a regular gang of these "ex-kids," as they are termed in the vernacular, and all are supposed to be looking for revenge. Until they get it there is still something of the prushun about them which makes them unwelcome in the old stager class. So they prowl about the community from place to place, looking eagerly for some weak lad whom they can decoy and show to the fraternity as evidence of their full membership. They never seem to realize what an awful thing they are doing. If you remonstrate with them, they reply: "W'y, you don't think we 've been slavin' all this while fer nothin', do you? It 's our turn to play jocker now," and, with a fiendish look in their eyes, they turn and stalk away. Ten years and more of tramp life have killed their better natures, and all that they can think of is vengeance, unscrupulous and sure. In this way the number of boys in Hoboland is always kept up to a certain standard. Every year a number are graduated from the prushun class, and go out into the world immediately to find younger children to take the places they have left. In time these do the same thing, and so on, until to-day there is no line of outlawry so sure of recruits as vagabondage. Each beggar is a propagandist, and his brethren expect of him at least one convert.

IV

THERE is not much that I can say of the children who go to the road voluntarily. I am sure that there are such, for I have traveled with them, but it has

TELLING "GHOST-STORIES."

been impossible for me to get into their life intimately enough to speak of it intelligently. Even the men constantly in their company can say but little about them. When asked for an explanation, they shake their heads and call them "little devils"; but why they are so, what it is that they are seeking, and where they come from, are questions to which they are unable to give any satisfactory replies. I know about twenty, all told, and, as far as I have been successful in observing them, they seem to me to belong to that class of children which the criminologist Lombroso finds morally delinquent at birth. Certainly it would be hard to account for their abnormal criminal sense on any other ground. They take to the road as to their normal element, and are on it but a short time ere they know almost as much as the oldest travelers. Their minds seem bent toward crime and vagabondage, and their intuitive powers almost uncanny. To hear them talk makes one think, if he shuts his eyes, that he is in the presence of trained criminal artists, and I have sometimes imagined that they were not children, but dwarfed men born out of due time. They undertake successfully some of the most dangerous robberies in the world, and come off scot-free, so that old and experienced thieves simply stare and wonder. The temptation is to think that they are accidents, but they recur so frequently as to demand a theory of origin and existence. They are, I do not doubt, the product of criminal breeding, and are just as much admired in the criminal world as are the feats of some *Wunderkind*, for instance, among musicians. Watch the scene in an outcasts' den when one of these queer little creatures comes in, and you may see the very same thing that goes on in the "artist's box" at some concert where a prodigy is performing. The people swarm around him, pet him, make him laugh and talk, till the proprietor finds him a valuable drawing card for the establishment. The child himself seldom realizes his importance, and, when off duty, plays at games in keeping with his age. The instant business is suggested, however, his countenance assumes a most serious air, and it is then that one wonders whether he is not, after all, some skilful old soul traveling back through life in a fresh young body. Indeed, there is so much in his case that appeals to my sense of wonder that I simply cannot study him for what he is; but there are those who can do this, and I promise them a most interesting field of observation. I know enough about it to believe that if it can be thoroughly explored there will be a great change in the punishment of criminals. These boys have in them in largest measure what the entire body of moral delinquents possesses in some degree; and when these baffling characteristics have been definitely analyzed and placed, penology will start on a fresh course.

It may be worth while to say what I can about their physical appearance. The most of them have seemed to me to have fairly well-formed bodies, but something out of the ordinary in their eyes, and in a few cases in the entire face. Sometimes the left eye has drooped very noticeably, and one boy that I recall had something akin to a description I once heard of the "evil eye." It was a gipsy who explained it to me; and if he was right, that a "little curtain," capable of falling over the eyeball at will, is the main curiosity, then this boy had the evil eye. He could throw a film over his eye in the most distressing fashion, and delighted in the power to do so; indeed, it was his main way of teasing people. He knew that it was not a pleasant sight, and if he had a petty grudge to gratify, he chose this very effective torment. Concerning the faces, it is difficult to explain just what was the matter. They were not exactly deformed, but there was a peculiar depravity about them that one could but notice instantly. At times I fancied that it was in the arrangement of features rather than acquired expression of the life; but there were cases where the effects of evil environment and cruel abuse were plain to see. I have sometimes taken the pains to look up the parents of a child who thus interested me, but I could not discover any similar depravity in their countenances. There was depravity there, to be sure, but of a different kind. I believe that the parents of these children, and especially the mothers, could tell a great deal concerning them, and the theorists in criminology will never be thoroughly equipped for their work till all this evidence has been heard.

THE foregoing is but a partial summary of several years' experience with the children of the road. It is far from being what I should like to write about them, but perhaps enough has been said to forestate the problem as it appears to one who has traveled with these children and learned to know them "in the open." Surely there is kindness and ingenuity enough in the world to devise a plan or a system by which they may be snatched from the road and restored to their better selves. Surely, too, these little epitomes of *Wanderlust*, and even of crime, are not to baffle philanthropy and science forever. I feel sure that, whatever may be the answer to the thousand questions which center in this problem, one thing can be done, and done at once. Wherever law is able to deal with these children, let it be done on the basis of an intelligent classification. In punishing them for their misdemeanors and crimes, let them not be tumbled indiscriminately into massive reform institutions, officered by political appointment and managed with an eye to the immediate interests of the taxpayer instead of the welfare of the inmates. The one practical resource that lies nearest to our hand as philanthropic sociologists is the reform of the reformatories. We may not hope to reach in many generations the last sources of juvenile crime, but we are deserving of a far worse punishment than these moral delinquents if, being well born and well bred, we do not set ourselves resolutely to the bettering of penal conditions once imposed.

First of all, we must have a humane and scientific separation of the inmates in all these reformatories. Sex, age, height, and weight are not the only things to be taken into consideration when dealing with erring children. Birth, temperament, habits, education, and experience are questions of far more vital importance, and it is no unreasonable demand upon the State that careful attention to each of these points be required in the scheme of such institutions. Put an ambulanter's child with a simple runaway boy, and there will be two ambulanters; associate a youngster with the passion to be tough with a companion innately criminal, and the latter will be the leader. The law of the survival of the fittest is just as operative in low life as in any other. In such spheres the worst natures are the fittest, and the partially good must yield to them unless zealously defended by outside help. It is suicidal to put them together, and wherever this is done, especially among children, there need be no surprise if criminals, and not citizens, are developed.

Second, the management of reformatories should be in scientific hands; and just here I am constrained to plead for the training of young men and women for the rare usefulness that awaits them in such institutions. It is to these places that the children I have been describing will have to go, and, with all respect to the officials now in charge, I believe that there are apt and gifted young men and women in this country who could bring to them invaluable assistance, if they could only be persuaded to train for it and to offer it. I do not know why it is, but for some reason these institutions do not yet appeal to any large number of students who intend taking service in the ranks of reform. The university settlement attracts many, and this is one of the finest manifestations of the universal brotherhood which is to be. Meanwhile, there is a moral hospital service to be carried on in penal and reformatory houses. Shall it be done by raw, untrained hands, by selfish quacks, or by careful, scientific students? Must the moral nurse and physician be chosen for his ability to control votes, or to treat his patients with skilled attention and consideration? If the treatment of physical disease offers attractions that call thousands upon thousands of young men and women into the nursing and medical professions, here is a field even more fascinating to the student, and so full of opportunity and interesting employment that it will be a matter of wonder if the supply does not speedily exceed the demand.

There is one thing more. Reformatories, planned, officered, and conducted according to the principles of scientific philanthropy, should be stationed, not at the end of the road, but at the junction of all by-paths that leads into it.

III

CLUB LIFE AMONG OUTCASTS

I

ONE of the first noticeable features of low life is its gregariousness. To be alone, except in a few cases where a certain morbidity and peculiar fondness for isolation prevail, is almost the worst punishment that can befall the outcast. There is a variety of causes for this, but I think the main one is the desire to feel that although he is forbidden the privileges and rights of a polite society, he can nevertheless identify himself with just as definite and exclusive a community as the one he has been turned out of.

His specialty in crime and rowdyism determines the particular form and direction of his social life. If he is a tramp he wants to know his partners, and the same instinct prevails in all other fields of outlawry. In time, and as he comes to see that his world is a large one,—so large, in fact, that he can never understand it all,—he chooses as he can those particular "pals" with whom he can get on the easiest. Out of this choice there develops what I call the outcast's club. He himself calls it a gang, and his club-house a "hang-out." It is of such clubs that I want to write in this chapter. I do not pretend to know all of them. Far from it! And some of those that I know are too vile for description; but the various kinds that I can describe, I have chosen those which are the most representative.

II

Low life as I know it in America is composed of three distinct classes, and they are called, in outcasts' slang, the "Kids," the "Natives," and the "Old Bucks." The Kids, as their name suggests, are boys and girls, the Natives are the middle-aged outcasts, and the Old Bucks are the superannuated. Each of these classes has clubs corresponding in character and purpose to the age of the members.

The clubs of the Kids are composed mainly of mischievous children and instinctively criminal children. As a rule, they are organized by boys alone, but I have known girls also to take part in their proceedings. The lads are usually between ten and fifteen years old. Sometimes they live at home with their parents, if they have any, and sometimes in lodging-houses. They get their living, such as it is, by rag-picking, selling newspapers, blacking boots, and doing odd errands fitted to their strength. None of them, not even the criminally inclined, are able to steal enough to support themselves.

To illustrate, I shall take two clubs which I knew, one in Chicago, and one in Cincinnati. The Chicago club belonged exclusively to a set of lads on the North Side who called themselves the "Wildcats." The most of them were homeless little fellows who lived in that district as newsboys and boot-blacks. They numbered about twenty, and although they had no officially elected leader, a little fellow called Fraxy was nevertheless a recognized "pres'dent," and was supposed to know more about the city and certain tricks than the rest, and I think it was he who started the club. He was an attractive lad, capable of exercising considerable influence over his companions, and I can easily understand how he persuaded them to form the club. For personality counts for as much in low life as it does in "high life," and little Fraxy had a remarkably magnetic one. He drew boys to him wherever he went, and before going to Chicago had organized a similar club in Toledo, Ohio.

The club-house of the Wildcats was a little cave which they had dug in a cabbage-field on the outskirts of the city. Here they gathered nearly every night in the week to smoke cigarettes, read dime novels or hear them read, tell tales, crack jokes, and plan their mischievous raids on the neighboring districts. The cave contained a brickwork stove, some benches, some old pots and cans, one or two obscene pictures, and an old shoe-box, in which were stored from time to time various things to eat.

The youngest boy was ten and the oldest fourteen, and as I remember them they were not especially bad boys. I have often sat with them and listened to their stories and jokes, and although they could swear, and a few could drink like drunkards, the most of them had hearts still kind. But they were intensely mischievous. The more nuisances they could commit the happier they were; and the odd part of it all was that their misdemeanors never brought them the slightest profit, and were remarkable for nothing but their wantonness. I remember particularly one night when they stoned an old church simply because Fraxy had suggested it as sport. They left their cave about nine o'clock and went to a stone-pile near at hand, where they filled their pockets full of rocks. Then they started off pell-mell for the church, the windows of which they "peppered 'n' salted" till they looked like "'skeeter-nettin's," as Fraxy said. The moment they had finished they scampered into town and brought up at various lodging-houses.

They never thieved or begged while I knew them, and not one of them had what could be called a criminal habit. They were simply full of boyishness, and having no homes, no parents, no friends, no refined instincts, it is no wonder that they worked off their animal spirits in pranks of this sort. Sometimes they used to take their girl friends out to the cave, too, and enlist them for a while in the same mischievous work that I have described; but they always treated them kindly, and spoke of them as their "dear little kidsy-widsies." The girls helped to make the cave more homelike, and the lads appreciated every decoration and knickknack given them.

Every city has clubs like this. They are a natural consequence of slum life, and to better them it is first necessary to better the slums themselves. Sunday-school lessons will not accomplish this; reading-rooms will not accomplish it; gymnasiums will not accomplish it; and nothing that I know of will accomplish it except personal contact with some man or boy who is willing to live among them and show them, as he alone can, a better life. There are many young men in the world who have remarkable ability, I believe, for just such work, if they would only go into it. By this I do not necessarily mean joining some organization or "settlement"; I mean that the would-be helper shall live his own individual life among these people, learn to understand their whims and passions, and try to be of use to them as a personal friend. If he is especially adapted to dealing with boys, he has only to take up his residence in any slum in any city, and he will find plenty to do. But whatever he does, he must not let them think that he is among them as a reformer.

III

THE club in Cincinnati was of a different kind. It is true that it consisted of young boys, and that some of them were boot-blacks and newsboys, but in other respects they were different. Their club name was the "Sneakers," and their hang-out was an old deserted house-boat, which lay stranded on the river-bank about a mile or so out of town. Some of them had homes, but the majority lived in lodging-houses or on the boat. When I first knew them they had been organized about three months, and a few of them had already been caught and sent to the reform school. Their business was stealing, pure and simple. Old metals were the things they looked for chiefly, because they were the handiest to get at. They had had no training in picking pockets or "sly work" of any particular sort, but they did know some untenanted houses, and these they entered and cut away the lead pipes to sell to dealers in such wares. Sometimes they also broke into engine-houses, and, if possible, unscrewed the brass-work on the engines, and I have even known them to take the wheels off wagons to get the tires. Their boat was their storehouse until the excitement over the theft had subsided, and then they persuaded some tramp or town "tough" to dispose of their goods. They never made very much profit, but enough to keep up interest in further crimes.

I became acquainted with them through an old vagabond in Cincinnati who helped them now and then. He took me out to see them one night, and I had a good opportunity to learn what their club was made of. Most of the lads were over fourteen years of age, and two had already been twice in reform schools in different States. These two were the leaders, and mainly, I think, on account of certain tough airs which they "put on." They talked criminal slang, and had an all-wise tone that was greatly liked by the other boys. They were all saturated with criminal ideas, and their faces gave evidence of crooked characteristics. How they came to club together is probably best explained by the older vagabond. I asked him how he accounted for such an organization, and he replied:

"Got it in 'em, I guess. It 's the only reason I know. Some kids always is that way. The divil 's born in 'em."

I think that is true, and I still consider it the best explanation of the Sneakers. They were criminals by instinct, and such boys, just as mischievous boys, drift together and combine plots and schemes. I know of

A GATHERING OF "OLD BUCKS."

other boys of the same type who, instead of stealing, burn barns and outhouses. Young as they are, their moral obliquity is so definitely developed that they do such things passionately. They like to see the blaze, and yet when asked wherein the fun lies, they cannot tell.

How to reform such boys is a question which, I think, has never been settled satisfactorily. For one, I do not believe that they can ever be helped by any clubs organized for their improvement. They have no interest in such things, and none can be awakened strong enough to kill their interest in criminal practices. They are mentally maimed, and practically belong in an insane asylum. In saying this I do not wish to be understood as paying tribute to the "fad" of some philanthropic circles, which regard the criminal as either diseased or delinquent—as born lacking in mental and moral aptitudes, or perverted through no fault of his own. Without any attempt to tone down the reproach of criminality, or to account for the facts by heredity or environment, it still remains true that in thousands of cases there is as direct evidence of insanity in a boy's crimes and misdemeanors as in a man's, and I firmly believe that a more scientific century will institute medical treatment of juvenile crime, and found reform schools where the cure of insanity will be as much an object as moral instruction and character-building.

IV

Club life among the Natives,—the older outcasts, —although in many respects quite different from that of the Kids, is in some ways strikingly similar.

There are, for instance, young rowdies and roughs whose main pleasures are mischief and petty misdemeanors, just as among the young boys in Chicago. But in place of breaking church windows and turning over horse-blocks, they join what are called "scrappin' gangs," and spend most of their time in fighting hostile clubs of the same order. They are not clever enough as yet to become successful criminals; they are too brutal and impolite to do profitable begging, and as rowdyism is about the only thing they can take part in, their associations become pugilistic clubs.

How these originated is an open question even among the rowdies themselves. My own explanation of their origin is this: Every community, if it is at all complex and varied, has different sets of outcasts and ne'er-do-wells, just as it has varieties of respectable people. In time these different sets appropriate, often quite accidentally, territories of their own. One set, for example, will live mainly on the east side of a city, and another set on the west side. After some residence in their distinct quarters, local prejudices and habits are formed, and, what is more to the point, a local patriotism grows. The east-sider thinks his hang-outs and dives are the best, and the west-sider thinks the same of his. Out of this conceit there comes invariably a class hatred, which grows, and finally develops into the "scrappin' gangs," the purpose of which is to defend the pride of each separate district. In New York I know of over half a dozen of these pugnacious organizations, and they fight for as many different territories. I have seen in one club young and old of both sexes joined together to defend their "kentry," as they called the street or series of streets in which they lived. The majority of the real fighters, however, are powerful fellows between the ages of eighteen and twenty-two. Sometimes they live at home, and a few pretend to do some work, but most of them are loafers, who spend their time in drinking, gambling, and petty thieving. They usually sleep in old tenements and cheap lodging-houses, and in the daytime they are either in the streets or at some dive supported mainly by their patronage.

I knew such a place in the city of New York, on the East Side, and not far from the Brooklyn Bridge. It was kept by an Irishman, and he had no customers other than those belonging to a "scrappin' gang" called the "Rappers." There were two rooms—one fronting on the street, and used as a bar-room; the other, in the rear, was the gambling- and "practisin'"-room. Here they came every night, played cards, drank stale beer, and exercised themselves in fisticuffing and "scrappin'." I visited them one night, and saw some of their movements, as they called the various triangles and circles which they formed as strategic guards when attacking the hostile gangs of the West Side. One of them they nicknamed the "V gag," and prided themselves on its efficiency. It was simply a triangle which they formed to charge the better into the ranks of their enemies, and it reminded me strongly of football tactics.

That same night they were to scuffle with a West-Side gang called the "Ducks," as one of their members had been insulted by one of the Duck gang. Battle was to be joined in a certain alley not far from Eighth

Avenue, and they started out, their pockets full of stones, in companies of two and three, to meet later in the alley. I accompanied the leader, a fellow called the "slugger," and reached the alley about eleven o'clock. He wanted me to give my assistance, but I told him that I could play war correspondent much better, and so was excused from action. And it was action indeed. They had hardly reached the battle-ground before the Ducks were upon them, and rocks flew and fists punched in a most terrific manner. Noses bled, coats were torn, hats were lost, and black eyes became the fashion. This went on for about fifteen minutes, and the battle was over. The Rappers were defeated fairly and squarely, but, as the slugger said, when we were all at the hang-out again, "we mought 'a' licked 'em ef we 'd 'a' had 'em over here."

Such is the "scrappin' gang." Every large city supports one or two, and London has a score of them. They make some of its districts uninhabitable for respectable persons, and woe to the man who tries to interfere with them. As their members die or grow old, younger fellows come forward, often enough out of the very boys' clubs I have described, and take the place of the departed heroes. This is what rowdies call life.

Like the famous *Studenten-Corps* in Germany, they need some sort of rough excitement, and the bloodier it is the happier they are. They have so much heart in them that no ordinary exercise relieves it, and they institute these foolish fighting clubs. It is possible that some sweet-natured philanthropist might go among them and accomplish wonders. In London the Salvation Army has done some splendid work with these same rowdies, and I know personally several who are to-day respectable working-men. But as for organizing polite clubs among them on any large scale, I think it impossible.

V

AMONG the other Natives, club life, as a rule, centers around the saloon, where they gather to exchange news bulletins and meet their cronies. There are varieties of these saloons, corresponding to the varieties of outcasts, and in Chicago there are over twenty, each one of which is supported by a different clique and species; but these are not exactly clubs. The saloons are meeting-places more than anything else, or a sort of post-office. In the main they are very much like any other saloon, except that their *clientèle* comes principally from the outcasts' world; and about all the life they afford is a boisterous joviality, which seldom takes definite shape. It is proper to say right here that criminal outcasts, as a rule, never form clubs so marked in individuality as the "scrappin' gang." The thief, the burglar, the pickpocket, and other "professionals," although gregarious and friendly enough, do not organize simply for the sake of sociability. When they combine it is more for the sake of business than anything else, and whatever social life they seem to need is furnished them at the saloon or some private hang-out. This is also true to a great extent of all the Natives who have passed their thirtieth year. At that age they are usually so sobered, and have seen so much of the world, that they cannot get much pleasure out of the clubs that the younger men enjoy. The "scrappin' gang" no more appeals to them as a pastime or a source of happiness than it does to an old rounder. They feel happier in simply sitting on a bench in a saloon and talking over old times or planning new adventures. Whatever excitement remains for them in life is found mainly in carousals. Of these I have seen a goodly number, but I must confess that after all they are only too similar to carousals in high life, the only noticeable difference being their greater frequency. They occur just about four times as often as anywhere else, because the outcast, and especially the criminal, is intensely emotional; he can never live very long without some kind of excitement, and the older he grows the more alluring become his drinking-bouts. When his opportunities in this direction are shut off by jail-walls, he improvises something else, which often takes organized form; but it must be remembered that such organizations are purely makeshifts, and that the members would rather sit in some low concert-hall or saloon and have an old-time drinking-bout, if circumstances were only favorable.

VI

The most interesting of these impromptu clubs is the one called in the vernacular the "Kangaroo Court." It is found almost entirely in county jails, in which petty offenders and persons awaiting trial are confined. During the day the prisoners are allowed the freedom of a large hall, and at night they lodge in cells, the locks of which are sometimes fastened and sometimes not. The hall contains tables, benches, daily papers, and, in some instances, stoves and kitchen utensils. The prisoners walk about, jump, and play various games. After a while these games become tiresome, and the "Kangaroo Court" is formed. It consists of all the prisoners, and the officers are elected by them. The positions they fill are the "judgeship," the "searchership," the "spankership," and general "juryship." To illustrate the duties of these various officials, I shall give a personal experience in a county jail in New York State. It was my first encounter with the "Kangaroo Court."

I had been arrested for sleeping in an empty box-car. The watchman found me and lodged me in the station-house, where I spent a most gloomy night wondering what my punishment would be. Early in the morning I was brought before the "squire." He asked me what my name might be, and I replied that "it might be Billy Rice."

"What are you doing around here, Billy?" he queried further.

"Looking for work, your Honor."

"Thirty days," he thundered at me, and I was led away to the jail proper.

I had three companions at the time, and after we had passed the sheriff and his clerk, who had noted down all the facts, imaginary and otherwise, that we had cared to give him about our family histories, we were ushered pell-mell into the large hall. Surrounded in a twinkling by the other prisoners, we were asked to explain our general principles and misdemeanors. This over, and a few salutations exchanged, a tall and lanky rogue cried out in a loud voice:

"The Kangru will now k'lect."

There were about twenty present, and they soon planted themselves about us in a most solemn manner. Some rested on their haunches, others lounged against the walls, and still others sat quietly on the flagstones. As soon as entire quiet had been reached, the tall fellow, who, by the way, was the judge, instructed a half-grown companion, whom he nicknamed the "searcher," to bring his charges against the newcomers. He approached us solemnly and in a most conventional manner, and said:

"Priz'ners, you is charged with havin' boodle in yer pockets. Wha' does you plead—guilty or not guilty?"

I was the first in line, and pleaded not guilty.

"Are you willin' to be searched?" asked the judge.

"I am, your Honor," I replied.

Then the searcher inspected all my pockets, the lining of my coat, the leather band inside my hat, my shoes and socks, and finding nothing in the shape of money, declared that I was guiltless.

"You are discharged," said the judge, and the jurymen ratified the decision with a grunt.

A young fellow, a vagrant by profession, was the next case. He pleaded not guilty, and allowed himself to be searched. But unfortunately he had forgotten a solitary cent which was in his vest pocket. It was quickly confiscated, and he was remanded for trial on the charge of contempt of the "Kangru."

The next victim pleaded guilty to the possession of thirty-six cents, and was relieved of half. The last man, the guiltiest of all, although he pleaded innocence, was found out, and his three dollars were taken away from him instanter; he, too, was charged with contempt of court. His case came up soon after the preliminaries were over, and he was sentenced by the judge to walk the length of the corridor one hundred and three times each day of his confinement, besides washing all the dishes used at dinner for a week.

After all the trials were over, the confiscated money was handed to the genuine turnkey, with instructions that it be invested in tobacco. Later in the day the tobacco was brought into the jail and equally divided among all the prisoners.

The next day I, with the other late arrivals, was initiated as a member of the "Kangaroo Court." It was a very simple proceeding. I had to promise that I would always do my share of the necessary cleaning and washing, and also be honest and fair in judging the cases which might come up for trial.

Since then I have had opportunities of studying other "Kangaroo Courts," which have all been very much like the one I have described. They are both socialistic and autocratic, and at times they are very funny. But wherever they are they command the respect of jail-birds, and if a prisoner insults the court he is punished very severely. Moreover, it avails him nothing to complain to the authorities. He has too many against him, and the best thing he can do is to become one of them as soon as possible.

Other clubs of this same impromptu character are

simple makeshifts, which last sometimes a week, and sometimes but a day, if a more substantial amusement can be found to take their place. One, of which I was a member, existed for six hours only. It was organized to pass the time until a train came along to carry the men into a neighboring city. They selected a king and some princes, and called the club the "Royal Flush." Every half-hour a new king was chosen, in order to give as many members as possible the privileges which these offices carried with them. They were not especially valuable, but nevertheless novel enough to be entertaining. The king, for instance, had the right to order any one to fill his pipe or bring him a drink of water, while the princes were permitted to call the commoners all sorts of names as long as their official dignity lasted. So far as I know, they have never met since that afternoon camp on the prairies of Nebraska; and if they are comfortably seated in some favorite saloon, I can safely say that not one of them would care to exchange places with any half-hour king.

A little experience I had some time ago in New York will show how well posted the Natives are regarding these favorite saloons. I was calling on an old friend at a saloon in Third Avenue at the time. After I had told him of my plan to visit certain Western cities, and had mentioned some of them, he said:

"Well, you wan' ter drop in at the Half in State Street when you strike Chi [Chicago]; 'n' doan' forget Red's place in Denver, 'n' Dutch Mary's in Omaha. They 'll treat you square. Jes left Mary's place 'bout a week ago, 'n' never had a better time. Happy all the while, 'n' one day nearly tasted meself, felt so good. There 's nothin' like knowin' such places, you know. 'F you get into a strange town, takes you a ter'ble while to find yer fun 'less yer posted. But you 'll be all right at Red's 'n' Mary's, dead sure."

So the stranger is helped along in low life, and the Natives take just as much pride in passing him on to other friends and other clubs as does the high-life club-man. It gives them a feeling of importance, which is one of their main gratifications.

VII

Of the Old Bucks,—the superannuated outcasts,—and their club life, there is very little to say. Walk into any low dive in any city where they congregate, and you can see the whole affair. They sit there on the benches in tattered clothes, and rest their chins on crooked sticks or in their hands, and glare at one another with bloodshot eyes. Between drinks they discuss old times, old pals, old winnings, and then wonder what the new times amount to. And now and then, when in the mood, they throw a little crude thought on politics into the air. I have heard them discuss home rule, free trade, the Eastern question, and at the same time crack a joke on a hungry mosquito. A bit of wit, nasty or otherwise, will double them up in an instant, and then they cough and scramble to get their equilibrium again.

Late at night, when they can sit no longer on the whittled benches, and the bartender orders them home, they crawl away to musty lodging-houses and lie down in miserable bunks. The next morning they are on hand again at the same saloon, with the same old jokes and the same old laughs. They keep track of their younger pals if they can, and do their best to hold together their close relationships, and as one of their number tumbles down and dies, they remember his good points, and call for another beer. The Natives help them along now and then, and even the boys give them a dime on special occasions. But as they never need very much, and as low life is often the only one they know, they find it not very difficult to pick their way on to the end. If you pity them they are likely to laugh at you, and I have even known them to ask a city missionary if he would not take a drink with them.

To think of enticing such men into decent clubs is absurd; the only respectable place they ever enter is a reading-room—and then not to read. No, indeed! Watch them in Cooper Union. Half the time their newspapers are upside down and they are dozing. One eye is always on the alert, and the minute they think you are watching they grip the newspaper afresh, fairly pawing the print with their greasy fingers in their eagerness to carry out the rôle they have assumed. One day, in such a place, I scraped acquaintance with one of them, and, as if to show that it was the literary attraction which brought him there, he suddenly asked me in a most confidential tone what I thought of Tennyson. Of course I thought a good deal of him, and said so, but I had hardly finished before the old fellow querulously remarked:

MIDNIGHT.

"Don' cher think the best thing he ever did was that air 'Charge of the Seventeen Hundred'?"

VIII

I HAVE already said that, so far as the older outcasts are concerned, there is but little chance of helping them by respectable clubs; they are too fixed in their ways, and the best method of handling them is to destroy their own clubs and punish the members. The "scrappin' gang," for example, should be treated with severe law, whenever and wherever it shows its bloody hand, and if such a course were adopted and followed it would accomplish more good than any other conceivable method. The same treatment must be applied to the associations of other Natives, for the more widely they are separated and thus prevented from concourse the better will it be. It is their gregariousness which makes it so difficult to treat with them successfully, and until they can be dealt with separately, man for man, and in a prison-cell if necessary, not much can be accomplished. The evils in low life are contagious, and to be treated scientifically they must be quarantined and prevented from spreading. Break up its gangs. Begin at their beginnings. For let two outcasts have even but a little influence over a weak human being, and there are three outcasts; give them a few more similar chances, and there will be a gang.

I would not have any word of mine lessen the growing interest in man's fellow-man, or discourage by so much as a pen-stroke the brotherly influences on the "fallen brother" which are embodied in neighborhood guilds and college settlements of the present, but I am deeply convinced that there is a work these organizations cannot, must not, do. That work must be done by law and government. Vice must be punished, and the vicious sequestrated. Public spirit and citizenship duly appreciated and exercised must precede philanthropy in the slums. Government, municipal and State, must be a John the Baptist, preparing the way and making the paths straight, ere the embodied love of man and love of God can walk safely and effectively therein.

IV

THE AMERICAN TRAMP CONSIDERED GEOGRAPHICALLY

SOME years ago I was sitting, one spring afternoon, on a railroad-tie on "The Dope"[1] when New York Barcas appeared on the scene. There was nothing very peculiar about Barcas, except his map of the United States. Not that he ever set up to be a topographer, or aspired to any rivalry with Johnston, Kiepert, or Zell; but, like the ancients, Barcas had his known and his unknown world, and, like them again, he described the land he knew just as if it was all the world there was. I came to know Barcas's map in this wise:

We were both talking about certain tramp districts in the community, and I noticed that his idea of north, south, east, and west was somewhat different from mine. So, in order that our conversation might not be troubled with petty arguments on geographical boundaries, I asked him to map out the country for me according to his "best light"; and this is how he did it. He took out his pencil and drew a line from

[1] The Baltimore and Ohio Railroad—called "The Dope" because it is so greasy.

the Canadian frontier through Chicago to St. Louis, and another line from the Atlantic through Washington to the same point, and called all the territory north of the last-named boundary the East. He drew still another line from St. Louis to the Pacific coast, and called all the States north of this and west of Chicago the West. His North comprised all Canada, but he considered the province of Quebec the most prominent tramp territory in this district. His South was all that remained below his equatorial line, but the eastern part of it he nicknamed Niggerland, while the western part, bordering on the Pacific Ocean, he called the Coast.

This was the extent of Barcas's geography when I knew him. He seemed to realize that there are other countries in the world besides this one which he and his *confrères* consider laid out for their own particular benefit; nevertheless, in daily life and conversation the other divisions of the world are so conscientiously ignored for all practical purposes that North America may safely be said to comprise the American tramp's general idea of the earth. He knows well enough that he has brothers in other lands, but he considers them so unlucky in being left to ply their trade outside of his own peculiar paradise that he feels it necessary to ignore them. For in spite of the constitutional Bohemianism of his nature, he is still far from being a cosmopolitan. If he has suffering brethren in other communities, his heart does not throb for their sorrow. No, indeed! He simply says: "Why don't they get out o' those blasted holes and come over here? This is the only country for the tramp."

There is a great deal of truth in this, and my purpose in this chapter is to give an account of tramp traits, successes, and failures in this land of freedom. I shall take up the various districts as Barcas indicated them, not, however, because his points of the compass are at all typical or representative. No; Barcas's map is not for general circulation, and for this very good reason it would probably be difficult to find ten vagrants whose views would coincide with his or with those of any other ten idlers. This is a peculiarity of the vagabond, and it must be excused, for it has its *raison d'être.*

THE NORTH

THIS district (Canada) hardly belongs to the real American vagabondage. It is true that the hobo crosses the frontier now and then, and makes a short journey into Quebec, but it can scarcely be called a trip on business. It is undertaken more for the sake of travel, and a desire to see "them fellers up in Canady," and the scenery too, if the traveler is a lover of nature, as many hoboes are. As a rule, Canada is left pretty much in the hands of the local vagabonds, who are called "Frenchies." I have never thoroughly explored their territory, and, unfortunately, cannot write as definitely and comprehensively about their character as I would wish to do. However, the following facts are true as far as they go.

The main clan of Canadian tramps is composed of French-Canadians and Indians. I have never met a genuine tramp of this class who was born in France proper, yet I can well believe that there are such. The language of these beggars is a jargon partly French and partly English, with a small hobo vocabulary added thereto. Only a very few American tramps can speak this queer lingo. I have met a gipsy now and then who at least understood it, and I account for this on the ground that a large number of the words resemble those in the gipsy dialect. *Pâno*, for instance, means bread in both languages.

To be a successful beggar in Canada, one must be able to speak French, for Quebec is one of the main tramp districts, and the local population uses this language principally. The "Galway" (Catholic priest) is perhaps the best friend of the Frenchies; at any rate, this has been my experience. He gives alms ten times where a peasant gives once, and when a vagabond can find a cloister or a convent, he is almost sure to be well taken care of. The peasants, it must be remembered, are about all the Frenchies have after the Galway. To show how wise they are in doling out their charity, it is only necessary to say that the usual Frenchy is content when he gets his three meals a day without working. And as for myself, I can say that I have gone hungry for over thirty hours at a stretch in Canada, and this, too, although I was careful to visit every house that I passed. But the Canadian tramp is evidently satisfied with small rewards, else he could not live long in his chosen district. As I know him, he is a slow-going fellow, fond of peace and quiet, and seldom desirous of those wild "slopping-ups" in American trampdom for which so much money is needed. If he can only have some outcast woman, or "sister," as he calls her, to accompany him on his travels, and to make homelike and comfortable the little tent which he often carries; and if he can have his daily *pâno* and his usual supply of *dohun* (tobacco), he is a comparatively happy fellow. He reminds me more of the European tramp in general character than any other human parasite I can think of; and I shall be exceedingly sorry if he ever gets a foothold in the United States, because he is a vagrant down to the core, and this can hardly be said as yet of most American tramps. It is almost impossible to touch his emotions, and he usually looks upon the world as his enemy. He can hardly be called a victim of liquor, but rather the victim of an ill-matched parentage. He is often on the mercy of the world before he knows how he came into it, and it is not wonderful that he should drift into a class where no questions are asked, and where even the murderer is received with some distinction. To reform such a man requires that the social polity itself be permeated by a higher order of ethics than governs it at present —a truth quite as applicable in certain districts of the United States as elsewhere.

THE EAST

THE tramps of this part of the country represent the main intelligence as well as "respectability" of the brotherhood. They also comprise the most successful criminal element. But of course the vocation of the great majority is simply begging. To tell exactly where they thrive, and to particularize carefully, would take a book by itself, and the most I can do is to give a very general idea of the district.

New England, as a whole, is at present poor begging territory for those vagabonds who are not clever and not able to dress fairly well. Boston is the beggar's metropolis as well as the New England millionaire's, and, until a few years ago, Bughouse Mary's Tramp Home was as much a Boston institution as Tremont Temple or the Common. One could find there tramps of all grades of intelligence, cleanliness, and manners. And even in the streets I have often been able to pick out the "begging brothers" by the score from the general crowd. But it must not be forgotten that a city offers privileges to beggars which the rural districts deny, and probably, if the police authorities were more diligent than they are now, even Boston could be rid of the great majority of its worst loafers. I must admit, however, that it will be difficult ever to banish the entire tramp tribe, for some of them are exceedingly clever, and when decently clad can play the rôle of almost any member of society. For instance, I tramped through Connecticut and Rhode Island once with a "fawny man."[1] Both of us were respectably dressed, and, according to my companion's suggestion, we posed as strolling students, and always offered to pay for our meals and lodging; but the offer was never accepted. Why? Because the farmers "considered themselves repaid by the interesting accounts of our travels, and talks about politics," etc. My friend was very sharp and keen, and carried on a successful trade in spurious jewelry with some of the

[1] A peddler of bogus jewelry.

foolish country boys, when he was not discussing the probabilities of the presidential election. I am sure that I could travel through New England to-day, if respectably clad, and be gratuitously entertained wherever I should go; and simply because the credulity of the charitable is so favorable to "traveling gentlemen."

One of the main reasons why Massachusetts is such poor territory for the usual class of vagrants is its jail system. In many of these jails the order and discipline are superb, and work is required of the prisoners—and work is the last thing a real tramp ever means to undertake. I cannot help looking forward to very gratifying results to trampdom from the influence of the present Massachusetts jail system. For anything which brings the roving beggar into contact with sobriety and labor is bound to have a beneficial effect. New York, New Jersey, Pennsylvania, Ohio, and Michigan are all fairly good tramp States, and all swarm with allowed beggars. The most remarkable feature of vagrancy in New York State is that wonderful town known among vagrants as the "City" and also as "York." This is the most notorious tramp-nest in the United States. I have walked along the Bowery of an afternoon, and counted scores of men who never soil their hands with labor, and beg on an average a dollar a day. Even the policemen of this city are often friends of beggars, and I have seldom met a hobo who was very angry with a New York "bull." As a rule, the police officer, when finding tramps drunk on door-steps or begging, says in a coarse and brutal voice, "Get out!" and possibly gives them a rap with his club, but it is altogether too seldom that the beggar is arrested. One rather odd phase of tramp life in New York city is the shifting boundary-line that marks the charity of the town. Several years ago Eighty-ninth Street was about as far up-town as one could secure fair rewards for diligent begging. Now one can see tramps, on a winter night especially, scattered all along One Hundred and Twenty-fifth Street, not because this street is the only "good one," but because it is so "good" that better profits are realized than in those farther down. And for clothes, I have always found Harlem more profitable than other parts of the city. New York city is also one of the best places in the country for "snaring a kid"—persuading some youngster to accompany an older beggar on the road. There are so many ragamuffins lying around loose and unprotected in the more disreputable quarters of the town that it is only necessary to tell them a few "ghost-stories" (fancy tales of tramp life) to make them follow the story-teller as unresistingly as the boys of Hamelin marched after the Pied Piper. Almost every third boy that one meets in American vagabondage hails from "York." This accounts for the fact that several tramps of New York birth have the same name, for even the beggar's ingenuity is not capable of always hitting upon a unique cognomen. I have met fully a dozen roadsters having the name of "Yorkey," "New York Bob," "New York Whitey," "New York Slim," etc., which makes it not only the fashion but a necessity, when hearing a city tramp's name, to ask which Whitey, which Yorkey, or which Bob it is, and a personal description is usually necessary before the fellow can be distinguished.

Over in New Jersey, I think, there are more tramps to the square mile than in any other State, excepting Pennsylvania. The neighborhood around Newark is simply infested with beggars, who meet there on their way into and out of New York city. They often have a hang-out on the outskirts of the town, where they camp quite unmolested, unless they get drunk and draw their razors, which is more than common with Eastern tramps. It is surprising, too, how well they are fed, when one remembers that they have "battered" in this community for years. It is in Pennsylvania, however, that the tramp is best fed, while I still maintain that he gets more money in New York city. I do not know of a town or village in the Keystone State where a decently clad roadster cannot get all that he cares to eat without doing a stroke of work in payment. The jails are also a great boon to the fraternity. In the majority of them there is no work to do, while some furnish tobacco and the daily papers. Consequently, in winter, one can see tramps sitting comfortably on benches drawn close to the fire, and reading their morning paper, and smoking their after-breakfast pipe, as complacently and calmly as the merchant in his counting-room. Here they find refuge from the storms of winter, and make themselves entirely at home.

Ohio and Indiana, although fairly friendly to tramps, are noted for certain "horstile" features. The main one of these is the well-known "timber-lesson"—clubbing at the hands of the inhabitants of certain towns. I experienced this muscular instruction at one unfortunate time in my life, and I must say that it is one of the best remedies for vagabondage that exist. But it is very crude and often cruel. In company with two other tramps, I was made to run a gantlet extending from one end of the town of Oxford, Indiana, to the other. The boys and men who were "timbering" us threw rocks and clubbed us most diligently. I came out of the scrape with a rather sore back, and should probably have suffered more had I not been able to run with rather more than the usual speed. One of my fellow-sufferers, I heard, was in a hospital for some time. My other companion had his eye gouged terribly, and I fancy that he will never visit that town again. Apart from the "timber" custom, which, I understand, is now practised in other communities also, these two States are good begging districts. There are plenty of tramps within their boundaries, and when "the eagles are gathered together," the carcass to be preyed upon is not far away.

The other States of the East have so much in common with those already described that little need be said of them. Chicago, however, deserves a paragraph. This city, although troubled with hundreds of tramps, and noted for its generosity, is nevertheless a terror to evil-doers in this, that its policemen handle beggars according to law whenever they can catch them. Instead of the tiresomely reiterated "Get out!" and the brutal club-swinging in New York, one gets accustomed in Chicago to "thirty days in the Bridewell." I know this to be true, for I have

A "TIMBER LESSON."

been in Chicago as a tramp for days at a time, and have investigated every phase of tramp life in the city. Of course there are thousands of cases where the beggar is not caught, but I maintain that when he is found he is given a lesson almost as valuable as the one over in Indiana. The cities in the East which the vagabond considers his own are New York ("York"), Philadelphia ("Phillie"), Buffalo, Boston, Baltimore, Chicago (here he is very often deceived), Detroit (another place where he is deceived), and Cincinnati.

Just a word about the Eastern tramp himself. His language is a slang as nearly English as possible. Some words, however, would not be understood anywhere outside of the clan. His personal traits are great conceit, cleverness, and a viciousness which, although corresponding in the main to the same in other parts of the country, is nevertheless a little more refined, if I may use that word, than elsewhere. The number of his class it is difficult to determine definitely, but I believe that he and his companions are many thousands strong. His earnings, so far as my experience justifies me in judging, range from fifty cents to over two dollars a day, besides food, provided he begs steadily. I know from personal observation that an intelligent beggar can average the above amount in cities, and sometimes in smaller towns.

THE WEST

VAGABONDAGE in this part of the country is composed principally of "blanket-stiffs," "ex-prushuns," "gay-cats," and a small number of recognized tramps who, however, belong to none of the foregoing classes, and are known simply as "Westerners." The blanket-stiffs are men (or sometimes women) who walk, or "drill," as they say, from Salt Lake City to San Francisco about twice a year, begging their way from ranch to ranch, and always carrying their blankets with them. The ex-prushuns are young fellows who have served their apprenticeship as kids in the East, and are in the West "looking for revenge," *i. e.*, seeking some kid whom they can press into their service and compel to beg for them. The gay-cats are men who will work for "very good money," and are usually in the West in the autumn to take advantage of the high wages offered to laborers during the harvest season. The Westerners have no unique position, and resemble the Easterner, except that they as well as the majority of other Western rovers drink alcohol, diluted in a little water, in preference to other liquors. On this account, and also because Western tramps very often look down upon Eastern roadsters as "tenderfeet," there is not that brotherly feeling between the East and the West in vagrancy that one might expect. The Easterners think the Western brethren too rough and wild, while the latter think the former too tame. However, there is a continual intercourse kept up by the passing of Westerners to the East, and vice versa, and when neither party is intoxicated the quarrel seldom assumes very dangerous proportions.

Of the States in the Western district, I think that Illinois, Iowa, Wisconsin, Minnesota, Colorado, Washington, and a part of California are the best for tramps.

Iowa is usually liked very much by roadsters, but its temperance principles used to be thoroughly hated, as were also those of Kansas. It is needless to say, however, that in the river towns a tramp could usually have all the liquor he could stand. I was in Burlington once when there was a Grand Army celebration, which the tramps were attending (!) in full force; and the amount of "booze" that flowed was something astounding for a "dry" State. Nearly every vagrant that I met had a bottle, and when I asked where it came from, I was directed to an open saloon! A great fad in Nebraska, Iowa, and Kansas is to beg from the hotels. I have received hospitality in these places when I could get absolutely nothing at the private houses. This is especially true when the cook is a negro. He will almost always give a beggar a "set-down" (square meal), and sometimes he will include a bundle of food "for the journey." Still another fad when I knew the country was to call at the penitentiaries for clothes. I saw a man go into the Fort Madison "pen" (Iowa) one day with clothes not only tattered and torn, but infested with vermin. When he returned, I hardly knew him, he was so well dressed. Stillwater Penitentiary in Minnesota also had a notoriety for benevolence of this sort, but I cannot affirm this by personal observation.

Wisconsin, although not exactly unfriendly to tramps, is nevertheless a "poor" State, because it has no very large city and is peopled largely by New-Englanders. Milwaukee is perhaps the best place for a beggar. The Germans will give him all the beer he wants, and feed him well besides, for they are the most unwisely generous people in this country. Where they have a settlement, a tramp can thrive almost beyond description. For instance, in Milwaukee, as in other Wisconsin towns, he can batter for breakfast successfully from six o'clock until eleven o'clock in the morning, and is everywhere sure of a cup of coffee. I once attempted in Milwaukee to see just how many dinners I could get inside the ordinary dinner-time, and after an hour and a half I returned to the hang-out with three bundles of food, besides three dinners which had already been disposed of. I could have continued my dining indefinitely, had my capacity continued.

San Francisco and Denver are the main dependence of tramps in the West. If one meets a westward-bound beggar beyond the Mississippi, he may usually infer that the man is on his way to Denver; and if he is found on the other side of that city, and still westward bound, his destination is almost sure to be "'Frisco," or at least Salt Lake City, which is also a popular hang-out. Denver has a rather difficult task to perform, for the city is really a junction from which tramps start on their travels in various directions, and consequently the people have more than their share of beggars to feed. I have met in the city, at one time, as many as one hundred and fifty bona-fide tramps, and every one had been in the town for over a week. The people, however, do not seem to feel the burden of this riffraff addition to the population; at any rate, they befriend it most kindly. They seem especially willing to give money. I once knew a kid who averaged in Denver nearly three dollars a day for almost a week, by standing in front of shops and "battering" the ladies as they passed in and out. He was a handsome child, and this, of course, must be taken into consideration, for his success was phenomenal.

"'Frisco" is even better than Denver, furnishing districts in which tramps can thrive and remain for a longer time unmolested. There are more low lodging-houses, saloons, and dives; and there is also here a large native class whose character is not much higher than that of the tramp himself, so that he is lost among them—often to his own advantage. This difficulty of identification is a help to roadsters, for there is nothing that pleases and helps them so much as to be considered "town bums," the latter being allowed privileges which are denied to strangers.

In the estimation of the tramp the West does not rank with the East. The railroads are not so "good"; there are fewer cities; even the towns are too far apart; in some districts the people are too poor; and taking the country as a whole, the inhabitants are by no means so generous. I doubt whether the average gains of Western beggars amount to more than twenty-five cents a day. In "'Frisco" and Denver, as well as in a few other large towns, begging is of course much more remunerative, but in the rural parts the average wage of a beggar is even below twenty cents a day, besides food; at least, this is the result of my observation. In general the Western tramp is rough, often kind-hearted, wild and reckless; he always has his razor with him, and will "cut" whenever there is provocation. The blanket-stiff is perhaps the least violent of all; his long walking-tours seem to quiet his passion somewhat, and overcome his naturally wild tendencies. The ex-prushun is exactly the opposite, and I know of no roadster so cruel and mean to the weak as this young fellow, who is, after all, only a graduated kid. This is not so surprising, however, when one recollects that for years he has been subject to the whims and passions of various "jockers," or protectors, and naturally enough, when released from his bondage, he is only too likely to wreak his pent-up feelings on the nearest victim. After a year or two of Western life he either subsides and returns to the East, or becomes more intimately connected with the true criminal class, and attempts to do "crooked work." Several of the most notorious and successful thieves have been ex-prushuns.

Just how many tramps there are in the West it is even more difficult to decide than in the East, because they are scattered over such wide territory. Experience makes me believe, however, that there are fully half as many voluntary idlers in this part of the country as in the East. And the great majority of them, I fear, are even more irreclaimable than their comrades in other communities. They laugh at law, sneer at morality, and give free rein to appetite. Because of this many of them never reach middle age.

THE SOUTH

TRAMP life here has its own peculiarities. There are white loafers known as "hoboes," which is the general technical term among white tramps everywhere, and there are the "shinies," who are negroes. The odd part of it all is that these two classes hardly know each other; not that they hate each other or have any color-line, but simply that they apparently cannot associate together with profit. The hobo seems to do better when traveling only with hoboes, and the shiny lives much more comfortably in his own clan. My explanation of this fact is this: both parties have learned by experience that alms are much more generously given to a white man when alone than when in company with a negro. This, of course, does not apply anywhere but in the South, for a colored tramp is just as well treated in the East and West as a white one.

My knowledge of the shinies is very meager, for I was compelled to travel as a hobo when studying vagrancy in the South, and I have never met a member of that class who knew very much about his negro *confrères.* From all that I can gather, however, I think that they resemble very closely the gay-cats, for they do work now and then, although their being on the road is usually quite voluntary, unless their natural laziness can be considered as a force impelling them into trampdom. Their dialect is as different from the usual tramp lingo as black from white, and I have never been able to master its orthography.

As the South in the main is only skimmed over by most white tramps, and as a few cities represent the true strongholds of vagrancy, it is unnecessary to give any detailed account of this region. Besides, it is only in winter that many tramps, excepting, of course, the shinies, are found here, and consequently there is not very much to describe, for they go into this part of the country principally to "rest up" and shun the cold weather prevalent in other districts. The chief destinations of wandering beggars in the South are New Orleans, St. Augustine, Jacksonville, Tallahassee, and Atlanta. Several towns in Texas are also popular "resting-places," but usually the tramps in Texas have begged their money in other States, and are there principally for "a great slopping-up," for which dissipation Texas furnishes much more suitable accommodations than any other State in the Union. The usual time for Eastern and Western tramps to start South is in October. During this month large squads of vagabonds will be found traveling toward "Orleans." I once was on an Illinois Central freight-train when seventy-three tramps were fellow-passengers, and nearly every one was bound for either Florida or Louisiana. These two States may almost be called the South so far as hoboes are concerned. New Orleans is especially a tramp-nest, and ranks second to New York in hospitality, according to my experience. In the older part of the town one can find beggars of almost every nationality, and its low dives are often supported by the visiting knights of the road. Begging, as they do, very fair sums of money, and being only too willing to spend it quickly, they afford these innkeepers of the baser sort very fair rewards for keeping up their miserable "hotels." A well-trained beggar can very often average a dollar a day in New Orleans if he begs diligently. But he must be careful not to be arrested, for the jails in the South are man-killing holes in many and many an instance. Even in the East and West several of the county prisons are bad enough, but they cannot compare in filth to some of the miserable cells of the South.

Jacksonville and St. Augustine are good hang-outs for tramps, and in the winter such visitors are very numerous. They make a very decent living off the transient tourists at these winter resorts. But success is so short and precarious there that many hoboes prefer New Orleans, on account of its steadier character, and seldom visit the other towns. Besides, to batter around the hotels in St. Augustine one should be respectably clad, and polite in manner and bearing, which, in most cases, involves far too much trouble.

The most generous people in the South are the poor, but not the negro poor, who, according to my experience, are by no means large-hearted. Take them in the East or West, and they are friendly enough, but on their native heath they are, as a rule, stingy. I have received much more hospitality from the "poor whites" than from any other people. The negroes, when I asked them for something to eat, would say: "Oh, go and ask the Missis. I can't give you anything"; and when I would call upon the "missis," she was not to be seen. But the poor white would invite me into his shanty, and treat me as well as was in his power. It was not much, I must admit; but the spirit was willing though the pantry was nearly empty. In West Virginia, for instance, I have been entertained by some of the "hill people" in their log cabins in the most hospitable manner. The obvious reason of this is a scarcity of tramps; when they are few, generosity is great, and the few get the benefit.

If the students of this particular phase of sociology will only look minutely and personally into the conditions under which trampdom thrives and increases in our country, Barcas's map may yet become famous. Charles Godfrey Leland once wrote an article entitled "Wanted: Sign-Posts for Ginx's Baby." It would seem that his prayer has been answered, and that this unwanted, unprovided-for member of society has found his way through forest and mountains, over rivers and prairies, till now he knows the country far better than the philanthropist who would gladly get on his track. If this topographical survey shall serve to bring him nearer what should be, and what I am convinced aims to be, a source of betterment for him, Barcas will not have lived in vain.

V

THE CITY TRAMP

VAGABONDS specialize nowadays quite as much as other people. The fight for existence makes them do it. Although a few tramps are such all-round men that they can succeed almost anywhere, there are a great many others who find that they must devote their time to one distinct line of begging in order to succeed. So to-day we have all sorts of hoboes. There are house-beggars, office-beggars, street-beggars, old-clothes beggars, and of late years still another specialization has become popular in vagabondage. It is called "land-squatting," which means that the beggar in question has chosen a particular district for his operations. Of course, a large number of tramps still go over all the country, but it is becoming quite customary for vagabonds to pick out certain States and counties for their homes. The country, as a whole, is so large that no beggar can ever really know it on business principles, and some clever beggars not long ago decided that it is better to know thoroughly a small district than to have only a general knowledge of the entire continent. Consequently our large cities have become overrun with tramps who make them their homes the year round, till America can almost compete with England in the number of her "city vags." There is no large town in the United States that does not support its share, and it is seldom that these tramps are natives of the towns in which they beg. In New York, for example, there are scores of beggars who were born in Chicago, and vice versa. They have simply picked out the city which pleases them most and gone there. In time they become so numerous that it is found necessary to specialize still further, and even to divide the town itself into districts, and to assign them to distinct kinds of begging. It is of these specialists in vagrancy that I intend to write in this chapter.

The lowest type is what is called in tramp parlance the "tomato-can vag." In New York city, which has its full quota of these miserable creatures, they live in boxes, barrels, cellars, and nooks and corners of all sorts, where they can curl up and have a "doss" (sleep). They get their food, if it can be called that, by picking over the refuse in the slop-barrels and tomato-cans of dirty alleys. They beg very little, asking usually for the stale beer they find now and then in the kegs near saloons. Money is something that they seldom touch, and yet a good many of them have been first-class criminals and hoboes in their day.

I used to know a tomato-can tramp who lived for several months in a hogshead near the East-Side docks of New York. I visited him one night when on a stroll in that part of the city, and had a talk with him about his life. After he had reeled off a fine lot of yarns, he said:

"Why, I remember jes lots o' things. I 's been a

TOMATO-CAN TRAMPS.

crook, I 's been a moocher, an' now I 's shatin' on me uppers [I am broke]. Why, what I 's seen would keep them blokes up there in Cooper Union readin' all winter, I guess."

This was probably true. He had been everywhere, had seen and done nearly everything which the usual outcast can see and do, and he wound up his life simply "shatin' on his uppers." No one will have any dealings with such a tramp except the men and women in his own class. He is hated by all the beggars above him, and they "do" him every chance they get.

A fair example of this class hatred came under my notice in London, England. I was walking along Holborn one evening when I was suddenly accosted by an old man who wanted me to give him a drink.

"I would n't ask ye," he said, "'cept that I 'm nearly dyin' o' cold. Can' cher help a feller out?"

There was something so pitiful about him that I decided to take him into a public house. I picked out the lowest one in the neighborhood. The place was filled with beggars and criminals, but they were all of a higher class than my friend. However, I called for his gin, and told him to sit down. It was soon evident that the old man was an unwelcome guest, for even the bartender looked at him crossly. He noticed this, and began to grumble, and in a few minutes was in a quarrel with some of the men. The bartender told him to be quiet, but he claimed that he had as good a right to talk as any one else. He was finally put out, although I made all the remonstrance I dared. I started to leave too, but was prevented. This made me angry, and I turned on the men, and said:

"What right have you fellows to treat me this way? I came in with the old man respectably enough."

"Oh, come up 'n' 'ave a drink," said one of the men. "Don't get 'uffy. Come up 'n' 'ave a bitter."

Then another said: "Say, was that old feller any relation o' yourn? 'Cause ef 'e was, we 'll fetch 'im back; but ef 'e wa'n't, 'e kin stay where 'e is. 'E don't belong in 'ere."

"Why is that?" I asked.

"Why, don' cher know that 'e ain't o' our class? 'E 's a' ole can-moocher. 'E ain't got no right 'ere."

"Well, do you mean to say that you own this place, and no one can come in who is not of your choosing?"

"The case is jes this, 'n' you know it: it 's our biz to do anybody out o' our class."

"Would you 'do' me if you had a chance?"

"Bet cher life!"

I got out safely soon after this, and had gained knowledge for the future.

But, hated as he is by the more successful vagabonds, the tomato-can tramp is just as kind-hearted and jovial as any of them. And for fair treatment I will risk him every time. As a rule, he is an old man, sometimes over seventy years of age. He dresses most outlandishly, seldom having any two garments of the same color, and what he has are tattered and torn. His beard and hair are allowed to grow as long as they can, and usually give him the appearance of a hermit. Indeed, that is just what he is. He has exiled himself from all that is good and refined, and is like a leper even to his brethren. It is just such a life as his, however, to which all tramps that drink, as most outcasts do, are tending. It matters not how clever a criminal or beggar a man may be, if he is a victim of liquor, and lives long enough, he is sure to end as a tomato-can tramp. There is a suction in low life which draws men continually lower. It is an inferno of various little worlds, and each has its own pitch of degradation.

The next higher type of the town tramp is the "two-cent dosser"—the man who lives in stale-beer shops. In New York he is usually to be found about Mulberry Bend, the last resort of metropolitan outcasts before dropping down into the "barrel-and-box gentry." This district supports the queer kind of lodging-house called by the men who use it the "two-cent doss." It is really a makeshift for a restaurant, and is occasionally kept by an Italian. The lodgers come in late in the evening, pay two cents for some stale beer or coffee, and then scramble for "spots" on the benches or floor. All nationalities are represented. I have found in one of these places Chinamen, Frenchmen, Germans, Italians, Poles, negroes, Irishmen, Englishmen, and "'Mer'cans," and they were all as happy as could be. They beg just enough to keep them in "booze," their food being found mainly at "free lunches." Like the tomato-can tramp, they have little intercourse with beggars above them. By this I mean, of course, that they know they will not be treated sociably outside of their class, and decide very wisely to remain where they belong. They rarely leave a town which they have picked out as a home, and some of them never even get out of their narrow district.

In Chicago, for instance, there is a "joint" near Madison Street in which some men simply live day and night, excepting the few hours they spend in looking for the pennies they need. In the daytime they sit on the benches and talk shop, and at night they lie on the floor. There is a watchman who cares for them at night; he sleeps near the door in order to let in any belated beggar. But he first lights his candle, and commands the beggar to show how much money he has. If it is five cents, the price of a mug of beer, he is allowed to enter.

In New Orleans I once saw a place somewhat similar, the only difference being that at night ropes were stretched across the bar-room for the men to lean on while sleeping. Some persons fail to note much difference in the lives of the two-cent dossers and the tomato-can tramps, but the two-cent dossers make a sharp class distinction out of their greater privilege. Personally, I should rather live in a barrel or box than in a joint, if only for the sake of cleanliness. The joint is simply a nest of vermin, and cannot be kept clean; whereas, if a man is careful and works hard, he can keep a barrel fairly habitable for himself, and with no other occupants. Still, I am sorry to say that few men who do live in barrels achieve or desire this success. The most unique feature of the two-cent dosser class is its apparent happiness. The men are always funny, and crack a joke as easily as they tell a lie. I remember most vividly a night in one of their joints in St. Louis. All night long some one was laughing and joking, and my questions always met a witty reply. I noticed, for instance, that several of the men were blind in one eye, and I asked the meaning of this.

"Ha! ha! Don' cher know? Why, it 's 'cause we 're lookin' fer work so hard."

Another man wanted to know whether I could tell him where he could get a "kid." I asked him what use he had for one.

"Oh, prushuns [kids] is val'able; when you 've got 'em, you 're treasurer of a company."

Nevertheless, these men very seldom have boys, because their life is too unexciting, and the lads will not stay with them. A prushun, as a rule, wants something livelier than loafing around saloons and corners, and consequently is rarely found in these two classes.

The other types of city vagabondage can be classified as the "lodgin'-house gang," with the exception of the room-beggar. I must therefore consider them in relation to their different styles of begging rather than living; for when once a beggar can live in any sort of lodging-house, he has a right to belong to the general crowd, no matter what he pays for his bed. The seven-center house, for instance, is considerably lower than the ten-center, but its being a lodging-house is sufficient to separate its inmates entirely from the two classes who live in boxes and beer-shops. And to make the classifying feature more intelligible, I shall give first a short account of the lodging-house in all its grades, omitting only those that are carried on by charity.

Beginning with the lowest, there is the seven-center, in which hammocks of a bad order are used as beds. The covering is very often the lodger's coat, unless he happens to have a blanket of his own. In winter there is a large stove in the middle of the sleeping-room, and this keeps things fairly warm. The usual lodger in this house is the town tramp, although the wandering hobo goes there too. I have also seen a few genuine seekers of work there, but never two nights running. One night is usually enough, and they sleep out in preference to mixing in such a crowd as the place shelters.

The ten-center is the next grade above, and is probably the most popular of all in the United States. It is built after various models, the commonest being the "double-decker," where the bunks are made of gas-pipe, one right above the other. In this case the bedding is a straw tick and a blanket; that is all, as a rule. Yet I have known sheets to be used. Another model is something like the forecastle of a ship. Around the walls several tiers of bunks are built, sometimes twelve feet high, and in the middle is the "sitting-room," with stove and chairs. Occasionally the only bedding is straw, there being no blanket of any kind. The class of men found in places of this type is hard to describe; the town tramp is there, and so is almost every other kind of vagabond. It is a sort of cesspool into which are drained all sorts of outcasts, and the only way to distinguish them is to know them personally. Young and old, the intelligent and the ignorant, the criminal and the newsboy, all are found in the ten-center.

The fifteen-center comes next, and is very much like the ten-center, except that its customers are a little more orderly, and that it furnishes lockers into which the lodgers can put their clothes. This latter point is really the *raison d'être* of the fifteen-cent lodging-house, according to my experience. At any rate, I have failed to see any other good reason for charging five cents more for the beds, which are usually no better than those in the ten-center.

In the other grades, at twenty and twenty-five cents a night a man can have a little room to himself; by "room" I mean a sort of cell without a roof, in which is a cot, a chair (sometimes), and a locker. I slept in one of these houses in the Bowery one night. The office and sitting-room were comparatively cozy, and the lodgers were respectable so far as dress and general manner were concerned. Up-stairs in the sleeping-apartments things were not so pleasant. There was a bad odor about everything, and the beds were decidedly unclean, as are most beds in most lodging-houses. I left word at the office that I wished to be called at seven o'clock in the morning, and my order was distinctly obeyed, for about half-past six I was wakened by a man poking me in the ribs with a long stick leveled at me from over the partition-wall. After the man had poked me with the stick, he said, "Eh, bloke, time to get up."

Some tramps consider this style, and it probably is in their cases, for they are accustomed to all sorts of places, and the twenty-five-center is their nearest approach to hotel life. Although I have probably overlooked some exceptional institutions in this general description of lodging-houses, I have nevertheless given a fair account of the usual homes of the "lodgin'-house gang." And, as I said before, the town tramp is mixed up in this gang so promiscuously that to pick him out of the general crowd necessitates a personal encounter. All that I can do now is to portray him in his various guises as a beggar. I shall take four types to do this—the street-beggar, the house-beggar, the office-beggar, and the old-clothes beggar. These are all well-known characters in city vagabondage.

The street-beggar is, I believe, the cleverest all-round vagabond in the world. He knows more about human nature than any other tramp of my acquaintance, and can read its weak points with surprising ease. I used to know a New York tramp of this kind who begged almost entirely of women as they walked along the streets, and he claimed that he could tell, the minute he had seen their eyes, whether it would pay to "tackle 'em." How he did this I do not pretend to know, and he himself could not tell, but it was true that he seldom judged a woman wrongly. Fifth Avenue was his beat, and he knew fully fifty women in that district who were sure to give him something. His main tricks, if I can call them that, were those of the voice rather than of the hand. He knew when to whine and when to "talk straight," and, best of all, he knew when to make people laugh. This is the highest accomplishment of the street-beggar, for when a person will laugh with him he is pretty sure to get something; and if he can succeed in picking out a certain number of "clients," as he calls them, who will laugh with him every week the year round, his living is assured. This is the business of the clever street-beggar; he must scrape acquaintance with enough people in his

A CITY TRAMP AT WORK.

chosen district to support him. It matters not to him whether he excites their pity or mirth so long as he gets their nickels and dimes. I knew a woman beggar of this sort whose main trick, or "capital," as she called it, was extreme faith in the chivalry of men. She would clutch a man by the coat-sleeve, and tragically exclaim:

"How dare you cast me off? Don't you know that I am a woman? Have you no mother or sisters? Would you treat them as you are treating me?"

Some men are so squeamishly and nervously chivalrous that they will be taken in by such a beggar every time.

Women very often make the keenest street-beggars. They are more original in posing and dressing, and if with their other talents they can also use their voices cleverly, they do very well. Speaking of posing reminds me of a woman who is usually to be found near the Alhambra music-hall in London. She dresses very quietly and neatly, and her entire manner is that of a lady. I believe that she really was one in her day, but liquor has made her a match-vender; and her clever pose and dress are so attractive that people give her three times the value of the matches which she sells them. This match-selling is the main trick of the London street-beggar. It is a trick of defense against the police, and at the same time a blind to the public. People think that men and women selling matches are trying to earn an honest living, and this is true sometimes; but, according to my observation, the majority of match-venders offer one hand to the public for alms, and carry their "lights" (matches) in the other.

The business of the house-beggar is obviously to know a certain number of good houses in his district, just as the street-beggar knows a certain number of people in his street or streets. And if he is a mendicant who can deal with women more successfully than with men, he must know just when to visit houses in order that only the women may be at home. If he is a beggar of this style, he usually carries a "jigger"—an artificially made sore, placed usually on an arm or leg. He calls at the front door and asks for "the lady." When she appears he "sizes her up" as best he can, and decides whether it will pay to use his jigger. If it is necessary, he prefaces this disgusting scene by an account of his hardships, and claims that he has been very badly burned. Then he shows his miserable sore, and few women are callous enough to see it without flinching. If they "squeal," as the tramp says, he is sure to be rewarded.

Another trick is to send around pretty little girls and boys to do the begging. A child will succeed at house-begging when an able-bodied man or woman will fail utterly, and the same is true of a very old man—the more of a centenarian he looks, the better. But better than any of these tricks is what is called the "faintin' gag." I myself had the benefit of an undertaking of this character in Indianapolis some years ago, and I know it works well. I got into the town one night, and was at a loss to know what to do, until I accidentally met an old hobo who was trying to make his living there as a city tramp. He had been in the place only a few days, and had not yet found his particular district. He was simply browsing about in search of it, and he suggested that we try a certain quarter of the town that he had not visited at all. We did try it, and, after visiting twenty houses, got only two pieces of bread and butter. This, naturally enough, made my partner angry, and he told me to go back to the hang-out while he went on another beat. I waited for him nearly an hour, when he returned with a "poke-out" (food given at the door) and a "sinker" (a dollar). I, of course, was surprised, and asked for details.

"Oh, I got 'em right 'nough," he said. "You see, after leavin' you, I was so dead horstile that I was ready for anythin', 'n' the first house I struck was a parson's. At first he did n't want to feed me at all, but I got into his settin'-room 'n' gave 'im a great story. I tole 'im that I was nearly a-dyin' with hunger, 'n' ef he did n't feed me, the s'ciety agen' cruelty to animals 'u'd prosecute 'im. Then I begun to reel a bit 'n' look faintin'-like, 'n' purty soon I flops right on the floor as ef I was dead. Then the racket begun. The parson called 'Wifey!' an' the both of 'em peppered 'n' salted me for about ten minutes, when I comes to an' looks better. Then they could n't feed me fast 'nough. I had pie, cake, 'n' a lot o' other things 'fore I wuz done, 'n' when I left the parson give me the sinker, 'n' 'wifey' the poke-out; hope to die ef they did n't. See? That 's the way ye got ter catch them parsons—right in the eye."

As the old-clothes beggar is only a subspecies of the house-begging class, he deserves mention under the same head. His business, as his name implies, lies principally in looking for old wearing-apparel, which he sells to dealers in such wares. Sometimes he even pays for his food in order to devote his entire time and talents to his specialty. In London, for instance, I know a trio of this sort who live in a cellar where they keep their "goods." I visited their place one afternoon, and one of the men was kind enough to let himself be interviewed about his business. My first question was how he begged.

"Well, o' course our first business is to wear bad togs. F'r instance, ef I 's beggin' fer shoes I wants to put on a pair thet 's all gone, else I can't get any more, 'n' the same when I 's beggin' fer coats 'n' 'ats. It 's no use tellin' people that you 're beggin' fer somebody else. They won't believe it."

Then I questioned him as to the sort of garments which were most profitable.

"Breeches. We kin sell 'em every time. 'Ats does pretty well too, 'n' ef we get good shoes we kin do a rattlin' business. One o' my pals made seven bob fer a week jes out o' shoes. Wimmenses' togs hain't up ter the men's; an' yet we does fairly well wid 'em too. In 'ats, f'r instance, we does fairly good, 'cause the gals knows where we lives, 'n' they comes right 'ere instid o' goin' ter the dealers. Petticoats is next best when we gets good ones, but we don't very often, 'cause these Whitechapel donners [girls] wants picter-like ones, 'n' we don't always get 'em. I wish we could jes stick ter beggin' fer men's togs, 'cause they 's the best. Jes gimme 'nough breeches, 'n' I won't complain."

In American cities also, men's clothing is the most profitable for beggars of this sort; very few tramps ask for "wimmenses' togs." In Germany, however, all sorts of old clothes are looked for, and the city tramps are great competitors of the Jews in this business. An old German Jew once said to me:

"I wish these Kunden [tramps] were all dead. They spoil our business right along, because they get their stuff for nothing, and then undersell us. That is n't right, and I know it is n't."

In Frankfort-on-the-Main I once knew a Swiss beggar who collected eighteen pairs of shoes in one week, not counting other things that he asked for also. And he claimed that, after trying various kinds of begging, he had found the most money in the shoe business. Of course, all this depends on a beggar's ability to make people believe that he is really deserving, for clothes-beggars, like a number of other specialists, must have some natural adaptation for their chosen calling.

This is also true of the office-beggar, or "sticker," as he calls himself. His specialty brings him almost entirely in contact with men, and he must be exceedingly clever to deal successfully with them. A man will argue with a beggar, if he has time, just twice as long as a woman will, and he will also give just twice as much money if he gives anything. So the office-beggar has good material to work on if he understands it. One of his theories is that, when begging of men, the "story" must be "true to nature"; that is, so simple and direct that there is no possibility of doubling on his track. For instance, he will visit a lawyer, tell his story, and then simply hang around as long as he dares. It is this waiting so patiently that gives him his name of "sticker." There are fully a hundred tramps of this sort in New York city alone. They have their separate beats, and seldom leave them unless they are worked out. I know one beggar who never leaves Newspaper Row and Wall Street except for amusement, and he makes, on an average, seventy-five cents a day. And I know another tramp whose business keeps him confined to Broadway between Barclay Street and the Battery, while his home is in the Bowery near Houston Street. Men of this stamp have evidently been lucky in the selection of offices where a certain sum of money will be given every week. Such good fortune is the ambition of every energetic city tramp. He wants something definite every day, week, and month, and as he gets it or fails to get it, rates himself successful or unsuccessful.

The aristocrat of city vagabondage is represented by what I call the room-beggar. He cannot be classified with the lodging-house men, because he has little to do with them, except socially, as at the saloon or music-hall, for instance. His home is entirely separated from theirs, it being a room, and sometimes even an apartment, which he rents for himself and family. If he is successful at his trade, and is careful to dress with some nicety, he can scarcely be distinguished from the usual citizen, except by the trained observer; the only mark about him being that peculiar glance of the eye common to all criminals and beggars.

The room-beggar has no unique line of trade that I have been able to discover; he goes into anything that pays, and the main difference between him and the majority of the men in the "lodgin'-house gang" is his greater ingenuity in making things pay. He is the brainy man of the city tramps, and the other beggars know it, and all look up to him, with the exception of the clever street-beggar, who considers himself his equal, as I think he really is.

No tramp, for instance, is so clever at the begging-letter "racket," and this means a good deal. To be able to write a letter to a perfect stranger and make money out of it requires a skilled hand, and a man educated in many lines. The public has become somewhat used to this trick, and will not be deceived every time; only men of an original turn of mind can do much with it. It is this originality that is the main talent of the room-beggar. He concocts stories which would do credit to a literary man, and sometimes makes nearly as much money as the daring thief.

Women are also found in this class, and do very well at times. In the city of Berlin, Germany, there lived a "lady" of this sort. She had two homes. One was a cellar in a poor quarter of the town, and the other was an aristocratic *étage* in the West End. She sent letters to well-to-do people of all sorts, in which she claimed to be *eine hochwohlgeborene Dame* in distress. She invited likely philanthropists to visit her in her cellar in order that they might see how unfortunate her position really was. People went, were shocked, and, as a result, she had her apartment in the West End. For about ten months this woman and her two daughters lived in real luxury, and one of the "young ladies" was to marry in "high society" about the time that the ruse was made public.

This is by no means a new trick, and yet people are

being continually swindled. Why? Simply because the beggars who undertake it are cleverer than the people fooled by it. That is the only reason. If charitable people would only commit charity to skilled hands it would be much easier to handle beggars. The tramp is a specialist; so why not leave specialists to deal with him? The whole trouble comes of our willingness to be more unpractical in our philanthropy than in our business.

There is one more city tramp that I must catalogue. It is the "sponger." His duty in life consists, he thinks, in simply living off the visiting knights of the road. He is a parasite fed by parasites, and hated by all self-respecting beggars. He is found wherever the traveling hoboes congregate, and there is no town in any country that I have visited where he does not flourish. In the Bowery his name is legion, and a hobo can scarcely visit a saloon there without meeting him. The wandering vagabond considers him the "bunco-man" of the beggars' world, and that is a good name. He will do anything to get money from a hobo, but I doubt very much whether he ever begs on his own hook. Exactly how he comes to exist no one knows, but I fancy that he is a discouraged tramp; he has found that he is not a born beggar, and has concluded that the next best thing is to live off men who are. If there were no beggars in the world, he would probably have to work for his living, for he could not steal successfully.

As for stealing, few town beggars ever go into that as a business. Of course, they will take things that do not belong to them if they are sure of not being caught, but this safety is so vain a hope that it is seldom "banked on." It is strange that the city tramp is not more of a thief, for probably no one knows more about the town's chances than he. Criminals are always anxious to have some acquaintance in his ranks, knowing only too well that the "town vag" can post them as no one else can.

Another thing rather more unpopular among town tramps than is usually supposed is joining a clique. In New York city, for example, there are various gangs of toughs who prowl about the town committing all sorts of depredations and making themselves generally feared. Even the policemen are now and then held at bay by them, and woe to the drunken sailor with his wages in his pockets who falls into their hands. I have seldom found the city tramp in such company. He knows too well the dangers of such crowds, prefers what he calls the "cut-throat principle," or each man for himself. There is too much slavery for him among toughs of the gang order, and he cannot move around as freely as he likes. Then, too, gangs are every now and then fighting one another, and that is usually harder work than the beggar cares for.

One of the most interesting things in the study of tramps is to get at their own opinions of themselves. To a certain degree they may be called rational beings. There is opinion and method and reason in trampdom, —no doubt of it,—and there are shades of opinion that correspond to varieties of method. The tramp of the prairies, the "fawny man" in New England, the city tramp in the Bowery, each has his point of view. If one catechizes or interviews the last named of these, he says:

"I 'm a beggar, and I know it. I know, too, that most people look upon me as a bad sort of fellow. They want to catch and punish me, and I don't want them to do it. They are warring against me, and I 'm warring against them. They think that I don't know how I should use my life, and I think that I do. Somebody must be mistaken; I think that they are, and I 'm doing my best to beat them. If they beat me, well and good; and if I beat them, well and good."

This is the talk of the real artist in low life; he is in the vagabond world because it pleases him better than any other. A little different is the point of view of the drunkard beggar:

"I 'm a fool, and I know it. No man with any sense and honor would live as I do. But the worst of it all is, I can't live otherwise. Liquor won't leave me alone, and as I 've got to live somehow, why, I might as well live where I can take care of myself. If people are fools enough to let me swindle them, so much the worse for them and so much the better for me."

To change such opinions as these is a hard task. The first can be corrected only when the man who owns it is discouraged. When his spirit is broken he can be helped, but not until then. The second is the result of long suffering through passion. Until that passion is conquered nothing can be done.

VI

WHAT THE TRAMP EATS AND WEARS

I

THE tramp is the hungriest fellow in the world. No matter who he is,—*Chausséegrabentapezirer*, moocher, or hobo,—his appetite is invariably ravenous. How he comes by that quality of his defects is an open question even in his own mind. Sometimes he accounts for it on the ground that he is continually changing climate, and then again attributes it to his incessant loafing. A tramp once said to me: "Cigarette, it ain't work that makes blokes hungry; it 's bummin'!" I think there is some truth in this, for I know from personal experience that no work has ever made me so hungry as simple idling; and while on the road I also had a larger capacity for food than I have usually. Even riding on a freight-train for a morning used to make me hungry enough to eat two dinners, and yet there was almost no work about it. And I feel safe in saying that the tramp can usually eat nearly twice as much as the laboring-man of ordinary appetite.

Now, what does he find to satisfy this rapacious craving? There are two famous diets in vagabondage, called the "hot" and the "cold." Each one has its advocates and propagandists. The hot is befriended mainly by the persevering and energetic; the cold belongs exclusively to the lazy and unsuccessful. The first is remarkable for what its champions call "set-downs," that is to say, good solid meals three times a day—or oftener. The second consists almost entirely of "hand-outs" or "poke-outs," which are nothing but bundles of cold food handed out at the back door.

Every man on the road takes sides, one way or the other, in regard to these two systems of feeding, and his standing in the brotherhood is regulated by his choice. If he joins the set-downers he is considered at least a true hobo, and although he may have enemies, they will not dare to speak ill of his gift for begging. If, on the other hand, he contents himself with hand-outs, he not only loses all prestige among the genuine hoboes, but is continually in danger of tumbling down into the very lowest grades of tramp life. There is no middle course for him to follow.

II

SUCCESS in vagabondage depends largely on distinct and indispensable traits of character—diligence, patience, nerve, and politeness. If a tramp lacks any one of these qualities he is handicapped, and his chosen life will go hard with him. He needs diligence in order to keep his winnings up to a certain standard; he needs patience to help him through districts where charity is below par; he needs nerve to give him reputation among his cronies, and he needs politeness to win his way with strangers and to draw their sympathy and help. If he possesses these characteristics, no matter what his nationality may be, he will succeed. If not, he would better work than tramp—he will find it much easier and twice as profitable. The poke-out beggar is deficient in every one of these qualities, and his winnings demonstrate it.

I made his acquaintance first about ten years ago. I had just begun my life on the road, and as I knew but very little about tramping and nothing about begging, it was only natural that I should fall in with him, for he is the first person one meets in the vagabond world. The successful beggars do not show themselves immediately, and the newcomer must first give some valid evidence of his right to live among them before they take him in—a custom, by the way, which shows that tramping is much like other professions. But the poke-out tramp is not so fastidious; he chums with any one he can, successful or not; and as I had to associate with somebody, I began with him. After a while I was graduated out of his rank, and received into the set-down class, but only after a hard and severe training, which I would not go through again—even for the sake of Sociology.

III

As a rule, the poke-out beggar has but one meal a day, usually breakfast. This is the main meal with all vagabonds, and even the lazy tramp makes frantic efforts to find it. Its quantity as well as its quality depends largely on the kind of house he visits.

His usual breakfast, if he is lucky, consists of coffee, a little meat, some potatoes, and "punk 'n' plaster" (bread and butter). Coffee, more than anything else, is what every hobo wants early in the morning. After sleeping out of doors or in a box-car, especially during the colder months, a man is stiff and chilled, and coffee is the thing to revive him when he cannot get whisky, which is by no means the easiest thing to beg. I have known tramps to drink over six cups of coffee before they looked for anything solid, and I myself have often needed three before I could eat at all.

The dinner of the lazy beggar is a very slim affair. It is either a free lunch in a saloon, or a hand-out. This latter consists mainly of sandwiches, but now and then a cold potato will be put into the bundle, and also, occasionally, a piece of pie. After the tramp has had one or two of these impromptu lunches he persuades himself that he has had enough, and goes off for a rest. How often—but on account of bashfulness, rather than anything else—have I done the same thing! And what poor dinners they were! They no more satisfy a tramp's appetite than they would a lion's, but the indolent fellow tries to persuade himself otherwise. I once overheard a typical member of the class discussing the matter with himself, or rather with his appetite, which, for the sake of argument and companionship, he looked upon as a personality quite apart. He had just finished a slim and slender hand-out, had tossed into the bushes the paper bag that held it together, and, when I saw him, was looking up into the sky in a most confidential manner. Soon, and as if sorry he could not be kinder to it, he cast his eyes pityingly on his paunch, and said in a sad tone:

"Poor devil! I feel fer y'u—bet cher life I do! But yer 'll have to stand it, I guess. It 's the only way I know fer y'u to git along." Then he patted it gently, and repeated again his sympathetic "poor devil." But not once did he scold himself for his laziness. Not he! He never does.

His supper is very similar to his dinner, except that he tries now and then to wash it down with a cup of tea or coffee. Later in the evening he also indulges in another hand-out, unless he is on a freight-train or far from the abodes of men.

Such is the diet of the lazy tramp, and, strange to relate, despite its unwholesomeness and its meagerness, he is a comparatively healthy fellow, as are almost all tramps. Their endurance, especially that of the poke-out tramps, is something remarkable. I have known them to live on "wind-puddin'," as they call air, for over forty-eight hours without becoming exhausted, and there are cases on record where they have gone for four and five days without anything to eat or drink, and have lived to tell the tale. A man with whom I once traveled in Pennsylvania did this very thing. He was locked into a box-car which was shunted off on an unused side-track a long distance from any house or place where his cries could be heard. He was in the car for nearly one hundred and twenty hours, and although almost dead when found, he picked up in a few days, and before long was on the road again. I saw him at the

World's Fair at Chicago, and he was just as healthy and happy in his own way as ever.

In some of the sparsely settled districts in Texas tramps have suffered most appalling deaths by such accidents, but so long as a beggar keeps his freedom I do not believe that even a lazy one starves to death in this country. I know very well that people do not realize this, and that they feed tramps regularly, laboring under the delusion that it is only humane so to do.

But although the tramp hates honest labor, he hates starvation still more, and if he finds it impossible to pick up anything to eat, he will either go to jail or work. He loves this world altogether too much to voluntarily explore another of which he knows so little.

IV

THE clothes of the poke-out beggar are not much, if any, better than his food. In summer he seldom has more than a shirt, a pair of trousers, a coat, some old shoes, and a battered hat. Even in winter he wears little more, especially if he goes South. I have never seen him with underclothes or socks, and an overcoat is something he almost never gets hold of, unless he steals one, which is by no means common. While I lived with him I wore just such "togs." I shall never forget my first tramp suit of clothes. The coat was patched in a dozen places, and was nearly three sizes too large for me; the waistcoat was torn in the back, and had but two buttons; the trousers were out at the knees, and had to be turned up in

London fashion at the bottom to keep me from tripping; the hat was an old derby with the crown dented in numerous places; and the only decent thing I had was a flannel shirt. I purchased this rig of a Jew, and thought it would be just the thing for the road, and so it was, but only for the poke-out tramp's road. The hoboes laughed at me and called me "hoodoo," and I never got in with them in any such garb. Nevertheless, I wore it for nearly two months, and so long as I associated with lazy beggars only, it was all right. Many of them were never dressed so well, and not a few envied me my old coat.

It is by no means uncommon to see a poke-out vagabond wearing a garment which belongs to a woman's wardrobe. He is so indifferent that he will wear anything that will shield his nakedness, and I have known him to be so lazy that he did not even do that.

One old fellow I remember particularly. He had lost his shirt somehow, and for almost a week went about with only a coat between his body and the world at large. Some of his pals, although they were of his own class, told him that he ought to find another shirt, and the more he delayed it the more they labored with him. One night they were all gathered at a hang-out near Lima, Ohio, and the old fellow was told that unless he found a shirt that night they would take away his coat also. He begged and begged, but they were determined, and as he did not show any intention of doing as he was bidden, they carried out the threat. And all that night and the following day he was actually so lazy and stubborn that he would not yield, and would probably be there still, in some form or other, had his pals not relented and returned him the coat. As I said, he went for nearly a week without finding a shirt, and not once did he show the least shame or embarrassment.

Not long after this experience he got into limbo, and had to wear the famous "zebra"—the penitentiary dress. It is not popular among tramps, and they seldom wear it, but that old rascal, in spite of the disgrace and inconvenience that his confinement brought upon him, was probably pleased that he did not have to find his own clothes.

Such are the poke-out tramps of every country where I have studied them, and such they will always be. They are constitutionally incapacitated for any successful career in vagabondage, and the wonder is that they live at all. Properly speaking, they have no connection with the real brotherhood, and I should not have referred to them here, except that the public mistakes them for the genuine hoboes. They are not hoboes, and nothing angers the latter so much as to be classed with them.

The hobo is exceedingly proud in his way,—a person of susceptibilities,—and if you want to offend him, call him a "gay-cat" or a "poke-outer." He will never forgive you.

V

ALMOST the first advice given me after I had managed to scramble into the set-down class came from an old vagabond known among his cronies as "Portland Shorty." He knew that I had been but a short time on the road, and that in many respects I had not met with the success which was necessary to entitle me to respect among men of his class, but nevertheless he was willing to give me a few pointers, which, by the way, all hoboes are glad to do, if they feel that the recipient will turn them to profit.

I met Shorty for the first time in Chicago, and while we were lounging on the grass in the Lake Front Park, the following conversation took place:

"Cigarette," he began,—for I had already received my tramp name,—"how long 'v' y'u been on the road?"

I replied: "About two months."

"Wall, how long d' y'u 'spect to stay there?"

"Oh, 's long 's I 'm happy."

"Ez long ez yer happy, eh? Wall, then, I 'm goin' to chew the rag wid y'u fer a little while. Now, 'f yer wants to be happy, here 's a little advice fer y'u. In the first place, make up yer mind jes wha' cher goin' to be. Ef y'u 'spect to work fer yer livin', why, get off the road. Moochin' spiles workin' jes ez workin' spiles moochin'. The two don't go together nohow. So 'f yer goin' to be a bum fer life, never think o' work. Jes give yerself entirely to yer own speshul callin', fer 'f y'u don't yer 'll regret it. 'N the second place, y'u wan' to decide what kind o' beggar yer goin' to make. Ef yer a thief, 'n' playin' the beggar jes as a guy, why, then y'u knows yer bizness better 'n I do. But ef y'u ain't, 'n' are jes browsin' round lookin' fer a berth, then I wants to tell yer somethin'. There 's diff'rent kinds o' beggars; some gits there, 'n' some does n't. Them what gits there I call arteests, 'n' them what does n't I call ban'crupts. Now, wha' cher goin' to be, arteest or ban'crupt?"

I replied that I was still undecided, since I had not yet learned whether I could make a success on the road or not, but added that my inclination would be toward the "arteest" class.

"That 's right," he began afresh. "Be an arteest or nothin'. Beggin' 's a great bizness 'f yer cut out fer it, 'cause y'u 've got everythin' to win 'n' nothin' to lose. Not many callin's has them good points—see? Now, 'f yer goin' to be an arteest, y'u wants to make up yer mind to one thing, 'n' that is—hard work. Some people thinks that moochin' is easy, but lemme tell yer 't ain't. Batterin', when it 's done well, is the difficultest job under the moon—take my tip fer that. Y'u got to work hard all yer life to make boodle, 'n' 'f y'u wan' to save it, y'u mus' n't booze. Drinkin' 's what spiles bums. If they c'u'd leave it alone they 'd be somethin'. Now, Cig, that 's good sound talk, 'n' you 'd better hang on to it."

I did, and it helped me as much as anything else in getting in with the real hoboes. I have known them, now, for ten years, and feel abundantly qualified to describe their diet and dress.

VI

In the first place, they eat three good warm meals every day—breakfast from seven to eight o'clock, dinner at twelve, and supper at six. These are the set-downs[1] in tramp life, and it is the duty of every

[1] In Germany and England the tramps usually eat their set-downs in cheap restaurants or at lodging-houses. They beg

professional to find them regularly. The breakfast is very similar to the poke-out tramp's breakfast, the main additions being oatmeal and pancakes, if the beggar is willing to look for them. They can be found with a little perseverance. There are also some hoboes who want pie for breakfast, and they have it almost constantly. I once traveled with a Maine tramp who simply would not consider his breakfast complete until he had had his usual piece of apple-pie. And he actually had the nerve to go to houses and ask for that alone. During our companionship, which lasted over a week, he failed but once to get it, and then it was because he had to make a train.

The dinner is a more elaborate affair, and the tramp must often visit a number of houses before he finds the various dishes he desires. I remember well a hunt I had for a dinner in St. Louis. A Western tramp was my comrade at the time, and we had both decided upon our bill of fare. He wanted meat and potatoes, "punk 'n' plaster," some kind of dessert (pudding preferred), and three cups of coffee. I wanted the same things minus the dessert, and I had to visit fifteen houses before my appetite was satisfied. But, as my companion said, the point is that I finally got my dinner. He too was successful, even to the kind of pudding he wished.

Not all tramps are so particular as my Western pal, but they must have the "substanshuls" (meat and potatoes and bread and butter) anyhow. Unless they get them they are angry, and scold everything

money to pay for them, rather than look for them at private houses.

and everybody. I once knew a vagabond to call down all sorts of plagues and miseries on a certain house because he could not get enough potatoes there. He prayed that it might be cursed with smallpox, all the fevers that he knew, and every loathsome disease—and he meant it, too.

There are a number of hoboes who occasionally take their dinners in the form of what they call the "made-to-order scoff." It is something they have invented themselves, and for many reasons is their happiest meal. It takes place at the hang-out, and a more appropriate environment could not be found. When the scoff is on the program, the vagabonds gather together and decide who shall beg the meat, the potatoes, the onions, the corn, the bread and butter, the tea and coffee, and the desserts, if they are procurable. Then each one starts out on his separate errand, and if all goes well they return before long and hand their winnings over to the cook. This official, meanwhile, has collected the fire-wood and the old tin cans for frying and boiling the food. While the meal is cooking, the tramps sit around the fire on the stolen railroad-ties and compare jokes and experiences. Pretty soon dinner is announced, and they begin. They have no forks and often no knives, but that does not matter. "Fingers were made before forks." Sometimes they sharpen little sticks and use them, but fingers are more popular. The table manners of the Eskimos compare favorably with those of these picnicking hoboes, and I have often seen a tramp eat meat in a way that would bring a dusky blush to the cheek of the primeval Alaskan. It is remarkable,

A WESTERN ROADSTER.

however, that no matter how carelessly they eat their food, they seldom have dyspepsia. I have known only a few cases, and even then the sufferers were easily cured.

Supper is seldom much of a meal among hoboes, and mainly because it has to be looked for, during the greater part of the year, just about dark, the time when the hobo is either preparing his night's hang-out, or making arrangements for his night's journey, and the hunt for supper often occasions unpleasant delays. But he nevertheless looks for it if he can possibly spare the time. He considers it his bounden duty to eat regularly, and feels ashamed if he neglects to do it. I have heard him scold himself for an hour just because he failed to get a meal at the proper time, although he really did not care for it. Bohemian that he is, he still respects times and seasons, which is the more surprising since in other matters he is as reckless as a fool. In quarrels, for example, he regards neither sense nor custom, and has his own private point of view every time. But at the very moment that he is planning some senseless and useless fight, he will look for a meal as conscientiously as the laborer works for one, although he may not need it.

For supper he usually has about what other people have—potatoes (usually fried) and beefsteak, tea or coffee, bread and butter, and some kind of sauce. For three months of my time on the road I had almost exactly this bill of fare, and became so accustomed to it that I was considerably surprised if I found anything else. I mention these various items to show how closely the tramp's "hot diet" resembles that of most people. A great mistake is made in thinking that these men, as a class, have to eat things both uncommon and peculiar. Some of them do, but all of the set-downers eat about the same things that the respectable and worthy portion of the community eats.

In Pennsylvania, the "fattenin'-up State,"[1] or "P. A.," as the hobo calls it, apple-butter is his chief delicacy. I have seen him put it on his bread, meat, and potatoes, and one beggar that I knew wanted it "raw." I happened to be with this man one afternoon in the town of Bethlehem, and while we were sitting on a little bridge crossing the canal on the outskirts of the town, a Pennsylvania Dutchman hove in sight. My pal, being a beggar who liked to improve every opportunity, immediately said to me, in a professional sort of voice:

"Keep quiet, Cig, 'n' I 'll tackle 'im."

The man soon passed us, and the beggar followed. He caught up with him in a moment, and as I had also followed, I managed to overhear a part of the conversation. It was something like this:

"I say, boss, can' cher gimme the price of a meal?"

"Nein; dat kan ich nit."

"Well, can you take me home 'n' feed me?"

"Nein."

[1] It is most interesting to talk with Eastern tramps in the West who are homeward bound. If they have been in the West long, and look rather "seedy," and you ask them where they are going to in the East, they invariably reply: "Gosh! P. A., o' course. We wants to fatten up, we does." And there is no better place for this than Pennsylvania.

"Well, say; can' cher gimme a cigar?"

"Nein"—in anger.

"Well, say,"—and he put his arm affectionately on the Dutchman's shoulder,—"let's go 'n' have a drink. Eh?"

"Nein."

"Well, you old hoosier, you, can you gimme some apple-butter?"

Even the Dutchman laughed, but he said, "Nein."

Besides the three meals which every hobo has regularly, there are also two or three lunches a day, which are included in the hot diet, although they practically belong to the cold one. The first is taken in the morning about ten o'clock, and is begged at breakfast-time, the second about three or four o'clock, and the third late in the evening. Not all hoboes eat these between-meal "snacks," but the majority beg them at any rate, and if they do not need them they either throw them away or give them to some deserving person, often enough a seeker of work. For although the tramp hates labor, he does not hate the true laborer, and if he can help him along, he does it willingly. He knows only too well that it is mainly the laboring-man off whom he lives, and that it is well to do him a good turn whenever it is possible. Then, too, the hobo is a generous fellow, no matter what else he is, and is always willing to share his winnings with any one he really likes. With the gay-cat and the poke-outer he will have nothing to do, but with the criminal, his own pals, and the working-man he is always on good terms, unless they repel his overtures.

As a number of tramps spend considerable time in

jails, it seems appropriate to tell what they eat there, also. Their life in limbo is often voluntary, for although a great many hoboes go South every winter, there are others who prefer a jail in the North, and so whatever hardship they encounter is mainly of their own choosing. And since some of them do choose jail fare, it is evident that those particular beggars find it less disagreeable than winter life "outside," either North or South. The usual food in these places is bread, molasses, and coffee in the morning, some sort of thick soup or meat and potatoes with bread for dinner, and bread and molasses and tea for supper. There is generally enough, also, and although I have often heard the tramps grumble, it was mainly because they had nothing else to do. Confinement in county prisons, although it has its diversions, tends to make a man captious and irritable, and the tramp is no exception to this. Occasionally he gets into a jail where only two meals a day are given, and he must then exercise his fortitude. He never intends to be in such a place, but mistakes will happen even in vagabondage, and it is most interesting to see how the tramp gets out of them or endures them. He usually grits his teeth and promises "never to do it again"; and, considering his self-indulgent nature, I think he stands suffering remarkably well.

VII

WHAT the hot-diet tramp wears is another matter, but a not vastly different one. His ambition, although he does not always achieve it, is to have new togs quite as regularly as the man who buys them with hard cash. He also tries to keep up with the fashions and the seasons as closely as possible.

But all this must naturally be regulated by the charity of the community in which he happens to be. If he is near a college, and knows how to beg of the students, he can usually find just what and about all he needs; but if he is in a country district where clothes are worn down to the thread, he is in a hard case. As a rule, however, he dresses nearly as well as the day-laborer, and sometimes far better. There are tramps of this type in New York and Chicago whose dress is almost identical with that of the majority of the men one meets in the streets, and to distinguish them from the crowd requires an eye able to read their faces rather than their coats. Such men never allow their clothes to wear beyond a certain point before begging a fresh supply. And if they are careful, and do not ride in freight-trains often, a suit will last them several months, for they understand remarkably well how to take care of it. Every tramp of this order and grade carries a brush inside of his coat pocket, and uses it on the slightest provocation. On the road I also acquired this habit of brushing my clothes as often as they showed the slightest soil. It is a trick of the trade, and saves not only the clothes, but the self-respect of the brotherhood.

Dark clothes are the most popular, because they keep clean, or at least appear clean, for a longer time. I once wore a suit of this kind for nearly three months, and although I used it rather roughly, it was so good at the end of that time that I traded it to a tramp for a coat and vest almost new. The way to make sure of having a serviceable suit is to gather together several coats, vests, and trousers, and pick out a complement from the best and most suitable of the lot.

I shall not forget an experience of this sort I had in a Western town. I had worked all day with my companion looking simply for clothes, and at night we had six coats, eight vests, four pairs of trousers, and two overcoats. Out of this collection we chose two fairly good suits, but the rest were so poor that we had to throw them away. One of the coats was a clergyman's, and when he gave it to me he said: "It may not fit you very well, but you can use it as an overcoat, perhaps." It was even then too large for me, and I gave it to the tramp, who wore it for nearly a month. His pals laughed at him and called him "Parson Jim"; but he made more money with that coat than he could possibly have made in any other. He posed as a theological student among the farmers, and was most royally entertained. But his luck gave out in a short time, for he went to prison in his clerical habit not long after.

Hoboes take most delight in what is called the sack-coat. "Tailed jackets" are inconvenient, especially when one is riding on the trucks of a train; the skirts are liable to catch on something and thus delay matters. It is the inside of a tramp's coat, however, that is most interesting. It is usually furnished with numerous pockets, one of them being called the "poke-out pocket," in which he stows away his lunches. The others are used for brushes, tattooing-tools, combs,

AN AUCTION.

white rags, string, and other little notions that may "come handy" to a traveler. But in none of the pockets will there ever be found one bit of paper which might identify the bearer or implicate him in any suspicious work. He is too "foxy" to ever allow his real name to crop out in any telltale evidence on his person, except, perhaps, when he may have been foolish enough to have it tattooed somewhere on his body.

He is proudest of his hat and shoes, and with reason. The former is usually a soft black felt, but stiff hats are also *à la mode*, and I have even seen a "stovepipe" on the road. It was unique, however, and the owner did a good business with it; his "clients" used to feed him simply on account of his oddity. The footgear consists generally of laced shoes, but boots have to be accepted now and then. Socks, although much in vogue, often yield to white-linen rags wound smoothly around the feet. This is particularly true among the tramps of Germany. They take long walks, and contend that socks chafe the feet too much. There is truth in this, and while I lived with them I followed their custom to the extent of wearing the rags next to my feet and then drawing the socks over them. And I was very little troubled with sore feet while I did so; but for the one week when I tried to go without the rags I suffered considerably.

Overcoats are worn by the hoboes who go South in winter, but tramps who spend the cold months in jail do not need them, and if they beg any, usually sell them. Underclothes in some form or other are worn all the time, not so much for warmth as for cleanliness. Even the cleanest hoboes cannot keep entirely free of vermin, and they wear underclothes to protect their outer garments, changing the former as often as they can, and throwing away or burning the discarded pieces. The tramp's shirt is always of flannel, if he can find it, and very often he wears two, either for the sake of trade or to keep warm. Other garments are doubled also, and one finds men wearing two coats, two vests, and two pairs of trousers. It is by no means uncommon to see a tramp who wears linen and cotton shirts with two or three layers on his back. As one becomes soiled he throws it away, and so on till the three are discarded.

There is one more indispensable article of a tramp's toilet, and it is called the "shaver." This is a razor incased in a little sack, generally leather, which he hangs around his neck with a string. It is used for fighting and shaving, and is very good as a "guy" for getting him into jail. I saw how this was done one day in western Pennsylvania. The time was late October, and three tramps who came into town decided that the local jail would be a good place in which to spend the winter. They wanted a ninety-day sentence, and knew they could not get it for simple drunkenness; so they decided to pretend drunk and make a row in order to be sentenced on two charges. They began their brawl in the main street, and flourished their razors in good style. The officers arrested them after a little fight made for appearance' sake, and the judge gave them four months—thirty days more than they expected. Their razors were confiscated, too, but they got others the minute they were released. It sometimes happens, however, that the shavers are not discovered, because the men are not properly searched, and, owing to this lack of careful inspection by officials, rows in jails have often ended seriously.

VIII

A FRIEND at my elbow, to whom vagabondage is a *terra incognita*, remarks just at this juncture: "You ought to tell just how the tramp gets his three set-down meals a day."

I can scarcely believe that in our own country there is any ignorance in regard to this matter. The house in the settled districts that has not been visited by the tramp in search of one of his three meals seems to me not to exist. But if anybody needs enlightenment on this point, the following incident will be of interest.

One June day, some years ago, I strolled into the hang-out in a little town in Michigan just as the bells were ringing for dinner. I was a stranger in the place, and as I wanted to find my dinner as quickly as possible, in order to make a "freight" that was due about two o'clock, I asked one of the tramps at the camp whether he knew of any "mark" (a house where something is always given to beggars) in the town.

"Well, there ain't many," he replied. "Town 's too small and the people 's too relijus. The best is that big college building up there on the hill, but they ain't always willin' even there. They go by fits. If they 's in the mood, they feeds you, 'n' 'f they ain't, they sicks the dog on you; an' it takes a pretty foxy bloke to know what moods they is in. I struck 'em onc't when I felt dead sure they was in the k'rect one, 'n', by the hoky-poky, I had to look fer a new coat 'for' I left the town—blasted mean dog they got there. But there 's another place not far from the old red buildin' where any bloke kin scoff if he gives the right song 'n' dance. It 's No. 13 Grove Street. Great ole squaw lives there—feeds everybody she kin; sort o' bughouse [crazy] on the subject, you know—likes to talk 'bout her Sammy, 'n' all that sort o' stuff. Dead cinch, she is. Better hit her up 'n' take a feed. Yer bound to get a good ole set-down."

I followed his advice, and was soon at the back door of No. 13 Grove Street. In answer to my knock there appeared a motherly-looking old lady who wanted to know what she could do for me. What a tale I told her! And how kind she looked as I related my sad experiences as a young fellow trying to work his way to a distant town, where he hoped to find friends who would help him into college!

"Come right in; we are just at table." Then she called to her daughter Dorothy, a pretty lass, and told her to lay a plate for a stranger. She and the girl were the only persons in the house, and I was surprised that they took me in so willingly. Women, as a rule, are afraid of tramps, and prefer to feed them on the back steps. But I had evidently found an exception, for when I had washed my hands and face and combed my hair on the little porch, I was invited into the cozy dining-room and offered a place beside the hostess. How odd it seemed! I almost felt at home, and had to be on my guard to keep up my rôle as a vagabond. For it was certainly a temptation to relieve myself then and there, and have an old-time chat on respectable lines. I had been so long on the road that I was really in need of some such comfort, but I dared not take advantage of it. So I answered their questions about my home, my parents, and my plans as professionally as I could, and spun my story, not entirely of fiction, however, and they smiled or looked solemn as the occasion fitted. They seemed to take a great interest in my doings, and always had a word of sympathy or advice for predicaments which I fabricated. And how they fed me! My plate was not once empty, and I ate and ate simply out of respect to their politeness. When I had finished they both asked me to rest awhile before taking up my journey again; so I sat in their interesting little sitting-room, and listened to their talk, and answered their questions. Pretty soon, and evidently thinking that it would help me to know about him, the mother began to tell me of a lad of hers whom she had not seen for several years, and as she fancied that he might possibly have traveled my way, she asked if I had met him. I wanted to tell her that I had, if only to give her a mite of comfort, but I knew that it would be more cruel than the truth, and I said "I was afraid we had not met." Then she spoke of certain features of face that we had in common, and asked the girl if she did not think so.

"Yes," Dorothy replied, "he reminds me of Sam—just about the same build, too."

I could not stand this, and told them I must be on my way. As I was leaving, the old lady asked me not to be offended if she gave me a little book. "Of course not," I replied, and she fetched me a conventional little tract about a prodigal son. I thanked her, and then she advised me to visit a certain lawyer in the town, who, she said, was in need of a helper, and there I might find a chance for an education without looking farther. And as if to prove my right to such employment, while standing on the porch at her side, she laid her motherly hand on my head, and said to Dorothy, with a smile on her kindly face:

"The lad has an intelligent head—something like Sam's. Don't you think so?"

Both looked sadly and solemnly in earnest, and I stole away, hoping never to see them again until I should know where their Sam might be found. I have looked for him on many a road since that June day, always with the determination that no other "wandering boy" should hear from me of this kind mother's hospitality, and I hope they have him now, for they certainly deserve surcease of sorrow on his account.

There are people like this in every town, and it is the tramp's talent to find them, and "when found make a note on." He thus becomes a peripatetic directory for the tramp world, which lives on the working world at a cost which it is worth while to consider.

IX

THAT tramps are expensive no one will deny, but how much so it is difficult to decide. I have tried to show that a large number of them eat and wear things which certainly cost somebody considerable money, but a careful census of the vagabond population alone can estimate the amount. No one can tell exactly what this tramp population numbers, but I think it safe to say that there are not less than sixty thousand in this country. Every man of this number, as a rule, eats something twice a day, and the majority eat three good meals. They all wear some sort of clothing, and most of them rather respectable clothing. They all drink liquor, probably each one a glass of whisky a day. They all get into jail, and eat and drink there just as much at the expense of the community as elsewhere. They all chew and smoke tobacco, and all of them spend some of their time in lodging-houses. How much all this represents in money I cannot tell, but I believe that the expenses I have enumerated, together with the costs of conviction for vagrancy, drunkenness, and crime, will easily mount up into the millions. And all that the country can show for this expenditure is an idle, homeless, and useless class of individuals called tramps.

PART II

TRAVELS

PART II

TRAVELS

PART II—TRAVELS

I

LIFE AMONG GERMAN TRAMPS

WILLIAM II of Germany is the ruler of about fifty millions of people. A small fraction comprises the nobility, while the great majority are commoners, and the rest, about one hundred thousand, are roving beggars. His Imperial Majesty is probably well acquainted with his nobles, and he thinks that he understands the commoners, but the tramp who passes his castle now and then is a foreigner at home. Yet he is found in every city, town, and village, and there is hardly a home in the empire which he has not visited. He tramps the public highways as freely and fearlessly as the laborer, and rides on the royal railways as boldly as a king. His business in life is to prey upon the credulity of the charitable, and to steal when the eye of the law is not on watch. In spite, however, of all this publicity, comparatively little is known of his real life and character. Various books and pamphlets have been written about him, but they have usually been grounded on second-hand information, as I have looked in vain for any account of a personal study of tramp life.

Being desirous of knowing the real facts in the case, I at first supplemented my reading by various conversations with beggars as they lounged around near my home in Berlin, and occasionally invited some of the more intelligent into my study, and plied them as cleverly as possible with all sorts of questions. But they invariably fooled me, and told the most romantic of tales, believing, probably, that they were what I wanted. Time after time I have said to them, "Oh, come now, give over this story-telling, and let me have something that is really true." But they seemed unable to comprehend my purposes, and, true to their national traits, it was not in them to take part in any scheme which they could not understand. How to get at what I desired was the question. I called at the Bureau of Statistics, hoping surely to find here carefully tabulated statistics of vagrancy; but I was disappointed.

Dr. Berthold,[1] who kindly told me all he knew, said that Pastor von Bodelschwingh was the man who had made the best census of trampdom, and he had claimed that there were 200,000 arrests in Germany each year for begging; that 100,000 of them represented irreclaimable vagabonds, 80,000 bona-fide seekers of work, and the remaining 20,000 the maximum number of reclaimable beggars. Dr. Berthold continued: "The only way to know the entire truth about the tramp is to live with him. I had the intention to do this myself, but I delayed it too long, and now I am too old." He was very kind and gave me some valuable hints,

[1] Dr. Berthold is a well-known statistician, writer, and authority on matters pertaining to German labor colonies.

but admitted that nothing very definite was known about the wandering beggar.

I finally decided to give up these fruitless investigations, and to become a tramp myself in order to achieve my ends. I felt fairly equipped for such an undertaking, having had a two years' residence in Germany, and having also played the tramp in my own country. My plan, however, was not to study the enforced vagrant, but rather the man who wanders because he desires to, and prefers begging to working. And in that which follows I have attempted to describe my experiences with voluntary beggars only.

Early in April I made ready for the journey. My outfit was a close copy of the fashions in trampdom, my clothes being both old and easy to bear. I took no pass with me, because, in the first place, I could not get a German pass, and, secondly, I was anxious to find out just what experiences an unidentified man must go through. If I were to repeat the experiment I should do differently. Having decided to begin my investigations in Magdeburg, there being various reasons why I should not play the beggar in Berlin, I left my home on the date mentioned, and hurried through the streets to the railroad-station, where I invested a few groschen in a fourth-class ticket. My first afternoon was consequently spent in what very closely resembles the common American freight-car, except that it is windowed and occasionally has planks braced against the sides to serve as seats. The floor, however, or a piece of baggage, is the more customary resting-place. A ride in this miserable box costs two pfennigs the kilometer, and the passengers are naturally of the lower order of travelers, including the tramps, who make almost as much use of fourth-class privileges as our own vagrants do of the freight-trains.

My companions on the first trip were a queer lot. In one end of the car was a band playing the vilest music for the few sechser (five-pfennig pieces) occasionally thrown down to them. Their only rival was a little tambourine girl, who danced and rattled her noisy instrument as if her life depended upon her agility, as no doubt it did. The other travelers were market-women, laborers, and journeymen, and a fellow called Peasant Carl, who was more of a tramp than anything else, in spite of the fact that he had a trade. We were soon talking on various subjects, and it was not difficult to lead the conversation to the subject of tramp life. Carl was considerably surprised to find that an American should be *auf der Walze* (on the road), and needed some proof ere he was convinced that I was a roadster. My old clothes and general forlorn condition were not sufficient, and I was compelled to tell him a story. Once satisfied on this point, he turned out to be a good friend, and among other valuable facts that he generously gave me were scraps from the German tramp vocabulary, which he said might "come handy," since I was a stranger. I found that *Kunde*, or customer, was the general word for vagrant, but as the term vaguely covers the thousands of traveling journeymen in the community also, another term has been invented for the genuine tramp, none other than *Chausséegrabentapezirer*, or upholsterer of the highway ditches. What could be more genuinely, deliciously German?

THE FOURTH-CLASS CAR.

As this dialect is rather unique, and as different from the German language proper as black from white, I am tempted to give a few more words, tabulating them, for comparison's sake, alongside their American equivalents:

English.	*German.*	*German Tramp Dialect.*	*American Tramp Dialect.*
Bread	Das Brod	Der Kramp	Punk.
Water	Das Wasser	Der Gänsewein	
To beg	Betteln	Abklappen	To Batter.
To walk	Laufen	Tibbeln	To Drill.
Policeman	Der Schutzmann	Der Putz	The Bull.
Gendarmes	Gendarmes	Der Deckel	
Village	Das Dorf	Der Kaff	Jerktown.
Whisky-flask	Die Schnappsflasche	Die Finne	The Growler.
Passport	Der Reise-Pass	Die Flebbe	
Hunger	Der Hunger	Der Kohldampf.	

This vocabulary will give a fair idea of the dialect. It is much more complete than the American, affording, as it does, ample means whereby entire secrecy can be secured in public places. It is spoken by both *Handwerksburschen* and tramps, and it is my opinion that the former were not the originators, as is sometimes averred, but have rather acquired a fair knowledge of it by associating year after year, on the road, with beggars.

On my arrival in Magdeburg, my friend Carl suggested that we go to Die Herberge zur Heimath, a lodging-house somewhat above the common grade, where we could at least have our supper, but where I could not lodge, having no pass. This institution must be distinguished from the ordinary Herberge, or low-class lodging-house, and has a history worth more than a passing paragraph. It is a sort of refined edition of the Salvation Army "shelter," and was founded on religious and humanitarian principles by Professor Perthes of Bonn, whose first enterprise of the kind at Bonn has been so widely copied that at least three hundred towns of Germany now furnish this comfortable and respectable refuge to the traveling apprentice or journeyman, and, if he will conform to its usages and requirements, to the tramp also.

Entering the main room of the Heimath, I was surprised to see Carl rap on a table and the men sitting at the same to follow suit. I found out later that this meant "Hello," and that the after knock indicated "All right." Shaking hands is also a customary greeting in German trampdom, but hardly ever in American vagrancy. Tramps also call one another "brother," and use the pronoun "thou" invariably in preference to "you." The inmates of the Heimath, I soon found, were drawn from three classes. First, the apprentice making his first journey, and usually a very stupid fellow. The tramp was here also, but only, I think, to prey upon the Handwerksbursche, for no whisky is sold on the premises, and prayers are held morning and evening, a custom which all true roadsters despise. The rest were men fairly well on in life, who work occasionally and beg the remainder of the time. I counted altogether sixteen recognized beggars (Chausséegrabentapezirer), but made no attempt to make their acquaintance, having decided not to study them in foreign quarters, but to seek them in their real homes. For Die Herberge zur Heimath is not a tramps' nest, although some Germans think so, and as soon as I had had a fair supper, for which I paid three cents, I left with Carl for another domicile. We were not long in finding the Herberge proper, or perhaps improper, where life is seen in all its dirtiest phases. Entering the common meeting-room, and saluting as usual, we sat down at a table where there were other tramps also. I was immediately asked: "Wo kommst Du her? Wo willst Du hin? Was hast Du für Geschäft?" I answered these questions as cleverly as I could, and was soon deep in various conversations. Before I had been talking long, I made the acquaintance of a beggar belonging to the class called *Kommando-Schieber.* These fellows beg usually within very small districts, and know every house that is "good" for a meal or a pfennig. My newly made friend was kind enough to instruct both Carl and me in regard to Magdeburg.

"This town is rather *heiss* [unfriendly]," said he, "but if you look out and beg very carefully you can get along. A great trick here now is to tip the *Portier* of good houses, and thus get the pull on every flat in the building. You 've got to look out for the *Putz,* though, for if you 're caught, you 're sure for twenty-four hours in the *Kasten* [prison]. Another scheme that works pretty well with us fellows who know the town is to send around begging letters. You can easily make quite a *Stoss* [haul] if you work the plan well. Still, it 's risky for strangers. If you 're going to stay here long, you 'd better make friends with the *Herbergsvater.* He 's a pretty good *Kerl* [fellow], and if you let him know that you 've got a little money, he 'll look out for you when the Putz makes his inspection now and then. There 's nothing, you know, like standing in with them that are *klug* [clever], and you can bet that fellow is. . . . What do you say to a schnapps, brother?"

He had earned his drink, for he gave me a great many hints which were necessary to successful begging. One of them was about getting a pass. "Now, if you can scrape a little coin together," he said, "I 'll tell you how to get a *Flebbe* that no Putz can find out whether it 's forged or not. You see that fellow over there near the window—well, he looks like a fool, but if you can give him five marks, he 'll get you a *Wanderbuch* that 'll pass you anywhere. But don't go at him too clumsily, you know; take the matter easy. Nothing like taking your time, brother, is there?" I agreed that this was orthodox tramp doctrine, and determined to think the matter over, which I did, and came to the conclusion that I might eventually get into more trouble with a false pass than without any. And later experience approved the decision.

My first night in this tramp-nest was one I shall never forget. I slept with an old beggar in a bed long since given over to other lodgers, who fought us that night as if we were Frenchmen. And the stench in the sleeping-room was similar to that in a pigsty. Any complaint, however, would have been useless, for the price paid was only three cents, and for that sum of money one could not expect very much. Then, too, the host asked for no *Legitimations-Papier*, and this was an advantage which must be set over against

HUNTING FOR HIS PASS.

most of the annoyances. Nevertheless, I was glad enough to turn out early in the morning and look for a breakfast, which was soon found, but thoroughly European in quantity. Carl continued begging even after his breakfast, while I remained in the lodging-house talking with some of the inmates. I was surprised to see how fairly well dressed the German tramp is. The men in the Herberge were clad much more respectably than their American *confrère*, and seemed to have a desire to appear as decent as possible. Their intelligence was also very fair, every one being able to read and write as well as cipher. This, however, is not so surprising, for they were by no means young. It is my opinion that the majority of German tramps are over thirty years of age. There are some boys on the road, it is true, but by no means the number found in American trampdom. And I am happy to say that my experience convinces me that their treatment by the elder men is much more humane than in my own country. There is not in the German that viciousness which seems ingrained in the character of the American vagrant. The latter is a more generous fellow, however, than the German, as I learned by practical experience. When some of the tramps returned to the Herberge in the afternoon, I tried their good fellowship by asking several for a sechser with which to buy a cup of coffee. I offered my very sore foot as an excuse for not having myself begged. But they were not touched in the slightest. One fellow said: "If you can't beg your own money, why, you 'd better get off the road, for no other Chausséegrabentapezirer will hustle for you." An

American beggar would, as a rule, have handed me a penny, if he had it. But these men sat drinking their beer, schnapps, and coffee, utterly incapable, at least then, of a bit of brotherly charity. They had plenty of money, too. During the day nearly every one had begged from ninety pfennigs to one mark twenty, while Carl returned about five o'clock with three marks in hand.

I think the usual wage for diligent begging is be tween one mark fifty and four marks, in addition to the three meals. Of course there are a few who are much more successful. One fellow at the Herberge, for instance, who had been in England and could speak English quite well, claimed that he begged forty marks in one week during the previous winter from the Americans in Dresden.

Another vagrant told a story of a man he had met in South Germany on the road with two hundred marks in his pocket, which he had collected in two weeks in Munich. It is a great amusement for the tramp off duty to figure out the possibilities of his calling, and to illustrate the same with stories. There was one beggar in the room who even kept an account of his income and expenses. I saw the record for March, and found that his gains had been ninety-three marks and a few pfennigs, not including the meals which he had had in various kitchens where the servants were friendly. I must say right here, however, that such success is found only in cities. For I sampled the charity of the country time after time, and it is worth a bare living only, or, as Carl was wont to say, "One can't get fat on it."

We were convinced of this as soon as we had left Magdeburg and started afoot for Brunswick. Carl begged in every village that we passed through, but he could seldom get more than twenty or twenty-five pfennigs, with numerous slices of bread. I made no attempt to beg money, but visited several houses and asked for food, so that my companions might not suspect me. I was fairly well treated, at least quite as charitably as I would have been in the United States, and I think that, taking the country as a whole, the rewards of begging in Germany are much higher than in either England or America. The people seem bound to give, although they have had beggars among them for centuries.

My second night on the road was quite as interesting as the first. I had stopped with Carl and two other men in a little village not far from Brunswick, where there was no Herberge, and only one inn, or *Gasthaus*, as it was called. We asked the woman in charge if we could lodge there for the night, but she was by no means friendly, saying we were unclean. She told us to go to the barn, where we could sleep for a groschen apiece. As there was nothing better to do, we followed her instructions, and spent the night, which was cold for April, on some bundles of straw. I was fairly well repaid for this unpleasant experience by the various conversations which I overheard. One tramp was philosophizing in a maundering way over his life on the road, and what first brought him there. He reasoned that as he was born lazy, the blame should be put on his parents, but he finally concluded that the *Schnappsflasche* also had had a hand in the business. Another companion said: "Why should I work, when I can beg more than I can possibly earn? Now, if I should follow my trade I could earn about eighteen marks a week. But as a beggar I can beat that by ten marks. No, brother; it is n't all the blame of the Schnappsflasche that we 're on the road. I, for one, am here because I can do better than anywhere else. Is n't that so?" And he nudged me for an answer.

"Well," I said, "we lads on the road seem to have more money than most laborers, but we seldom have a decent place to lay our heads. For instance, what sort of place is this we 're in now?"

"Yes, that 's true," he returned; "but then we 're never sick, always happy, and perhaps we 're just as well off as anybody else. You forget that we never work, and that 's a great thing in our favor. Those lads who have their homes have to work for them, and don't you forget it. It 's my opinion that the home is n't worth the labor."

I think this latter opinion is very general in German vagrancy, and is one of its main causes. Liquor, however, is just as much of a curse in Germany as elsewhere, and brings more men into trampdom than is usually estimated. The Schnappsflasche is in nearly every tramp's pocket, and he usually empties it twice a day. It is a wonder to me how he can do it, for the schnapps is almost pure alcohol, and burns the throat terribly. Yet I found just outside of Brunswick a female tramp, nearly sixty years of age, who could empty *Die Finne* in a single "go," and seemed healthy too. This woman was the only feminine roadster I met during the journey, and I think she is one of the very few.

About noon of April 14 I arrived in Brunswick with Carl, who was on his way to Bremen, where he intended shipping as a coal-trimmer to New York, if possible. He was disgusted with Germany, he said, and felt that America was the only place for his nervous activity. He was somewhat surprised, however, as I was too, to find in Brunswick three American negroes who seemed to think quite the contrary of their country. One was an "actor," and the other two were ex-waiters, and they were traveling about the community and getting their living by dancing and singing in the streets and saloons. Charley, the actor, said: "We 're doin' pretty well; have our three squares a day, and all the booze we want. Can't do better than that at home." I explained this to Carl, as none of the negroes spoke German; but he could not be convinced that gold was not lying loose in the streets of American cities. In the afternoon his hatred of Germany was not quite so intense, as he begged a mark and a half in about two hours. One man that he visited was a member of "The Society against Begging and Vagrancy," and had a sign to that effect on his gate-post; but Carl found him, it seems, a generous Samaritan. This interested me considerably, for I had heard good reports of this society and its members, as well as of its success in fighting vagabondage. I asked several fellows what they thought of the organization. One tramp claimed that he always visited its members,—at least, those having signs on their gates,—for he was quite as apt to be well treated as not. Others were drastic in their criticisms, and said that the society would let a man starve rather than feed him. Carl, I think, was about right when he said that some members of the society fed vagrants, and some did not, and it was all according to chance.

From Brunswick a crowd of tramps, including myself, rode in a fourth-class car to a little station called Peine, in the direction of Hanover. A few of the men remained here in order to take in the *Verpflegung-Station* until the next day. This station, of which there are about two thousand in Germany, is a place where a man professing to be penniless can have a night's lodging, together with supper and breakfast, for a few hours' work. I moved on toward Hanover with fifteen other men who were bound in the same direction. They all had money, and no love for the Verpflegung-Station. We tramped along at a pace of about five kilometers to the hour—the usual gait of tramps when they are compelled to use the highways. They can beg food enough on the road, and thus the walking is not so disagreeable, for the German roads are superb.

At one little village where we stopped for refreshments the crowd took the place by storm, and the people were actually frightened into giving us bread and meat. It is true that the men were rather violent and used threatening language, yet there was no need to fear them, as they could hardly have attempted to do any great harm. For the German tramp, as a rule, though a great talker and "blower," is a coward, after all, and when answered rather roughly usually

ON THE ROAD.

subsides. At the village of Lehrte we again boarded a train, and rode into Hanover late in the evening. Some of my companions went to the Heimath, but the majority hunted out the common Herberge, and I followed the crowd. I was treated in the same fashion as at Magdeburg, and was asked no questions about a pass. There was great excitement in the Herberge over several little auctions, which the tramps were conducting for their own benefit. Some had coats, vests, and trousers to sell, while others were crying up the virtue of old buttons, collars, cuffs, neckties, and even pocket-books, the latter being found in almost every tramp's pocket. He finds them companionable, he says, whether he has any money or not. Several coats sold for five and ten cents apiece, while trousers brought higher prices. Knives were also on the market, and fully a dozen changed hands. I was struck in these auctions by the absence of Jews. In fact, I met only three during the trip, and they were extremely well dressed. I fancy that a tramp's life hardly offers inducements to men of their predilections. Yet one would think that no work and a fair reward for begging might satisfy even their trading propensities.

The trip from Hanover to Bremen was uninteresting, with only one incident worth recording. Five of us stopped on Easter night at one of the large bonfires that the peasants had built, just outside of Hanover, to commemorate the great holiday. When we arrived they were carousing most jovially, and seemed only too glad to welcome other companions; so we all took part, and danced around the fire, sometimes with the peasant girls, and then again by ourselves or singly. The peasants took no notice of the fact that we were tramps, and shared their sour milk and brown bread with us as if we were their best friends. One old fellow took such a fancy to Carl that he actually gave him a sechser. I was surprised to see him accept it, for the old man needed it much more than he did. This illustrates very truthfully the utter lack of friendly consideration in the character of the German tramp. One of the American species would have returned the penny with thanks, for he is a generous fellow, and can appreciate other interests than his own. But the Chausséegrabentapezirer has the least tender feeling of any beggar of my acquaintance. Even as a boon companion he falls far below the standard, and would never be tolerated in American trampdom. I can now understand why the great majority of German beggars in America are compelled to "flock" by themselves, and to choose companions from their own ranks. Their selfishness bars them out of the true brotherhood.

In Bremen poor Carl suffered a keen disappointment. He found that he could not ship as a coal-trimmer without a pass permitting him to leave the country. I advised him to seek work, and to earn money enough to pay his passage to New York. His trade was not overcrowded, and he had had a chance to labor in nearly every town we had visited, and I knew that he could succeed in Bremen. He finally decided to follow my advice; but the resolution weakened him so that I fear for a week at least he was a sorry-looking fellow. When we separated, he said,

"Auf Wiedersehen in Sheekago in '93." Indeed, nearly every tramp that I met intended to cross the ocean in '93, and to take part in Germany's exhibit at the fair. Of course they did not all succeed, but some most certainly did.

While I was sitting in the Heimath in Bremen, who should come in but a policeman and a detective. They passed around among the laborers, journeymen, and vagrants, asking a few questions, and looking occasionally at the men's passes. I was in somewhat of a tremor, and expected to be quizzed also. But, as luck would have it, they passed me by, and I escaped a searching. They arrested one tramp, but he was the only unfortunate I met during my travels. I learned afterward that he was sentenced to two days' imprisonment. An American beggar would have told the judge that he could stand on his head that long, but the German took it more seriously. From Bremen I decided to go south, and compare my experiences in northern Germany with tramp life in the vicinity of Cologne. I left Bremen with seven men on the train, and traveled the first day as far as Osnabrück, where I made an unnecessary halt, for I found nothing new or interesting there. There were plenty of tramps, it is true, but they had no news to impart, except that Osnabrück was a poor town. One youngster could hardly say enough against its hospitality. He claimed that he had even begged of the clergymen, and all that he received were "a few paltry pfennigs." I must admit that the boy was not far from correct in his judgment, for I visited several houses, and all I got was a dry piece of bread, which was given me by an old woman wiser than she was generous. Learning that I was a foreigner, she must needs know all about my ancestors, where I had come from, and where I was going. And then she made me listen to a long account of her boy in Piper City, —she was not sure whether it was in North or South America,—and asked me if I had ever met him. I told her that I had not, and she was nearly dumfounded. She thought that in the United States, "where there were so few people," everybody should know everybody else. I left her to her surprise and chagrin.

The city of Münster was my next stopping-place, and a greater contrast to Osnabrück could hardly exist. At the Herberge I learned that the town was considered one of the best between Hamburg and Cologne. The evidence was certainly convincing, for the tramps had all the liquor they could drink, as well as numerous bundles of food. Two fellows were doing a good business in exchanging their bread and *Wurst* (sausage) for groschen which others had begged instead of something to eat. I invested a few sechser in these wares, and was most bountifully repaid, receiving half a loaf of bread and two good-sized sausages for two and a half cents of our currency. This custom is very prevalent in German trampdom, and will illustrate the machinery of vagrancy. Some men will beg only for food, while others devote most of their lives to looking for money, and in almost any Herberge, even in the Heimath, these two parties can be found trading as if they were in a market. They scold, "jew," and fight one another while the trade is progressing, but when the bargain is finished good

DANCING AROUND A BONFIRE.

fellowship is again resumed. The joviality in the Herberge after the "market" was as boisterous and companionable as if there had not been the slightest trouble. Even the innkeeper took part, and danced around the room with his guests as if he were as much of a tramp as any of them. I think he had been a roadster sometime in his life, for he entered into the schemes and plans as earnestly as the law allows. Some of the men were discussing the number of charitable families in Münster, and more especially those "good" for money. One man, in order to make his point, enumerated by name the families friendly to beggars. The innkeeper, not agreeing with him, gave his own census of the Münster people, and it was most interesting to hear from his lips just what citizens were worth visiting and what not. Having conducted a tramp hotel in the city for years, he had found it to his interests to gather and dispense information useful to his customers. He could tell exactly what house was "good" for a meal or a hand-out, and could also map out the districts sure to yield pfennigs, groschen, or half-mark pieces. It is needless to say that such a man is invaluable to beggars. They hold him dearer than any other member of the clan, and pay him most liberally for his wisdom by spending nearly all of their money in his inn. This they can afford to do, for without his information and protection they would encounter hardships and difficulties insurmountable. During my stay at the Herberge, the proprietor sent out as many as eight fellows to different parts of the town, well posted and equipped for successful begging. Three of these men returned while I was still there, having averaged three marks and a half apiece in about five hours. If they had worked for this length of time their wage would have been about one mark apiece.

The journey from Münster to Düsseldorf is so tiresome afoot, and there is so little of interest lying between the towns, that I made the trip by rail, with three companions bound for Bavaria. These men had been tramping around in northern Prussia for nearly two months, and were thoroughly disgusted with their experiences. This was not surprising, however, for the Bavarian as well as the Saxon tramps think there is no prosperity outside of their own provinces, and, wander as much as they may in foreign parts, usually return to their own fields, feeling that they made a mistake in leaving. Begging in these provinces is also much more remunerative than anywhere else in Germany. Even the religion in Bavaria favors mendicancy, and it is only necessary to stand on a Sunday morning in front of some church to make a very fair haul. The tramps loaf around in the neighborhood of the churches and *stossen* (tackle) the poor Catholics as they pass in and out, usually getting a pfennig at least. One old roadster, thankful that he had lost a leg in the war of 1870, was unusually successful; but I heard afterward that he had been in the city for years, and probably the people take care of him as a sort of relic. He was rather clever, too, and had formed some sage opinions on charity and poverty. "The poor people," he said, "are the best friends we have. They give ten times where the rich man gives once." This is an indisputable fact.

In Cologne, where I arrived on April 21, the tramps were planning trips into southern Germany, Switzerland, and the Tyrol. I had intended to make at least one of these excursions, but I was tired, nauseated, and homesick. I made quick work with the towns of Elberfeld, Essen, Barmen, and Dortmund, and once settled down in Berlin, with almanac and gazetteer before me, found I had been fifteen days *auf der Walze*, had traveled over one thousand kilometers, studied more than seventy towns and villages, and met three hundred and forty-one voluntary vagrants, all of them, however, less voluntary than I.

The German tramp, if these experiences justify me in judging him, is a fairly intelligent fellow of not more than average tramp education, more stupid and less vicious than his American *confrère*, and with the traits of his nationality well stamped upon him. He is cautious, suspicious to a degree, ungenerous, but fairly just and square-dealing in the company of his fellows. He is too much of a Bohemian to be a Social Democrat, but has not enough patriotism to be easily fired with enthusiasm for his Kaiser. He loves schnapps and hates what he calls the *verdammte Heiligkeit* such as Die Herberge zur Heimath seeks to cultivate. He has generally served his three years in the army, but will dodge the recruiting officer by skipping his country whenever possible, if he has not. Besides this pervasive lack of patriotism, he has other dangers for the country. In the February riots in Berlin (1891) he was out in force, not for labor rights as against capital, but lending his shoulder to the wheel which he fondly hoped might turn in the direction of a general overthrow of the existing social state and order.

In regard to the public on which the German tramp lives and thrives, it is only necessary to say that it is even more inanely generous than its counterpart in the United States. With all its groans under taxes, military and otherwise, it nevertheless takes upon itself voluntarily the burden of the voluntary vagrant—the man who will not work. This is the more surprising when one recollects that the entire theoretical treatment of beggars in Germany is founded on the supposition that each one is a bona-fide seeker of labor. The community practically says to the culprit: You can make use of our Verpflegung-Stationen, where you can work for your lodging and meals, and have also a half-day to search for work, if you can identify yourself as a seeker of labor. We not only offer this, but also attempt to guarantee you, through the efforts of our philanthropists, a casual refuge in Die Herberge zur Heimath, while you are out of work. And if, through untoward circumstances or through your own carelessness and weakness, you have fallen so low that the Stationen and the Heimath cannot take you in because your identification-papers are irregular, and you appear more of a vagabond than an unfortunate laborer, we then invite you into the labor colonies, founded also by our philanthropists, where you can remain until you have earned good clothes and proved yourself worthy. But if we catch you begging, we will punish you as a vagrant; consequently you would do better to make use of all the privileges we offer, and thus break no laws. This is the theory, and I consider it a good one. But the man who will not work passes through these institutions as freely as the man who will, owing to the lack of determined discrimination on the part of the officers, and the desperate cleverness of the offenders.

II

WITH THE RUSSIAN GORIOUNS

I

IT was not my intention, in going to Russia, to tramp there. I planned merely to see St. Petersburg and Moscow, work for a while on Count Tolstoi's farm at Yasnaya Polyana, and then, after a short trip in the south, return to Berlin. I did all these things according to expectation, but I also made a tramp trip. It happened in this way: I had no more than reached the Russian capital when the tramp was forced upon me. As I jumped into the cab with my friend, who had come to the train to meet me, he pointed out about twenty tattered and sorry-looking peasants, marching by us under police escort.

"There go some Goriouns," he exclaimed—"look quick!"

I had only to follow the men with my eyes to know that they were Russian tramps.

"What are the police doing with them?" I asked.

"Oh, they probably have no passports and are to be sent back to their villages."

"Are there many tramps in Russia?"

My friend laughed. "Thousands of them. You

can hardly go into a village without meeting them. They are one of the greatest problems Russia has to deal with."

I soon saw also that I could not even approach a church without being accosted by them. They stood on the steps and at the doorway of every one I visited, and invariably begged of me, saying, "Radi Krista" ("For Christ's sake"). Even at Yasnaya Polyana, fifteen miles from the nearest town, and several minutes' walk from a highway, the Gorioun put in an appearance. I was there ten days, and at least one called every morning. They all seemed to know about Count Tolstoi's gospel, and came to his home, sure, at least, of something to eat. On the highway, at some distance from the house, I saw bands of ten and twenty marching by every day, and they often camped at a bridge which I crossed on my walks.

This continual meeting the tramp and hearing about him naturally made me curious, and I wondered whether it would be possible to make a journey among them. I knew enough Russian at least to make myself understood, and could understand much that was said to me. The great question, however, was whether, as a foreigner, I should be allowed to make such a trip. I talked with Count Tolstoi one day about the matter, telling him some of my experiences in other countries, and asking his advice.

"Why not?" he said, in his jovial, pleasant way. "Of course you will have hard work in understanding their dialects, and you can hardly expect to be taken for one of them, but otherwise you ought to get on easily enough. From your pass and other papers the police will see that you are nothing dangerous, and if anything should happen, all you have to do is to send to St. Petersburg. I should like to make such a trip myself, if I were younger. I 'm too old now. Once I went on a long pilgrimage and saw a good deal of the life, but of course you will see much more if you go directly into the tramp class. If you decide to make the trip, I wish you would find out how they look upon the authorities, and whether they really believe in what they call their religion. It ought to be very interesting to talk with them on these topics, and perhaps you will be able to gather some useful material —only you will not be permitted to print it here in Russia"; and he smiled.

I finally decided to make a trial trip, and was fortunate in finding a Moscow student who was willing to accompany me for a few days. He had tramped perforce in some of the southern provinces, and being much interested in the tramp class in the Vitebsk government, consented to go with me if I would begin my investigations there. I was fortunate also in having brought a tramp outfit with me. It had already seen service in England, Germany, and Italy, and I had taken it along for work in the fields at Yasnaya Polyana. It was a little better than the usual Gorioun dress, but I should really have been ashamed to put on anything shabbier. My friend the student was clad in a patched university uniform, which all of his class have to wear in Russia, and he looked like pictures I have seen of ragged Union soldiers in Libby Prison. We both had a little money in our pockets, and it was not our intention to beg for anything more than bread and milk, and not even for these things unless it was necessary to make good our pose. We reasoned that the peasants of whom we should have to ask for them needed them much more than we did, and I am glad to say that neither of us on this trip, nor I on others, which were sometimes made alone, asked for much that we did not pay for.

Our credentials for the journey consisted of our passports, some university papers, and an open letter which I had received in St. Petersburg from Prince Chilkoff, the Minister of Ways and Communication. It was addressed to the director of the Siberian Railway, but I kept it by me for the sake of identification, and it helped me through many a predicament, although the officials to whom it was presented could never get it through their heads how I, an Amerikanski tramp, could be in the possession of such an almighty document. There were times, I fear, when they were tempted to arrest me as an impostor, but they never did—a good fortune which I can only explain on account of the singularity of the situation. The Russian "system" was evidently not prepared for so weird a creature, and I was allowed to pass as an anomaly.

With the Moscow student I tramped for three days in the Vitebsk government, between the towns of Polotsk and Dünaburg, as dreary a stretch of country as is to be found anywhere in our West. It was warm August weather, and the sun came down on us in all its Russian fierceness. There were times when I simply had to get under a tree to keep from sunstroke. At night we slept out of doors, or in haystacks and barns. The peasants always offered us the hospitality of their cabins, as they do to all tramps, but we could not bring ourselves to put up with the vermin we should have found there. In winter, on the other hand, the Gorioun is glad enough to curl up over their stoves, and I suppose that we also should have been, had the weather been cold. As it was, most of the vagabonds we met slept outside, as we did, and we always had plenty of company. On this trip we met two hundred, traveling in bands and families. They invariably wanted to know where I came from, which is the first question they ask, after the greeting, "Strassvuitye," and I told them the truth on each occasion. "America—America," they would say in their simple way. "What government is that in?" meaning what Russian province. I could not make them understand that it was not in Russia at all, which to them is the entire world, but they called me "the far-away brother," and I was probably considered a new species in their class. I never had the feeling that they accepted me as one of their own,—it would have been strange if they had,—but they, at any rate, dubbed me "brother," and this was as much as I could ask. They always wanted to share their simple fare with me, and I soon saw that there was but little danger in associating with them.

II

There are two types of tramps in Russia, and they may be classified as the authorized and the unauthorized. The first are the so-called religious mendicants, who are protected by the church and tolerated by the police; the second are the common vagabonds. It is these last who constitute, from the Russian point of view, the tramp problem. The religious beggars are considered an inevitable church class, and are taken care of almost as conscientiously as the priests. The common tramps, on the other hand, are looked upon as a very unnecessary burden, and ever since the conversion of Russia to Christianity, laws have been passed and institutions founded for their suppression and reform. It is estimated that in European Russia alone they number over nine hundred thousand, and in Siberia their class represents an even greater proportion of the population.

Their national name among themselves is "Gorionns"—mourners, or victims of grief. The word is an invention of their own, but is supposed to come from the Russian word *gore*, meaning sadness. In Russian proper they are called *brodiagi*. If you ask them why they do not work,—and the great majority are perfectly able to do so,—they reply in the forlornest voice mortal ever heard: "Master, I am a Gorioun—a victim of sorrow." They seem to have accepted the philosophy that a certain number of human beings are foreordained to a life of misery and sadness, and they pose as members of this class. On many of their passports I saw such expressions as "Burned out," "Has lost all his relatives," "Has no home," "Will die soon," "Is possessed of the pitiful spirit," and others of a like nature, which they bribe officials to write, or themselves forge. I could have had similar explanations put on my own passport. There are tramps who make a regular business of this kind of imposture, and it is another evidence of how difficult it is to make even a passport tell the truth. In Germany the same trick is practised by tramps, and in both countries the beggar can buy false passes which the police cannot detect. I saw several in Russia which looked exactly like the genuine thing, and, had I wished to appear to be a Russian, could have bought one any day for ten rubles.

In looks and dress the Gorioun acts out to a nicety the story which his papers are supposed to substantiate. Never have I seen such sad faces as these men and women have when begging. At heart they are capable of considerable fun and boisterousness, but they affect a look of despondency, which many of them retain even when off duty. In other respects they resemble very closely the ordinary peasant, or *muzhik*. They all have an immense shock of hair, parted in the middle and chopped off roughly at the edges. The face is generally covered with a huge beard, which gives them a backwoodsman look not always indicative of their character. In America, for instance, they would be taken by tramps for "Hoosiers," but, in their way, they are just as clever and sharp as the hobo who would laugh at them. Indeed, I know of no hobo who can equal them in facial trickery and disguise, and wherever this is the necessary qualification for successful begging they are past masters. Their clothes are invariably rough and patched, and if by some chance they get a good suit it is pawned or sold immediately. The usual peasant shirt or blouse takes the place of a coat, and the trousers are tucked into the boots also in peasant fashion. A tea-pot hangs at the belt, and a bundle, containing all their possessions, is slung over the shoulder. Thus they tramp about the country from village to village, year in and year out, and are always distinguishable from the fact that on meeting a *Gospodinn* (gentleman), or any one else of whom they can beg, off come their greasy caps, down go their great shocky heads, and they say, "Radi Krista."

When tramping on the highway, they average about fifteen miles a day, but a great many never make over five. One old man on the Kursk road, between Tula and Orel, told me that he was satisfied if he covered three versts a day,—a verst is two thirds of a mile, —and he expected that it would take him the entire autumn and part of the winter to reach Odessa, whither he was bound. In this respect the Goriouns are like all other vagabonds; they love rest, and if they find a good place, stick to it as long as possible. In the country they make their homes with the peasants, sleeping in summer in sheds and haystacks, and in winter in the peasants' cabins. Plagues though they are, the peasant always gives them shelter, and it very seldom happens that they die of cold or starvation in districts thickly populated. I could have stopped for days in every village I passed through, and the peasants would even have protected me from the police if it had been in their power. Their own life is so hard that it comes natural to take pity on the tramp, and they all have the feeling that favors thus shown prepare a place for them in the heaven of their imagination. Indeed, the Gorioun plays on this feeling in begging of them. I often heard him say, in asking for alms: "It will help you out above"; and his humble friends seemed pleased to be thus assured.

Men predominate in the Gorioun class, but in no other country that I have visited are there so many women and families "on tramp." They are all mixed up together, men, women, and children, and no great effort is made to keep even the families intact. I was told by tramps that in the peasants' cabins there is very little separation even between the peasants and the vagabonds, and on cold nights they all curl up in a heap on the tops of the great piles of masonry which serve them as stoves. In large cities they live in lodging-houses and night-shelters. In St. Petersburg these places are found mainly in what is called the "Siennaia," about five blocks behind the Kazan cathedral. There are entire alleyways and courts in this district given up to the Gorious, and in one house alone, Dom Viazemski, over ten thousand lodge every night. They have the right to return to their planks at any time during the day, and speak of them as their homes—their *dom*. The cost of a "spot" on the benches is thirty-five copecks (about twenty cents) a week, in advance.

The life that goes on here is pretty much the same as in lodging-houses everywhere, but there are a few peculiar features to be noticed. In the first place, there is a chief, or *ataman*, of the Goriouns of each room, and he is given the rights and privileges of a bully. He is the strongest and most daring of all, and his companions allow him to play "the almighty act," as the hobo would say, in their confabs and councils. Any tramp who refuses to knuckle

SLEEPING IN A BARN.

down to him is considered either a spy or a rival candidate, in which latter case he must fight it out with fists, and sometimes with knives. If he is successful he takes the ataman place, and holds it until some one else dislodges him. In case he is taken for a spy he is shunned by all concerned, and I was told that every year several men are killed on this suspicion. When an actual raid by the police is planned, the ataman generally gets wind of it beforehand, and all lights are put out before the police arrive. They can then accomplish very little, and while I was in St. Petersburg several of their attempted raids ended unsuccessfully.

Another queer custom is the way each man takes care of his boots. In every country the *Schuhwerk*, as the Germans say, is prized, perhaps, more than any other part of the wardrobe, but the reason in St. Petersburg is unique. Thanks to his boots, the Gorioun can be enrolled as a torch-bearer or mourner at funerals, and this is one of his most lucrative employments. The agencies which manage funerals recruit from the tramp class so many mourners for each interment; about thirteen thousand are employed in this way every year. The agencies furnish the suitable clothes and pocket-handkerchiefs—everything, in fact, but the shoes, which the tramp must be able to show on his feet, or he will not be hired. When a funeral is "on," the tramps gather at the Nikolski market, and are selected by an employee of the agency. Those chosen are conducted to the house of the deceased, and there, under a porch, in a shed, or even in the court, ten, twenty, or thirty of them, according to the elaborateness of the funeral, undress themselves entirely, even in the dead of winter, and put on the mourner's garb. Their own clothing is rolled up in a bundle and taken to the cemetery in a basket, where, after the ceremony, it must be put on again. The promised wage for this service is forty copecks a man, but with tips and drinks it usually amounts to a ruble. The St. Petersburg street-gamins have a way of crying out, "Nachel li?" ("Hast thou found it?") to the Gorlouns as they file along—an allusion to their daylight torches. Some very funny scenes take place when the boys get too saucy; for the men forget, in their anger, the solemnity of the situation, and, dropping their torches, run after the boys, much to the consternation of the agency and the family concerned.

The funeral over and the money in their pockets, they return to the lodging-house for an uproarious night spent in drinking *vodka*. When the last drop is gone, they fall over on their planks senseless, and to see them in this condition makes one fancy he is looking on in a morgue. They lie there as if dead, and the stench in the room could not be worse if they were actually in a state of decay. One would think, under such circumstances, there must be a heavy percentage of sickness and mortality among them, but I think this is not true. I saw a number of crippled and deformed beggars, but otherwise they seemed a fairly healthy lot, and never anywhere have I seen such herculean bodies. Many of them looked as if they could lift an ox, and in one of the few squabbles that I witnessed, they knocked one another about in a way that would have done honor to professional pugilists. However, these knock-down fights are not frequent. For a people so degraded they are phenomenally sweet-tempered; in England and America, tramps with their strength would be measuring it on all occasions.

In the lodging-houses, as in the peasants' cabins, men and women are mixed up together, and there seems to be no effort at all to keep them separated. They say that they are married, or "belong to the family," and the *Starosta* (proprietor) allows them to keep together. Their children—and each couple has its full share—are used for begging purposes; indeed, they are the winning card of the Russian tramp. If they are deformed or crippled, so much the better.

The food of these tramps is probably the simplest bill of fare known among European vagabonds. On the road they seldom have more than black bread and milk, and even in towns they are satisfied with the addition of a dish of potatoes. Meat they know very little about, and it almost never occurs to them to spend their money for a good steak; they prefer to buy vodka. Of course there are exceptions to this rule; in every country there are beggars who keep up with the latest styles and indulge in a gourmet's dishes, but they are not common in Russia.

There is another trait of the Gorionns to record—their clannishness. In almost every government of the empire they are organized as compactly as a trade-union, and even in St. Petersburg, strict as the police are, they have their peculiar *artel*. It was impossible for me to become a member of these corporations. I should have had to knuckle down very submissively to some ataman, or bully, and this I was not willing to do. It would also have been necessary to learn the different dialects, and I had all I could do to make use of my small Russian vocabulary. Each artel has its own peculiar lingo, and it is almost as hard to learn as Russian itself. Even the native inhabitants know very little about such dialects, and the students who traveled with me had as much difficulty as I did in understanding them. Fortunately, however, the tramps can also speak Russian, and we generally conversed with them in this language. I give here what I learned about their various artels, but it is in no sense an exhaustive report. There are many of which I heard nothing, and it would take a book to describe them all.

In Moscow one of the most notorious clans is the so-called "Gouslitzki," or "Old Believers," who came originally from the district of Bogorodsk. They are mixed up with the regular working population of the town and have no particular sign by which a stranger could distinguish them, but their business is entirely criminal. They counterfeit money, forge passports and baptismal certificates, beg and steal, and the police have to keep a continual watch over them. Ostensibly their business is manufacturing trinkets, colored images, and toys, but these are merely subterfuges to gain them the privilege of standing on the sidewalks as hawkers. In their lodging-houses—and there are several supported by them alone—they live under the direction of a head man whom they must obey, and a certain percentage of their day's earnings has to be contributed to a common fund. From time to time this fund is divided equally among all the members of the organization, but it is almost immediately given back as "renewed stock." The Gouslitzki are unlike most of their class in being very parsimonious, and they have the reputation of drinking very little—some not at all. They speak two languages, Russian and a dialect which is practically their mother-tongue. They have been settled in Moscow for generations, and the police find it impossible to drive them out.

The "Chouvaliki," another well-known gang, are mainly peasants, but they come also from the Moscow government, being settled in the districts of Veresisk and Mozhaisk. It would be very peculiar in America to see a band of farmers starting off on begging and marauding trips, but this happens in Russia, and the Chouvaliki are of this class. In the census of Russia they are put down as peasants, and they do pretend to work a part of the year, but they are known from Moscow to the Don as the begging Chouvaliki. They go on the road twice a year, and exploit by preference the governments of Tamboff, Voronesh, and so on down to the Don. The Russians call them brigands, and tell frightful stories about their robberies, but the Goriouns spoke of them merely as beggars, and I fancy this is what they are. On returning from their trips, which last sometimes several weeks, they spend in one orgy all the money they have taken in.

It is in White Russia, and above all in the government of Vitebsk, farther north, that the tramps form these beggars' organizations. During my journey through the Vitebsk government I heard of them right and left, and it is this district that contributes largely to the criminal population of St. Petersburg. The rich Ukraine is also a notorious haunt. At Kharkoff, for instance, I got into a regular nest of them, called "Tchortoff Gniezda" (Nest of Devils). They live there in dirty little cabins and underground caves, a close community with its ataman and common funds. They start out in the morning on their begging trips, and return at night for debauches, those who have been most successful inviting their *rakli*, or pals, to celebrate with them. There is a careful division, or *douban*, of all the spoils taken in during the day, and each one receives his share, minus the contribution to the common tribe.

In Kazan, the Tatar town on the Volga, there is an artel of beggars whose origin goes back to the taking of Kazan by Ivan IV, and they are known all over Russia as the "Kazanskia Sieroty" (the Kazan Orphans). Although Mussulmans, they beg "in the name of Christ" ("Radi Krista"). They will beg even from other beggars if they do not belong to their organization, and consider everybody their prey who is not an "Orphan." They can only be compared to the tramps who exploit the governments of Samara and Saratoff, and those coming from fifteen villages of the districts of Saransk and Insarsk, in the government of Penza. These last, although officially peasants, are all organized into narrow begging corporations, and call themselves "Kalousni," which comes from their dialect word *kalit*, meaning "to reap," or, as they would say, "to beg." In Moscow, on the other hand, the generic dialect term for beggars is "Zvonary," which comes from *zvonit*, also meaning "to beg."

The Kalousni, or "Reapers," start out on their begging trips in their wagons immediately after harvest. All of them who can move, excepting the very oldest and youngest, depart for "the work," as it is called. Those who have no blind or deformed children of their own rent them in neighboring villages. The village of Akchenas is the center of this trade, and peasants send their deformed children there to be marketed off. In the Galitzin village, in the government of Penza, amounting to three hundred cabins, five hundred of the inhabitants are peasant beggars; in Akchenas, one hundred and twenty cabins, there are only four persons who are not "Reapers"; in Germakoff, another hamlet of the district, there is not an inhabitant who does not go kalit (begging). The return of these bands to their homes is celebrated by fêtes and orgies. The main one is on November 8, St. Michael's day, when they spend every copeck they have collected. The next trip takes place in winter, and they return to their villages by Lent. The third return is just before Pentecost.

Although I did not tramp in Siberia, I traveled there and heard much of the local tramps. They are not so definitely organized as in European Russia,—many travel entirely alone,—but I saw and heard of several categories. On the highway between Ekaterinburg and Tiumen the traveler is accosted by beggars known as the "Kossoulinski." They live exclusively by begging, and in summer sleep out of doors along the route between the towns mentioned.

At Ekaterinburg there are also unnamed gangs of young men and little boys and girls who are continually begging of the inhabitants. They are generally the children of deported convicts, or those of peasants who were driven by famine out of neighboring districts.

If I could have got into the wooded parts of Siberia I might also have madé the acquaintance of that queer product of Siberian prison life, the runaway convict tramp. Early in the spring he makes a dash for liberty, sometimes being shot down in the attempt, and then again succeeding. He runs to the woods and lives there until autumn, when, if there is no hope of getting back to European Russia, he gives himself up and returns to prison again. In the spring, "when the birds call him," as one of his songs pathetically relates, he makes another dash for the trees. Only at night does he venture into the villages, and then merely for a moment to snatch the food left for him on the window-sills by the generous-hearted peasants. He grabs the bread, or whatever it is that they have set out, and then scampers back to the woods like a wolf.

III

RELIGIOUS beggars in Russia are a class by themselves. In giving alms to them the average Russian thinks that he is making so much more likely his welcome in heaven, and they, of course, stand by him in the conceit. If you give them a ruble they will swear that you are going to heaven, and even twenty copecks make one's chance pretty good.

The most easily distinguished type is what is called

the religious lay mendicant. He is always standing around the churches in St. Petersburg and Moscow, and everybody who has visited these cities will recall him. He is generally an old peasant, begging for some village church, and the police or church authorities give him the necessary passes and stamped documents. He stands at a church door or near some shrine, bareheaded and with a little plate in his hand, covered with cloth on which is embroidered the cross. This is a *passe-partout* wherever he goes, and serves as an excuse for entering restaurants, railway-stations, and other public places. As a Russian gentleman said to me: "You can't drive a man out with the cross in his hand," and he is consequently allowed to go pretty much where he pleases. Unfortunately, however, it is not very difficult to imitate him, and there are a number of Gorious in Russia, posing as religious lay mendicants. They counterfeit the necessary papers, buy the plate and cross, and then beg with all their might. Occasionally they are discovered and severely punished, but the winnings from this kind of begging are so tempting—sometimes as much as ten rubles, or five dollars a day—that they are willing to run the risk. There are also monk beggars who proceed in the same way as those of the lay order, except that they wear monk costumes. It is consequently not easy for the common tramp to imitate them, but it has been done.

Authorized and permitted though these monks are, there is but little need for them to beg, for their convents are almost without exception rich. The more they have, however, the more they want, and so the monks are sent out to beg of poor and rich alike. An amusing story is told of how one of these convents was relieved of some of its superfluous wealth. During the Crimean War Nicholas I borrowed ten million rubles from the Laura monastery at Kieff, and gave in exchange his note like any other mortal. Alexander II, after coming to the throne, made a tour of the provinces and visited Kieff, where, according to custom, the first thing he did was to call at the Laura. He was received by the metropolitan and clergy in great array, and during the ceremony the note of Nicholas was presented to him, of course for payment, on a beautiful plate. He took the bit of paper, read it carefully, and then, holding it high in the air, said in a very solemn voice: "Behold the most touching proof of the patriotism of Russia's clergy when she has need of them! I cannot better thank you than by giving you, as a glorious memento, this autograph of my august father." And that ended the matter for all time.

The pilgrims are another type of religious beggar. They also are mainly old peasants, who have made a vow to go afoot to some distant shrine, often a thousand miles away. They take with them only money enough to buy candles to place at the altars where they worship en route, and trust to the mercy of the people they meet for food and shelter. No peasant would refuse them hospitality, and they are taken in whenever they appear. Money is never offered them, because it is known that they will not accept it. All they want is food enough to keep body and soul together, and this they feel free to ask for.

These pilgrimages are very frequent in Russia, and are always the result of a vow, made sometimes many years before. Each famous monastery, like the Soloviecki, near the White Sea, the Troitzke, near Moscow, the Laura, at Kieff, and many others, has its days of "grand pardon," which attract pilgrims from the farthest points of the empire. They travel invariably on foot, and occasionally in bands, but the typical pilgrim goes alone. His destination is sometimes even Jerusalem. This is often the case among devoted monks, who make this the last act of a life consecrated to the church. The peasants feed and shelter the pilgrim, and he is one of their main objects of veneration.

There is one more class of authorized beggars in Russia—the nuns. These women, with long robes and pointed bonnets, generally travel in couples. They beg on what is called the "contract system." An arrangement is made with a convent by which they are allowed to exploit certain districts, and they agree in return to give the convent a certain percentage of their winnings; all over this amount belongs to them personally. They are taxed according to their ability, the percentage varying from one to three rubles a day. When they are young and pretty, which they sometimes are, they do very well. As a Russian who has often given to them said to me: "You can't give copper to a pretty woman," and they know wonderfully well how to make their attractions tell. They are acquainted with all the "good places," and learn quickly to discern the generous giver. There is no doubt, however, that much is given them without any thought of the church or religion, and it is an open secret in Russia that there is a great deal of corruption among them. I myself saw them in a state of intoxication several times, and their conduct was not at all in keeping with their religious calling.

IV

SOMETHING remains to be said about the causes of vagabondage in Russia and what is being done to suppress it. The religious mendicants must be left out of the discussion, for they are not supposed to be a part of the problem. It is the Gorioun class that the Russians are particularly anxious to be rid of, and it is they who correspond to the tramp class in more Western countries.

The love of liquor is the main cause of their degradation. Two thirds could be made respectable men and women if they were free of their passion for drink, and until they are, I see no hope of bettering them. They will even steal from the churches, religious as they are, if impelled by thirst for vodka, and it is simply impossible for an employer to have anything to do with them. In St. Petersburg a large number of them are discharged mechanics and day-laborers, who know perfectly well how to earn their living, but have lost position after position on account of their loose habits. The minute they get a week's wage, they go off and spend it for drink, and then there is no place for them.

Besides this strictly individual cause, there are certain economic facts which help to explain the situa-

A LODGING-HOUSE.

tion. The lowering of railroad fares has started a regular hegira of peasants toward the towns, where they imagine that they are to make their fortunes. We think in America that a great deal might be done to change the lot of outcasts if they could be led back to the country and settled on farms, but Russia teaches us plainly enough that this alone will not suffice. There must be something besides country air and surroundings to offset the attractions and temptations of city life. In Russia it has been found that after the peasant has once experienced these attractions he is never happy on the farm.

Over seven thousand peasant tramps are sent away from St. Petersburg every year, but a still larger number find their way back. There is a case on record where a man was sent away one hundred and seven times and returned after each expulsion. When one takes into consideration that the majority of all those thus sent away receive new clothes before leaving, it is easy to see what an expense they are to the town, and the most of them sell their new clothes at the first opportunity. This is one of the weakest points in all the Russian methods with tramps. The police return vagabonds to their villages, expecting them thus to be kept away from city temptations, but the trouble is that they cannot hold them there. They run back to the towns the first chance they get, and then there has to be another expensive expulsion. Lately some of the governors of inland districts have petitioned the police to stop doing this, explaining that tramps thus returned corrupt their village companions.

Besides returning a beggar to his village, there are

also light punishments. If he is arrested for the first time in St. Petersburg, he is brought before a commission, by which he is questioned and then handed over to a more special committee, before which he must submit to another cross-questioning. If he can prove that he has been driven to beg by poverty alone, he is recommended to the care of the poor authorities of his district. If he has been arrested several times before, he is taken immediately to a justice, by whom he is condemned to a punishment, varying, according to circumstances, from a month's to three months' hard labor in prison. These are only such beggars as have been caught in the act, so to speak, and have papers certifying to their identity. Those who are found without passports are taken in hand by the police alone. If nothing very bad is found against them, they are allowed to go free, if some one will stand sponsor for them; in this case they must send to their home authorities for a passport, and if it is received they can remain in the town for a period of three months. It is possible with good conduct to have this term of probation prolonged to nine months, but after that, unless very good reasons are given, the man must return to his village.

There are also reformatory and charitable institutions which seek a regeneration of the tramp on philanthropic grounds. Recently a number of workhouses have been put up in the largest towns, and great hopes are placed in these very praiseworthy undertakings. The present empress has taken them all under her personal protection, and there is every likelihood that they will be well supported. The effort is thus made to offer every tramp a chance to work; they are to serve as a test-house where the Gorioun can show what he really is. He is not compelled to make use of them, but if it should be discovered that he knew about them and still begged, he would be punished very severely.

Both men and women are received, and they can earn their daily bread by working for it. Lodging must be found elsewhere, but children can be left during the day in a crèche belonging to the institution. Father John of Kronstadt is credited with having founded the first of these workhouses, but it is only lately that they have become popular. If well managed they ought to do good, for the great question in Russia, as well as everywhere else, is to find out who the really deserving are, and the workhouses can be of great assistance in developing the facts. How much they will aid in lessening the professional vagabondage of the country remains to be seen. If the police—and everybody knows what powers the Russian police have—are unable to accomplish this, it is hardly likely that the workhouses can do much more. Indeed, I fear that nothing can root out entirely this class in Russia. It is too old and settled to give up the struggle without a long resistance, and there are traditions dear to all Russians which will forever aid the Gorioun in his business. A Russian prince with whom I talked about the possibility of getting rid of the tramp class said to me: "It is simply out of the question. We are all beggars, every mother's son of us. The aristocrat begs a smile of the czar, and others ask for honors, positions, decorations, subsidies, and pensions, and it is these beggars who are the most persistent of all. Russia is the land of *na tchai* ["for tea," like *pour boire* in French, and *Trinkgeld* in German], and no laws or imperial ukase will ever make it any different."

III

TWO TRAMPS IN ENGLAND

THE British tramp had long been an object of curiosity with me. I felt that I knew his American cousin as well as it is possible to know him by living with him, and I had learned the ways of the German *Chausséegrabentapezirer*. Among my friends in the university at Berlin was a student of philosophy who also regarded the English tramp with interest so great that he was willing to make a tramp journey with me to discover and study him. He doubted somewhat his ability to pass for an undeveloped vagrant, but decided to try it. We suffered, I am proud to say, no diminution of our friendship in this curious comradeship in a new field.

One February day we drew up our agreement, and on the same day left for Hamburg. There we took ship for Grimsby, on a boat carrying mainly steerage passengers. Our fellow-travelers were twenty-two homeward-bound sailors, an old woman, and a young girl on her way to London to marry a man with whom she had fallen in love by telegram—at any rate, so she said.

We were all cooped up together in a nasty little

hole absolutely without ventilation. I felt sorry for the women, and they, in their kind-hearted way, said that they were sorry for me, "because I looked so sick-like." But I anticipate a little.

While we were still lying at the dock we had an amusing experience. Just as the gang-plank was nearly ready to be hauled in, two detectives came on board. I was surprised that they had not appeared before; for it is one of Kaiser Wilhelm's strong points to see that none of his young men, or "dear servants," as he calls them, get out of his domain before they have done their duty in his army. The sailors laughed at them, and told them to go home; meanwhile Ryborg and I were supposedly asleep. That there was method in this drowsiness I cannot deny, for Ryborg had no really current pass, and we were both fearful of being detained. We were finally discovered, and when one of the officers asked me if we were sailors, I rather naturally said, "Yes," being half asleep, and having seen that they had not disturbed the true seamen.

The man was determined to see my passport, however, and the long sheet of paper amused him considerably. He called it *ein mächtiges Ding*, and I patriotically told him he was right, and that it was about the "greatest thing" he had ever handled. He failed to see the point, and poked Ryborg. Then I quaked a little, but laughed inwardly too, when Ryborg handed him his student's card; for it did seem odd to find a student of philosophy in that miserable den. The detective thought so too, and claimed that he did not exactly understand the situation.

"Are you a sailor, a workman, an American, or what?" said the officer.

"Ich bin—ein Studierter" ("I am—a learned one"), gasped Ryborg.

That settled the matter. The detectives walked off, and we were left for the following thirty-two hours to our North Sea misery, which was of such a character that, when we landed, we vowed never to go to sea again.

Grimsby was uninteresting, so we went straight on to Hull. As this was the point where our vagabondage was properly to begin, I soon had my eye on watch for what American tramps call a "town bum." I found one in a main street, and introduced myself thus:

"I say, Jack, can you tell us where the moochers hang out in these parts?"

"You 're a Yank, ain't you?" said he.

This I acknowledged, at the same time asking, "Why?"

"Because I know a lot of blokes over in your country, an' I 'm thinkin' o' goin' over myself. How d' you think I 'd like it?"

"Tiptop," I answered; "but you know they 're givin' the likes of us ninety days in Chicago now."

"O-oh, well, p'r'aps I 'll go over later," was his rejoinder; and then he told me where the moochers were to be found.

"You see thet corner? Well, just turn thet, an' keep hoofin' along till you come to an alley. Go up to the top, then down on your right to the bottom, an' ask roun' there somewhere for Blanket Row. You 'll find all the moochers you want there; but look out for the Robert and the Dee [the policeman and the detective]. They 'll give you seven days if they catch you moochin'."

We found Blanket Row all right, and, luckily enough, at No. 21, a kip-house (lodging-house), or doss-house, as some call it, nicknamed "The Dog's Home." It looked rather uninviting, and we gazed at it carefully before entering. After a little consultation we made up our minds to go in, so we walked through a long and dirty passage, pushed open a creaky, rickety door, and found ourselves in a smoky, dirty hole containing about fifty moochers. I was greeted with: "Hello, Yank! Where 'd you come from?"

The voice came from the fire, and I walked over from the door, and found as miserable a specimen of vagrancy as one often sees. I sat down, and told him a long "ghost-story" (yarn), and he returned the favor in the same coin. When he was convinced that I was one of the fraternity, he pointed out various things of interest.

"Them fires," said he, "is where you cook your scoff [food]. You can make tea, too, any time you like, provided, of course, you 've got the tea. You 'll find all the pots, cans, pans, and boilers in that corner; they b'long to the missus, but we use them. Them cupboards over there is where you put your grub, ef you 're stayin' here any time; they cost a tanner [sixpence] apiece, but they ain't worth hawkin'. My stomach 's the only cupboard I need. That piece o' paper on the wall 's the only sort of picter they 've got in the place."

I looked over at the wall, and saw upon it a notice to the effect that smallpox was in the district, and that persons would be vaccinated free of charge at a place specified.

All this while Ryborg was doing his best to play tramp, and the stories he told, the tough way in which he tried to tell them, the half-and-half effects they achieved, and his general out-of-place condition, were almost as interesting to me as the real moochers. I overheard him telling one of the men that he was "a sailor by inclination, but a tough by temperament."

One of the tramps had taken a fancy to him, and was determined to be hospitable, so he boiled a large can of tea, and made poor Ryborg drink, drink, drink, till he had actually taken two quarts of the beverage at one sitting. He told me afterward that he had made up his mind, if any more were offered him, to pour it into his pocket, and trust to luck not to get caught.

The Dog's Home in the second story consisted principally of beds. The price of each is threepence a night, and this is the common price all over Great Britain, except in the so-called "Models," where a penny more is charged simply for the very deceitful name. I am sorry to say that the house was not much cleaner in the second story than in the first, if the tramps told us the truth. They all agreed in saying that the place was "crummy" (infested with vermin); consequently we decided to sleep elsewhere; for we wanted a good night's rest, and there was nothing especially to be gained by staying there.

We lived in the "home" in the daytime, however, and were on the watch for everything of interest. As for the "sweet charity" of Hull, I learned that most of the moochers were satisfied when they could beg a "bob" (shilling) a day besides "scoff," and some seemed happy on fourpence a day. The old men and the young boys were most successful in begging. There were vagrants of middle age, and some much younger, who did fairly well; but they lacked the determined spirit of the grandfathers and the kids. I had noticed this before in America, and suppose it is because the very old and the very young tramps realize that they must rely on their begging for subsistence, while the vagrants of twenty-five and thirty know that they have an alternative in work when luck goes against them, and are consequently less in earnest.

My companion and I, being somewhat better dressed than most of the lodgers, were objects of considerable interest. Our hats, peculiarly American in style, were the main curiosities. They proclaimed our nationality wherever we went. Never in my life have I been so bothered with stares. One day I took off my hat in a small crowd of people, and asked a bystander if he saw anything peculiar about it. He admitted that he did not; but still the citizens of Hull guyed me unmercifully, and, for that matter, so did their countrymen elsewhere.

I had been accustomed in America to dress fairly well when tramping, and the very clothes I was wearing in England had seen service at home and in Germany also; therefore I was quite unprepared for their comical reception by the British. There was only one man in the Dog's Home who appreciated our

AN ENGLISH TYPE.

style, and he was a countryman not so very long out of America. He was a most interesting fellow; had been both workman and tramp at home; but one day bade good-by to Hartford, Connecticut, and decided to go abroad. He came to Glasgow on a cattle-ship, expecting to get a return pass on his arrival, but was deceived, and put ashore with only four shillings in his pocket. Naturally he was angry, and made up his mind to see Scotland, England, and Wales at the expense of Scotchmen, Englishmen, and Welshmen. It was a courageous thing to do, if not a moral one; and, perhaps, it was not so very wicked, for his one ambition seemed to be to see the Tower of London. He had been "on tramp" about two months, had had some interesting experiences, and had become somewhat opinionated. Hearing that he had been in Scotland, I was interested to know whether he liked the country and had learned any of the tramp dialect that one might need there.

"To tell the truth, mate," he said, "I was too drunk. You see, I got hold of a fellow in Glasgow who had some boodle, and we chummed it together till the boodle was gone; and the only thing I can tell you about Glasgow or Edinburgh is that they 've got a fine pile of stone in Edinburgh, right in the main street, to the memory of that story-writer—you know his name—what is it?"

I suggested "Scott," and he went on:

"Yes; that 's it—Scott. Well, since I 've been out of Scotland I 've had some hard times, and I 'd 'a' been in Ameriky long ago if I had n't pawned my rubber boots. I tell you, Jack, I 'd ruther be lynched in our country than die a natural death over here; and as for moochin' and lodgin', why, I can beg in five minutes in New York more money than I can here in a day. As it is, I 'm a little bit of a wonder to some of these fellows, because I 'm so dead struck on havin' the pleasures of life. I look for 'em till I get 'em, you know, and so fur I 've had my bob a day, besides chuck. And that 's more than some of these blasted gay-cats can say. Did you ever in your life see such badly faked bums? They make me think of prehistoric gorillas. Half the time only a few parts of their bodies are covered in, and yet they think they can batter more when togged that way. How 's that for bein' bughouse [crazy], eh? Oh, well, you can laugh all you want to; but by the time you 've seen two per cent. of what I 've seen, you 'll say, 'Thet Yank war n't fur from bein' right.'" He promised to have another talk with me at the World's Fair.

The fellow was correct about the clothes and the filthiness of the English moocher. Generally he dresses in a way that in America would be thought indecent and in Germany criminal. He is too lazy to clean up, if he had the chance, and harbors vermin as if he liked them. It is not surprising that lodging-houses are so unclean; for if the proprietors of these places should admit only decent tramps, their houses would be left without occupants in a very short time. This is not an attractive theme, but it is one for the practical reformer to treat; for I am convinced that when a man becomes callous in regard to filth, his reformation will be far to seek. And there is nothing that can make a purely temporary vagrant a thoroughgoing one so surely as the inability to keep himself clean in person.

One little incident in the Dog's Home is worth telling, for it illustrates a trait that is international among tramps. A kid had in some way offended an older moocher, and the man was on the point of striking him, when the Hartford tramp stepped forward and said: "You would n't hit a kid, would you?"

The man started back and answered: "Well, I ort n' to, I know; but he plagued me like a reg'lar little divil."

That is a trait in trampdom, and even among criminals, that I have noticed wherever I have been. My own case illustrates it also. I am somewhat smaller than the average man, and I have no doubt that I have often enough offended some of my cronies; but never in all my experience have I had a real row or been struck by a tramp. I remember once quarreling with a vagabond until I became very hot-headed. I was preparing boldly for action, when the great, burly fellow said: "I say, Cigarette, if ye 're a-goin' to fight, I 'm a-goin' to run." Such sentiment is fine anywhere, and doubly fine when found, as it is so often, in the life of the vagrant beggar.

From Hull, Ryborg and I walked to York, visiting nearly every kip-house on the way, as this place is the best for studying English moochers. In the kip at Beverley we learned that Mr. Gladstone was always good for a bob—a statement that I very much doubt; for if it had been widely known, the Grand Old Man would have gone to the workhouse, so numerous are English beggars. Another story told there was that of the "hawker tramp." He had a little girl with him, and the two evidently did a very fair business.

"We 've just come from Edinbro," said the old man, "and altogether we ain't done bad; but we 'd been nowhere 'thout the bible.[1] You see, now'days in England, to beg much of a swag a feller has got to have some sort of a gag, and the hawkin' gag is as good as any. We've had shoe-strings, pencils, buttons, and lots of other things in stock; but all the good they 've done us, and all the good they do any moocher, is to get him into a house or pub with a good excuse. When he 's once in, he can beg good enough; and if Robert comes along, he can claim that he 's simply peddlin'. See? Besides, I 've got a license, in order to be safe; it only costs five bob, an' is well worth havin'. If you 're goin' to beg much in these parts, you 'd better git one, too."

This is the "hawkin' gag," and very popular it is, too. In America it has almost exhausted itself, with all the other peddling tricks, excepting always the "mush faker," or umbrella peddler and mender, and the "fawny man," or hawker of spurious jewelry. In England simple and artistic begging is by no means so well done as in America. The English moocher has to resort to his "gag," and his "lurks" are almost innumerable. One day he is a "shallow cove" or "shivering Jimmy"; another he is a "crocus" (sham doctor): but not very often is he a successful mendicant pure and simple. He begs all the time, to be sure, but continually relies on some trick or other for success.

[1] The "bible" is tramp slang for the hawker's little parcel of things which he is supposed to peddle.

On arriving at York, we went at once to Warmgate, the kip-house district, and picked out the filthiest kip we could find. The inmates were principally in pairs; each moocher had his Judy (wife), and each little kid had his little Moll (sister). These children are the very offspring of the road, and they reminded me of monkeys. Yet one has to feel sorry for them, since they did not ask for life, and yet are compelled to see its meanest and dirtiest side. Their mothers, when they are not drunk, love them; and when they are, their fathers have to play mothers, if they are not drunk themselves. Never in my life have I seen a more serio-comic situation than in that York kip-house, where two tramps were rocking their babies to sleep. Moochers—Bohemians of the Bohemians—fondling their babies! I should far sooner have looked for a New York hobo in clergyman's robes. But tramping with children and babies is a fad in English vagabondage.

From this I turned to listen to a very domestic confab between a Judy and her mate. She had just washed her face, and made herself really pretty. Then she sat down on a bench close to her man, and began to pet him. This bit of discourse followed:

"Just go and get a shave now, Jim. I 'll give you a wing [penny], if you will, for the doin' o' 't."

"Bah! What 's the matter uv my phiz, anyhow?"

"Naw; you doan't look purty. I can't love you thet way."

"Blast yer love, anyhow! Doan't keep a-naggin' all the time."

"Please, now, git a scrape. I 'm all washed up. You mought look as decent as I do."

"Lemme alone; I 'm on the brain [I 'm thinking]."

"Well, you mought have me on the brain a little more than you do. Did n't I git you out o' bein' pinched the other day?"

He looked at her, relented, patted her head, and went for a shave.

The surprise to me in all this was the genuine wifeliness of that Judy. She was probably as degraded as womankind ever gets to be, and yet she had enough humanity in her to be really in love.

Just a word here as to tramp companionship in England. Among the men, although one now and then sees "mates," he more often meets the male vagabonds alone, so far as other men are concerned. Women, too, do not often ally themselves with other women. But between the sexes partnership is common; though seldom long-lived, it is very friendly while it lasts. The woman is practically the slave of the man; he is the supposed breadwinner, but the Judy does more than her share of the begging all the while.

We went by rail from York to Durham, for there was little of interest to be found between the two points. Everywhere it was the cities far more than the country that furnished the most amusing and instructive sights. On the train a rather pleasant-looking man, overhearing our conversation, asked Ryborg who we were.

"You 'll excuse me," said he, "but your intelligence does seem a little more valuable than your clothes;

and would you mind telling me what you are doing in England?"

As he seemed a candid sort of fellow, Ryborg began very frankly to tell him our mission, and I took up the story when he was tired. It was difficult for the stranger to express his astonishment.

"What!" said he. "Do you mean to say that you 've left good homes behind you, and are over here simply to study tramps? What good will it ever do you?"

"Well," said Ryborg, "it 's one way of seeking the truth."

"I declare, you 're the rummest pair of fellows I 've ever seen," he returned; and he looked after us curiously as we got off the train at Durham.

Here we gave the vagabonds a wide berth, on account of smallpox; three tramps had been taken out of a kip-house that very day; so after a night's rest we moved on to Newcastle, stopping for a few hours on the way at the dirtiest kip that we found in England. One of the inmates, a powerful poser as a bully, was terrorizing an old man.

"I say, granddad, get me a light, will you? Be sharp, now!"

OLD MAN. I 'm too rheumatizin'-like. Caan't you get it yerself?

BULLY. Naw, I caan't. I waant you to get it. Hustle, now!

OLD MAN. I sha'an't do it. I ain't yer Hi Tittle Ti-Ti, an' I waant you to rec'lect it, too.

BULLY. See here, pop; what date is to-day?

OLD MAN. Fifth of March.

Bully. Well, pop, just twelve months ago to-day I killed a man. So look out!

The old man brought the light.

Newcastle, from the vagabond's point of view, exists principally in Pilgrim Street. I visited three kips there, saw eighty-four new faces, and learned something about the wages of beggars in England. Four moochers gave me the information. They were quarreling at the time. Number One was saying: "It 's a lie. I 'd git off the road in a minute ef I could only beg what you say I can. Ef I hustle I can git four bob a day, and I 'm willin' to fight that I can, too."

Number Two said: "You never mooched four bob in your life; you knaw you 're happy when you git ten wing a day. I 'm the only moocher in this 'ouse, an' I want you to know it. I beg 'xac'ly five bob in eight hours; an' ef I begged twenty-four hours, 'ow much 'd that be?"

Number Three here put in: "Tired legs an' 'n empty stomach."

Number Four: "Keep still, ye bloomin' idjits!"

None of them could beg over two bob a day, and they knew it. There are beggars in England who can average nearly half a sovereign a day, but they are by no means numerous. Most of them are able to get about eighteen pence or two shillings; that is all.

Our Newcastle friends told us that the road between there and Edinburgh was not a profitable one. They claimed that the people were too "clanny-like," meaning too stingy. The Durham district they called

A MOOCHER

the "bread and cheese caounty," while Yorkshire was the "pie and cake neighborhood." Accordingly, we took ship for Leith.

A fellow-passenger, half hoosier and half criminal, made up his mind that I was a crooked man. "Don't come near me," he said; "you 're a pickpocket, an' I can feel it."

I said: "How can you tell?"

"By your hand-shake and the cut of your phiz."

And throughout the trip he continued to regard me as a species of bogy-man, while Ryborg he considered a most reputable traveler. So he was and is; but he made some of his most criminal faces on that same voyage, nevertheless. One of them, I particularly remember, seemed to say, "I can't eat, can't sleep, can't do anything"; and his under lip would fall in a most genuine manner. He was often eloquent in his representations of my ability to pose as a tramp; but I am sure that nothing I can do would so quickly throw even the vigilant off the track as that face of my companion.

We went into Scotland without any prejudice; but we had scarcely been in Edinburgh three hours when an English roadster tried to make me believe terrible things of the "Scotties," as he called the Scotch tramps. "The Scotties are good enough to mooch with," said he, "an' ain't bad people in some ways till they 're drunk; an' then they 're enough to make a cat sick. Why, Yank, they can't talk about anything then but Bobbie Burns. It 's Bobbie did this, an' Bobbie did that, till you 'd think the sun did n't rise an' set on anybody else. I wish the feller had n't ever lived."

The poor man had evidently never read Bobbie's "Jolly Beggars"; for if he had he would have long since made a pilgrimage to Ayr.

Edinburgh can almost be reckoned as one of the best mooching towns in Great Britain, and if I were a beggar casting about for a life-residence, I think I should select this beautiful city, and that from my own personal experience. There is something deliciously credulous in the true citizen, and the university makes it a specially good place for clothes. Our first meal in the town we found at a "refuge" in High Street. We paid a penny apiece for a quart of good thick soup and half a loaf of bread. It was the largest quantity of food I have ever had for so little money; but it should be remembered that it was a charity. Cheap-restaurant living, in both Scotland and England, is more of a theory than a reality. For twopence I have had a dinner at a Herberge in Germany that I could not get in Great Britain for five; and for ten cents I have had *table d'hôte* with four courses in Chicago that I could not get in London for a shilling.

The cheapest restaurants that I know of in the United Kingdom are the cocoa-rooms; but a tramp can live three times as cheaply in the kip-house, if he cooks his own food. Tramps fully realize this, and it is seldom that they go near a cocoa-room. One old moocher said to me, when I questioned him on the subject, "I 've been in them places time and again, but I never get my stomach's worth in them"—a statement to which I can add my own similar testimony.

When traveling from Edinburgh to Glasgow, the tramp has two routes—one by way of Bathgate, the other by way of Linlithgow. Neither of them is a good begging highway. The people along the road are, as the German tramp would say, *ausgepumpt.* Nevertheless, it must be traveled afoot, for railway fares in Great Britain are much too high for the beggar's purse.

Ryborg and I determined this time to separate, he going through Bathgate, and I by way of Linlithgow. In this way we covered more ground, and at the same time Ryborg had the desired opportunity to play the tramp alone. His argument for the experiment ran in this wise: "To save my life, I don't seem to be able to talk with these beggars more than two minutes at a time, and I 'm really afraid that I am spoiling your scheme. You see, if they discover that I am not what I pretend to be, our work is in danger; so I 'll try this trip alone, and see if I can't get a little more into the tramp spirit." We promised to find each other in front of the general post-office in Glasgow.

On the whole journey I found but one interesting moocher, and that a moocheress. She traveled my way for about two hours, and as she smoked my cigarettes she gave me a little of her biography. She had lived just fifty years, did not know when she entered trampdom, had no recollection of her parents, and believed mainly in "booze," as she called it. She prided herself on being a fighting woman, as do a great many of the English Judies.

"Why, I 'm a reg'lar Charley Mitchell," said she, "when I want to be."

"Would n't you rather be a John L. Sullivan?" said I, to test her patriotism.

"Oh, yes, ef I wuz Amerikin; but I 'm English—I 'm patriotic, I am."

"Then," said I, "you would n't want to be Lackie Thompson."

"D' you want t' insult me?" said she. "Naw; I would n' be anything Scot-like."

"How is it, Judy, that you are in Scotland, then?"

"Oh, I 'm just lookin' fer me mate. I lost him in Edinburgh, an' 's soon 's I find him, I 'm goin' back to England." Just before I left her she said: "Tell me how you draw thet smoke in. I 've heard thet it 's real good; but how d' you do it?"

I told her how to inhale the smoke of a cigarette. She tried it, choked, and promised herself by all the gods of her poor heaven never to try it again. English Judies are great smokers, but they use clay pipes, as a rule.

Glasgow is the best kip town that we found. Its lodging-houses are known all over Great Britain, and as soon as I was well within the city I asked for a "Burns Home." There are several of these in Glasgow, all belonging to Mr. Robert Burns, who was once a working-man, but is now a wealthy proprietor. He built his homes mainly to make money, but also to furnish poor workmen a cheap and fairly respectable sleeping-place. I stayed at the Watson Street Home, and although there were many workmen in the place, there were also numerous vagabonds. In the "sitting-room" there must have been about a hundred and fifty people, and some of them had been loafing around Glasgow for months. I made friends with one of these old residents, and he did me some good service. He had been in America, had been well treated there, he said, and so wanted to treat me well. I asked him about the industrial intentions of the lodgers at the "home."

"Well," said he, "it 's hard to tell about all of them Some of these fellows sit in this room from morning till night, and never are seen to beg a copper; yet they live, too. Others do a little work now and then as 'sandwich-men,' and other little jobs, while there 's a few of us do nothing but beg."

"Is Glasgow a good town for moochin'?" I asked.

"Well, that depends on the moocher. There 's enough charity here, and some to spare, if you know how to look for it. I never get over half a crown a day, but I can tell you a dozen places where you can get your dinner. Scoff 's always more plenty than money."

"D' you mind tellin' what 's the main gag in Glasgow just now, for raisin' money?" I queried still further.

"Well, I think gettin' vaccinated 's about the best thing goin' just now."

"What d' you mean?"

"Well, you see, smallpox 's on the boards; the people are scared; bums are likeliest to get the sickness; so it 's been arranged that any man who will get himself vaccinated can have a week's kip free. Some blokes 've been jagged [vaccinated] two or three times."

This same vagabond did me another good turn down near the docks. We were walking along a street when three town tramps came along and guyed my hat. My companion noticed it, and as I had told him that I had been considerably martyrized in this way before, he turned round sharply on the guyers, and thundered out:

"Who 're you lookin' at? Ef you 're tryin' to guy this Yank, you 'd better stop. Ef you don't, there 'll be a fight."

I said: "Let 's run, if you really mean that."

"Not much! I 'm English, you know; and I can knock out any Scotchman that comes around, and I 'm in the mood for 't right now."

The town bums took him at his word, and left. I said to him: "You English fellows seem to have things pretty much your own way here."

"Yes," he answered; "we English fellers know how to bluff. We 've been bluffin' the world now for a good many years."

"You forget the United States," I could not help interjecting.

"Beg pardon, Yank; beg pardon!"

Ryborg and I met at the post-office, according to agreement. He had seen so few tramps along the way that he was still in doubt as to his abilities. He remained courageous, however, and I proposed a trip to Dublin. This meant Irish Sea, no appetite, and general ill health. But off we sailed to see Ireland. We stayed nine hours, and then sailed back to Liverpool. On the way I saw more of Ireland in a dear old Biddy than I did in Dublin. She claimed that she saw Ireland in me also—a discernment truly penetrating, considering that the Irish in me died out about two hundred years ago.

In Liverpool our tramp work began again in good earnest, and I was fortunate in meeting there an old friend—Manchester Charley. We went around the Horn [1] together a few years ago, and got very well acquainted, as tramps will on such journeys; but we did not expect to meet next in Liverpool, though I knew Charley had left the States for London. He seemed glad to see me, and yet a little ashamed of me, too. My shoes were rather played out, and in other respects, also, I was somewhat below the American tramp grade. Charley noticed this, and his first greeting was, "Shall I get you a new pair of shoes?" I explained the situation as best I could, but Charley could not understand how I could "lower myself so." I told him that I was certainly better dressed than most of the tramps I had met along the road, whereat he laughed most scornfully.

"Why, Cig," he said, "the fellers you 've been bummin' with are nothin' but skugees [a species of gay-cat]. You have n't seen a first-class hobo yet, I 'll bet."

That was true, if one takes the American hobo as the standard, and I admitted it. Then he introduced three of his companions, saying: "Here are some of the real article."

They were very clever-appearing vagabonds, and very well dressed, too. I acknowledged their vast superiority as politely as I was able to do, and asked Charley how it had come about that I had so missed the genuine beggars, as I had all the while been on the lookout for them.

[1] The Horn is a bit of railway in Iowa, extending from Red Oak southward for about twenty miles, then northwest for twenty more. It is used principally for long trains, as the main line from Red Oak to Pacific Junction is too hilly.

Charley said: "The fact is, there are not many of us in England. Up at London you 'll find more than anywhere else, but we ain't anywhere near as strong as you fellers in the States."

"Why is this? You certainly ought to be," I returned.

"Well," he replied, "this is how it is. The country is full of these half-and-half bums. They go everywhere, and the people get tired of them; so when a really sharp moocher comes along, he has to run his chance of bein' classed with them chaps—that is, if he begs at houses. If he does as I do,—sends letters of introduction,—his luck will probably be better. Here in Liverpool, for instance, we do fairly well at the letter racket; but we could never make a livin' at all if we had to batter the way most beggars do."

Later in the day Charley explained matters more fully, and it turned out, as I expected, that he did "crooked work" also, both he and his comrades. I said to him at parting: "I could succeed in England, too, if I wanted to do that sort of business; but that is n't legitimate mooching."

"It all depends," he answered. "A tramp ought to do anything he can, and there 's no feller so able to dodge the Dee as a bum if he plays the beggar and is a crook besides."

This is a fact; but still it is not true hoboing or mooching, this being a beggar only in appearance. Some men do it constantly, I know; but the real tramp, wherever he is found, will rarely go into anything outside of begging and cheating. Thieving he leaves to more experienced hands.

Liverpool fairly swarms with the lowest class of tramps, and we many times voted Manchester Charley's testimony correct. They live off any one they can capture, even "visiting brethren," and are cordially hated by them.

We planned to separate in our journey to London, after the manner of our last trip in Scotland. Ryborg was to take his way through Crewe, Birmingham, Warwick, and Oxford; I was to visit Chester, Shrewsbury, Hereford, Bristol, and Bath. We were to meet at the end of a week in Reading, and journey on to London together. My own experiences on the way were very common. I saw only a repetition of what I had become familiar with in the other parts of England: "prehistoric gorillas," a few rather clever beggars, about twenty kip-houses, and more than two hundred vagrants. Nearly half of them, however, were seeking work. Two nights I slept in straw-stacks, and each time I had fully a dozen companions. They called themselves "free dossers," and in one way they were rather amusing—in fact, a new species of tramp: they were determined not to spend a copper of what they begged.

It seems that these fellows start out from London early in the spring, and batter all summer. In the autumn they return to London with their swag and spend the winter in some comfort. On their travels they either beg what they need or go without. If they cannot beg a lodging, they sleep in barns, brick-yards, and straw-stacks; and from early in March till late in September they do not squander a single halfpenny that comes in their way. I had never before met this variety of vagabond, and I doubt very much whether they would be allowed to associate with the real American hoboes; for the true tramp likes more generosity among his fellows, and when he meets a stingy brother he is likely to give him a wide berth.

Once in Reading, Ryborg and I met at the appointed corner, and he gave the following account of himself:

"In the first place, I had a mean road, and saw but few vagabonds. I had only three experiences. The first was not far from Crewe. I was practising to become a beggar, and I tried to smoke a pipe. For a while I made out very well, and accomplished a lot of smoke. I thought I should get on well now in kip-houses. But the second pipe played me a mean trick. I felt bad all over, and staggered along the road most unbecomingly for either a gentleman or a beggar. I gave it up. My second experience was with a crazy tramp. He traveled with me for nearly an hour, and I could find nothing interesting in him except his habit of wetting his middle finger and rubbing it on his cheek-bone. This he did constantly; but though I questioned him carefully, I could get nothing out of him. Finally he got angry with me, and leaned up against a fence till I left him. My last adventure happened when a workman gave me fivepence. He thought I was an honest and unfortunate laborer, and after we had talked awhile he handed me the money, saying very politely, 'Perhaps this will help you on your travels.'"

Our first night in London was spent in a German Herberge in the East End. The second night we slept

A REST BY THE WAYSIDE.

in a Salvation Army shelter in Whitechapel Road. At this last place we paid twopence each for our beds —boxes, I should say. They look like coffins with no bottoms except the floor. Yet they are comfortable enough, considering the price. The blankets are of leather, and if a man keeps his clothes on he can sleep warmly enough. On entering the shelter, we went to the rear of the building, where some of the lodgers were smoking their pipes and recounting their day's experiences. Everything was as orderly as possible, although many of the men were out-and-out vagabonds. I devoted myself to an old man who had a very bad cough. He spoke kindly of the Salvation Army, and had only one complaint to make.

"These Salvationers," said he, "forget one thing: they forget that we men are tired. In the meetings they want us to sing 's loud 's ef we 'd just got out of bed. They say, 'Come on, men; sing away, be happy —sing, now!' But how 's a man goin' to sing after he 's mooched and walked all day, I should like to know? I ain't no enemy of the Salvationers, but I wish they 'd remember that we get fagged out."

Ryborg and I went into the meeting, and as long as I live I shall never forget the sincerity of its leaders. They were not especially wise or delicate, but they were in earnest all over. One of the "soldiers" handed us hymn-books, and said, "Cheer up, men; better times a-comin'"; and the entire spirit of the meeting was of the same good fellowship. I felt then what I had felt often before, that the Salvation Army, in spite of its many mistakes, is, after all, one of the most consistent agencies for the betterment of the class it seeks to uplift. The leaders of this meeting believed in their hearts that we should be "lost" unless something interposed to "save" us, and they were determined to save us if they could. In other words, the Salvation Army actually believes in hell, and is "hustling" to keep men out of it.

We went to bed about ten o'clock, but I slept very little. The lodgers coughed nearly all night, and it was impossible to rest in such a racket; but as some of the men said, it was better than sleeping out.

The next two nights of our stay as tramps in London were spent in the Notting Hill casual ward, or "spike," as it is called in tramp parlance. There are twenty-four of these wards in London, and they are well scattered over England at large also. Their object is to afford wanderers a place where they can get food and lodging for a night or two by earning it. The usual work required is stone-breaking and oakum-picking. We had delayed visiting these places until we should arrive in London, as they are all very much alike, and we cared for only one experience of their hospitality. As I knew that this Notting Hill ward is considered one of the best in all England, we went there. Two years before I had visited this ward as a "gentleman." I had a letter from the president of the Board of Guardians, and I was treated most kindly. But on this March evening I went in as a tramp, and, as was to be expected, my treatment was entirely different.

We appeared at the door of the ward about half-past seven. A little window was raised, and I stepped forward to state our business. Unconsciously I leaned against the sill of the window, which offended the inspector in charge considerably.

"What 's your name?" he thundered. Still leaning on the sill, I gave him my name honestly enough. He then remarked to some person inside that we were not accustomed to such places, evidently, and called out, "Stand back, will you!" Back I stood. He cried out again, "Take off your hat!" My hat came off instanter. Still again: "You come in here as if you was a meeleeonary. You 're not; you 're a casual." I was as meek as could well be. Ryborg was itching to grab the inspector with his long arms. The next question was as to where we had slept the night before.

"Straw-stack," I replied.

"None of your impudence! You slept out—why don't you say so? Have you got any money?"

"A ha'penny, sir."

"Hand it in!" In it went. Then I had to tell my trade, which was that of a sailor; and naturally the next question was as to where I was bound.

"To Ameriky, sir, if I can ever get there."

"You 're goin' to tramp it, are n't you?"

"Yes, sir; that 's my intention"; but for the life of me I could not see how I was to reach America that way. I was so frightened that I would have told him anything he wanted.

When he was through with us, a kind-hearted attendant took us in hand, gave us some gruel and bread, a bath, clean night-shirts, and then a cell apiece, in which we slept very well.

As there were only four inmates that morning, we

were needed for the cleaning up, and so escaped stone-breaking, which I dreaded exceedingly, and were put at various light occupations—or rather I was. Ryborg was the victim of his strength. Our breakfast consisted of the same dish as our supper of the night before. I was soon busy as general fireman, scrubber, knife-cleaner, coal-carrier, dish-washer, and helper of my sister-sufferer, Mrs. Murphy, as she washed her task of towels and shirts. At noon we had pea-soup and bread. I enjoyed it, but Ryborg did not. The poor fellow was feeling badly; he had had to scrub nearly twenty cells, and the bending over incident to such a feat had nearly broken his back. At dinner he said plaintively, "Flynt, I want to go home." "So do I," I replied; "but I fancy we 're wanted here till to-morrow morning." This proved to be the case; but he felt better in the afternoon, and got through comfortably, wheeling nearly a ton of stone from some of the cells to the general pile. He earned his keep, if ever any poor prisoner did.

I fear I was more shiftless, for about the middle of the afternoon the attendant who was with me at the furnace said: "You might as well rest; just keep your eye on the fires, that 's all." It was kind of him; and as I had at least earned my pea-soup and gruel, I took his advice. He was kinder to me, I think, because I gave him a corn-cob pipe which he had had to take away from me the night before. During the day he had asked me several questions about it, and I said: "It's a very decent sort of pipe—coolin'-like, you know."

"Does n't Mark Twain always smoke one o' them pipes?" said he.

"Blest if I know," said I; "but I can well think it."

"I 'm a great friend of Mark Twain," he pursued; "an' I 'm a-thinkin' o' gettin' one o' them pipes, jest out of respect for him."

"Well," said I, "permit me, in the name of your respect, to present you with my pipe; besides, you 've got it, anyhow."

He thanked me profusely, and promised to keep it forever. Later in the day he reported it to be just as I had said, "sort o' coolin'-like." And he was a good friend to me all the rest of my stay in the Notting Hill station.

On Wednesday morning we were turned loose with our two ha'pennies. We were both so happy that we decided to get off the road that very day.

We had been tramps for three weeks, and had walked most of this time fully fifteen miles a day; so we looked up my friend at the Temple, and in a few hours were respectable again. That same day I took my tramp clothes out to the casual ward, and presented them to my friend the attendant. I had told him the day before that I expected to get new togs soon, and he had put in a plea for my old ones. Good luck to him and them!

SOMETHING definite ought to be said here, I think, regarding the character of the English moocher, and as Ryborg is new in trampdom, and as his impressions are likely to be sharper than mine, I have asked him to write out, in a few words, his general opinion of the tramps he met in this three weeks' journey.

Most of the tramps we met during our trip in England impressed me as being a trifle insane. There is a peculiar dullness and lack of nervous energy about them that distinguish them very noticeably from the working-men. Still, they have a marked sagacity in getting up tricks to secure their food and lodging, and in getting out of work. Their life, together with ill-nourishing food, would tend to produce a mild form of insanity. There is surely a peculiarity about their mental structure that I have observed nowhere else.

They are fond of philosophizing about themselves, and in a comical way. One of the worst vagabonds I saw told me that he considered himself as fine a fellow as any one, and that he had two brothers who were well-to-do, but he could not stick to one thing long enough to lay up money. He said that it never did anybody any good to knock about, unless his mind was so formed that he could learn by it. He did not see that he was not the equal of anybody in perseverance, and he was not able to understand why it was not considered very noble to live by begging and by peddling without a license.

Some attribute their pauper condition to a roving disposition; others lay their misfortunes to a cruel fate; but it is very evident that the passion for drink is at the bottom of ninety per cent. of the vagrancy in England.

The tramps do not seem at all discontented or unhappy. They complained sometimes that people were stingy, but almost all of them looked well fed. There are a few of them who really want work, but the majority are not very anxious for a job. As one of the men in the kip-house said one day, after there had been a good deal of discussion on the subject: "Well, there 's more talk about work in this house than there 's doin' of 't."

Most of the tramps we met were well informed, and fully half of them had been in America, or the "States," as they say. They also keep up to the times on political issues and pugilistic and police news. In one of the lodging-houses I heard the keeper of the place reading the police news of the week to an interested circle of beggars. I was struck by a remark of one of the fellows, that the sentence of the court was not so severe as one culprit had deserved.

They are a very hospitable set to their own kind. I never entered a kip without a seat being offered to me, and in many cases they gave me a bowl of tea and a bit of bread. I never saw any quarreling over the cooking-utensils or the corner of the fireplace. Though they are without doubt the dirtiest and the raggedest and the poorest of men, I was everywhere treated by them with politeness, so far as they understood politeness; in fact, they were often far more courteous than the steamer and other officials under whose charge I came during the journey.

These conclusions are identical with my own. Excepting workhouses, casual wards, one or two "ticket systems," and jails, there seems to be no great amount of legal machinery for the treatment of vagrancy in England. The workhouses are places where any one who can prove that he is penniless may be taken in indefinitely. The casual ward has already been explained. The ticket system is simply the issuing of tickets, at police stations, to vagrants in need of food, the tickets calling for so much bread, and perhaps a lodging. Sometimes the ticket must be worked for, and sometimes it is gratis. The jails are mean places to get into, the discipline being severe, and work being exacted of the prisoners.

Sentences for begging range from seven days upward, but most of the tramps with whom I talked spoke of seven days as the usual punishment for simple begging, unless the offender could be proved to be an old stager.

As regards the punishment of the confirmed beggar in England, there seems to me to be but one thing to say: it is too slight and trivial. The professional beggar should be shut up indefinitely. There are plenty to laugh at this suggestion, I am aware. Well and good. Just so long as they laugh, the beggars will laugh also; and it is my opinion that the beggars will come out ahead.

IV

THE TRAMP AT HOME

IN an article which appeared in the "Contemporary Review" for August, 1891, I made a first attempt to relate some of my experiences in tramp life in the United States, and endeavored to describe a true knight of the road. It was a short paper, and there was a great deal left unsaid that might have been said, but it was a truthful report as far as it went. To one intimately acquainted with the hoboes I doubt whether the article would have seemed inaccurate, but it was so judged by some critics, and a number of my statements were challenged. Among other criticisms made, it was said that I had mistaken the character of the "American tramp" in three particulars: first, his nationality; second, his numbers; third, his unwillingness to work. It was also assumed that an Englishman was responsible for the supposed false statements.

I was in New York at the time, and having ten days at my disposal before leaving for Europe, I decided to retrace some of my old routes and have another view of the situation. This chapter is a report of my experiences on the journey, and I have confined myself to the rehearsal of bare facts without further comment, believing that the reader will moralize and philosophize whenever necessary.

It was about five o'clock on the afternoon of a cool September day that I left my friend's home clad as a tramp, and started for the night boat for Albany. I wore an old suit of clothes, a flannel shirt, a good pair of shoes, and a respectable hat. I had paid special attention to the shoes and hat, for it is a piece of tramp philosophy that the two extremities of a beggar are first looked at by the person of whom he is begging. While riding from Harlem down to the landing-place of the steamer, I laughed to myself while thinking how the tramps would envy me my nice head- and foot-gear. I wondered, too, whether I should be allowed to return with these coverings.

At the ticket-office I paid one of my three dollars for a ticket on the boat to Albany. I made this heavy draft upon my slight exchequer because I was afraid to beat my way on the railroad between the two cities. I knew of old how roadsters are hated by the residents of both banks of the Hudson River, and not being at all sure that I should be successful in making the journey from New York to Albany in one night as a "dead-beat" on a freight-train, I felt safer in buying a second-class ticket on the steamboat, and beginning my journey in the morning at Albany.

I fear that the reader would have laughed at my calamity had he seen me after landing at Albany. Then I was a tramp indeed, for the other two dollars had disappeared from my pockets while I was sleeping with a motley crowd of Italians on some boxes thrown promiscuously about the hold of the steamboat. There was now no possibility of dilettantism. I had to go head over heels into the beggar's life. I am glad now that it was so, but for the moment I was downhearted, for I had leaned on those two dollars as possible friends if my begging courage should fail me at the crucial moment. But this was past, my bridges were burned, so I began my journey in earnest.

I sauntered lazily over to West Albany, for it was still early, and arrived as the people were lighting their breakfast fires. I waited until it seemed that the fires should have done their duty, and then began. I visited several houses. Sometimes the man of the house said that his wife was sick, or that he was out of work himself; and sometimes they told me to get out—that they had already fed one tramp.

My fifth call was at the home of a German woman who claimed that she had fed beggars in the Fatherland. She invited me in, placed a nice warm breakfast before me, and then we began a conversation in German about life, labor, and beggars. She was sorry for me, and said that I looked too young to be a beggar. I told her a tale. It was one of those stories in which the ghost of a truth still lingers—such as tramps know so well how to tell. I shall never know exactly how much of it she believed, or what she thought of me, as I told her that I was the outcast of a *hochwohlgeboren* family in Germany. I know, however, that she was sympathetic, and that she took me in, whether she did the same for my romance or not.

After breakfast I started for Troy. I knew that I

should meet with plenty of loafers during the walk, and I preferred chatting with them on or near the highway. For Albany has a penitentiary. There is not a well-informed tramp in the United States that does not know about that prison; it has punished many a vagrant, and the Albany policemen are no friends to beggars. Syracuse Tom will bear me out in this statement, for he winters in Albany with his kid every year; but he does this simply because he is so well posted. Of course other tramps visit Albany as well, for it is a well-known town for "refreshments"; but only a few can thrive long there by begging only for money.

On my way to Troy I found a camp of thirty-three tramps. They were living off the charity of Albany. They had all been in for breakfast, and were now returned to the hang-out to chat and scheme. Some were discussing Albany prisons, its policemen, saloons, and general hospitality. Others had built a fire, and were boiling their shirts in a borrowed kettle to kill the vermin. Still others were planning Southern tours. Some had decided to winter in St. Augustine, some in Jacksonville, and a few were talking of the best routes to New Orleans.

One of the fellows recognized me. He must needs know where I had been so long, and why my hands were so white. "Cigarette," he said, "have you been a-doin' time? Where did you get yer white colors?" I told Yorkey that I had been sick, and had been back on the road only a few days. He would not believe me, and I am afraid that he took me for a "crooked man," for he said: "Cig, you 've not been in the sicklugger all this while, and I hain't seen your register for many a day. No, my young bloke; you can't fool me. You 've been up a tree, and you can't deny it."

I could not convince him of my innocence, so we dropped the subject, and I told him that I was bound for Buffalo, where I had friends who would help me to brace up and get off the road. I assured him that I knew now what a foolish business "bumming" was, and that I was going to make a grand effort to get work. Even this he would not believe, and he insisted that I was going West to some town where I knew that the tramps were going to have a "drunk." He tried to persuade me to go South with him, and claimed that Yonkers Slim was going to meet him in Washington with some money, and that the bums intended to have a great "sloppin'-up" (drinking-bout). I made him understand that I was determined to go West. Then he gave me some advice which was typical.

"Young feller, you 're goin' to a pretty poor country. Why, when I left Buffalo two weeks ago, the bulls [police] were more than pinchin' the tramps right in the streets, and givin' them ninety days. The only decent thing about a journey up that way is the New York Central Railroad. You can ride that to death. That 's the only godsend the country has. Jes let me tell you, though, what towns it cuts through, and then you 'll squeal. Now, there 's Schenectady. You can chew all right there, but divil a cent can you beg. Then comes Fonda, and you must know what a poor town that is. Then you 've got Utica, where you can feed all right, for any fool can do that, but you can't hit a bloke for a dime in the streets without a bull seein' you and chuckin' you up for fifty-nine days in Utica jail. And you must know well enough what that jail is this time o' year—it 's jes filled with a blasted lot o' gay-cats [men who will work] who 've been on a booze. After Utica there 's Rochester, a place that onc't was good, but is n't worth pawnin' now since that gay-cat shot a woman there some time ago. After Rochester, what you got? Buffalo—the most God-forsaken town a bum ever heard of."

Here I interrupted my lecturer to say that I had heard of Buffalo as a good "chewing town." He turned upon me fiercely. "What d' you want? D' you only want to chew? Don't you want boodle, booze, togs, and a good livin'? Of course you do, jes like ev'ry genooine hobo. It 's only a blasted gay-cat that 'll fool around this country now. Cig, you 'd better come South with us. Why, las' year the blokes more than sloughed in money around the Ponce de Leon Hotel in St. Aug'stine. We kin git there in a week if we ride passenger-trains. You 'll hustle for an overcoat if you stay here much longer, an' I 'll bet my Thanksgivin' dinner that every bloke you meet up the road is bound South. You 'd better foller their coat-tails." I thanked Yorkey, but satisfied him that I was determined to get to Buffalo. "Well, so long, Cigarette," he said, when I left the camp for Troy.

Between Troy and Cohoes I found another camp of tramps. Here were forty-two men and boys who were enjoying what tramps term a "sloppin'-up." Some of them had just returned from the hop-country, and had gathered together the fellows in their vicinity, and were now drinking keg after keg of beer. Thirteen kegs had already been emptied. These men seemed well satisfied with their treatment around Troy, and the majority of them had been there for nearly a week. One half-drunken loafer from Milwaukee was so anxious to praise the town's hospitality that he was haranguing some of his comrades most zealously. "I 've boozed around this town," he said, "off and on for the last seven years, and I 've not been sloughed up yet. There 's only one or two bulls in the town that 's after tramps, and if a bloke is anyway foxy he can slip them all right. Two years ago I fooled around here for two months, and had my three square meals every day, and booze too, and I was never touched. You can't hustle pennies, o' course, as well as you can down in the City [New York], but you can batter for clothes, chuck, and booze all right enough. I know as many as ten saloon-keepers in the town that 'll give me a drink and ask no questions. Yes; Troy 's all right, and it 's only a rotten gay-cat that 'u'd say it wa'n't. The only mean thing about the town is that it 's slow. Us hoboes must be on the march, and it 's not in us to fool round a jerk town like this 'un too long. It 's tiresome, blokes."

A hunt for supper in Cohoes afforded me a great deal of amusement, for I was entertained by an alderman's wife. At any rate, she told me, while I was eating my supper in the large restaurant dining-room, that her husband, eating his supper in a private room on the floor below, was a village father and a hater of tramps. "But don't worry," she said; "he shall not bother you while I 'm around. I always feed a hungry man, and I always shall. I can't understand how some people can turn away from the door any one who claims to be hungry. If I should do this, I would expect to be hungry myself before long." A freight-train passed by the house while I was at the table, and my hostess noticed my anxiety to be aboard of it. "Never mind," she said; "there 'll be plenty of freights along a little later, and this is a good place to catch them, for there is a grade here, and you can keep away from the station, where you might be arrested." I remembered this woman throughout my journey, and every tramp that I met bound in this direction was advised of her house. I think it would hardly be so good another year.

From Cohoes to Schenectady is only a short ride, and it seemed as if I had been asleep in the box-car only a few minutes when Ohio Red, who was with me, cried out, "Cigarette, we 're in the yards; let 's get out." We slept in a box-car overnight. This is an odd way of resting. The coat, vest, and shoes are taken off, then the shoes are made into a pillow, the vest is laid over them, and the coat is thrown over the shoulders. So sleep most of the tramps during the warm months.

After an early breakfast, we went over to the hang-out on the eastern side of the town. Thirteen rovers were already there, cooking a conventional meal. They had begged meat, potatoes, bread, and coffee, and had stolen some other vegetables, besides a kettle, and were now anxiously watching the fire. Two more vagrants, who had been looking for cigar-stubs in the town, came in later. Their pockets were well filled, and they divided equally their findings. This "snipe" chewing and smoking is the most popular use of to-

A DIVISION.

bacco in trampdom, and is even preferred to "store brands" of the weed, which are easily begged. About dinner-time a man came out to the camp, and offered every one of us the job of shoveling sand for a dollar and a half a day, the work to continue into November. He might better have stayed away. The tramps told him that they had just left as good a job as that in Buffalo, and were now looking for three dollars a day!

At nightfall sixteen tramps, including myself, boarded a freight-train bound west. I was now on the main line of the New York Central, and had no further need to fear any large amount of walking. During the night ride I had an interesting talk with the brakeman at my end of the train. I was in a "gondola" (open car), and he espied me from the top of a box-car, and came down. "Hello, young fellow!" he said. "Where are you travelin' to?" "Just up the road a bit, boss," I answered. "Well, let 's go to the other end of the car, where we won't catch the cinders; I 've got one in my eye now filin' it to pieces. Can you take it out, d' you think?" he asked. I held his lantern on my arm, and looked for the cinder, which was soon out. Just then the train whistled for Fonda, and the brake-man said: "You want to lay low here, for there 's a watchman in the yards. I 'll bring you a bit to eat out of my pail after we pull out." He returned, when we were again started, with a parcel of food, and began to speak of the towns up the road. "Utica," he said, "if you intend gettin' your breakfast there in the mornin', is sort of a snide place, this time of the year. You see, the hop-pickers are around there, and the police always arrest a lot of 'em, and you fellows are likely to be jugged too. This town that we 've just left, however, is the meanest one on the road. I was comin' through here about a week ago, and did n't know there was a bum on the train. The watchman scouted around, and found three of 'em in a box-car, and yanked 'em all up. If I 'd known they were round, I 'd 'a' posted 'em about this town, but I had n't an idea they were there. I hate to see a lad get pulled for ridin' a train, because I 've been broke myself, and I know what it is to be on the road. I 'll always carry a man on my train if I can. But of course you know that sometimes the con [conductor] is a mean devil, and we can't do anything that 'll give him a grudge ag'in' us; if he should see a bum on the train, he might report us. So you see what risks we run. But I 've given many a lad a ride, and I 'm always willing to be square to a square plug [fellow]." This is a typical kind-hearted Eastern brakeman, and the tramps like him.

In Utica I made the acquaintance of a roadster called "Utica Biddy." I met him at the tramp camp just outside of the town, near the R., W. & O. R. R. tracks, where twenty-six other loafers were waiting for three of their fellow-travelers to return from the hop-country, in order to help spend their money. Biddy is one of the best-known tramps on the New York Central, and he gave me more information about the districts around Syracuse and Utica than I could possibly have accumulated single-handed. While riding in a box-car from Utica to Syracuse we had a long conversation, and the following is the substance of what he told me:

"I 've been a bum on the division of this railroad

from Albany to Syracuse for the last four years. I 've had my three squares every day, and in winter I 've had a bed every night. I know you 'll hardly believe this, for some of you beggars come up to this country and curse it because you don't get on the spot what you want. Now, I 'll give you a few pointers about these towns. We 've just left a town [Utica] where I can go to over a score of houses and get a square meal whenever I want it. Of course I was born there, and that may make a bit o' difference, but I can do the same in Rome, Albany, and Syracuse. I 've been on this beat so long and have watched my chances so carefully that I know now just where to go when hungry. I hear a great many tramps kick about Utica, its policemen and snide houses. But if a lad will just knuckle down for a month or so and hunt out the good houses, make himself acquainted with the tough policemen and keep out of their way, find good barns for a doss at night, and make a business of bummin' carefully, there 's not a town on the Central that ain't good. The trouble with you strange blokes is this: you come up here, booze, draw your razors when you 're drunk, do too much crooked work, and o' course the people get hostile. Why, see how many lads are workin' my racket over in Pennsylvania. You know yourself that on the Pennsy [Pennsylvania Railroad] line there are tramps who not only bum within a division, but inside of subdivisions, and can chew whenever they like. But they do this 'cause they 're foxy and have had their boozin' knocked out of them. Now, those lads that we left back in Utica will more than likely get sloughed into jail when they get to boozin'. You can't expect the people to stand such stuff as that. And these are the kind of fellows, too, who jigger our ridin' on this railroad. They get drunk, and if they want to ride and can't find an empty car, they break a seal [a car seal], and then there 's the devil to pay about the tramps tryin' to rob the cars. If the bums would only keep sober once in a while, there would n't be a tramp pinched once a month. The bulls around here don't care to yank a tramp unless they have to. But what can they do when they find a bloke paradin' the streets with a jag on? They pull him in, o' course, or else the people would kick. I 'll gamble that he would n't be touched, though, if he were simply huntin' a meal."

In Syracuse, Biddy, in order to prove his acquaintance with the town, told me of a house where I was certain of getting something to eat. I followed his instructions, and got exactly what I went for—a good dinner. The great excitements in Syracuse, I found, were a big drunk and the State fair. I have never seen such a number of tramps together at one time. Between De Witt and Syracuse there was a camp of fifty, and there were twenty empty beer-kegs lying around in the grass. Some of the fellows were sick, others had sick clothes, and many of the rest were in fine shape for a free fight. There were two well-dressed tramps whom I immediately recognized as "fawny men"—fellows who sell bogus jewelry for more than it is worth. One of these men was a notorious roadster of American birth, who, for purposes best known to himself, went by the name of "Liverpool George." He is the most successful fawny man that I have ever met. He earned twenty-two dollars in one day at the fair by selling for two dollars apiece rings which can be bought in Buffalo for two dollars a dozen. The tramps call this worldly success.

Before I left Syracuse there came to the camp another batch of tramps numbering sixteen. They had just returned from the hop-country, and their money was well poised for another "shot at the growler." During my stay of three days at the camp and vicinity, the men were intoxicated almost all the time. They would even go into town half drunk to look for something to eat. Yet I heard of no arrest while I was there. About a mile from the hang-out, and east of Syracuse, there were two barns in which the tramps slept. It was most amusing to see the loafers returning to their nests in the hay-loft night after night. Sometimes I listened to comical tales until the early hours of the morning. I was also the spectator of a number of fights. One particular barn where I spent two nights, near Syracuse, was a regular arena for fisticuffing and squabbling. The men were so cross and ill-tempered after their recent galas that they would quarrel on the slightest pretext. One fellow gave his companion a black eye because he told him that he "ought to hustle better togs" (clothes). Another poor excuse for a knock-down was that a fellow had said that "tramps were bughouse" (crazy).

The journey from Syracuse to Buffalo was very prosaic. I rode from Syracuse to Rochester with a kid and two colored tramps. The boy was in search of his "jocker," or protector, whom he had lost in Albany. From various registries at watering-tanks, he expected to find him in Canal Street, Buffalo. At Port Byron a female tramp, with her companion, Milwaukee Jim, entered the box-car in which we were riding. I learned from him that I must be very careful in my conduct at Rochester. I decided to leave the town as quickly as possible after arrival. On the eastern outskirts of the place I met a gang of twenty-three tramps walking to Fairport, ten miles distant, in order to escape any possible arrest in the Rochester railroad yards while catching a freight-train bound east. Between Rochester and Churchville I found still another frightened crowd numbering twenty-seven. They were waiting for nightfall before entering the city to board a train for Albany.

The kid continued with me on the journey to Buffalo, and I enjoyed a talk with him in the car about his life on the road and what inducements it offered. He was only sixteen years of age, but as bright and well versed in tramp lore as many an aged roadster. He became interested in tramp life in the Illinois Reformatory. Some of his companions at the school, who had been with tramps, told him of their experiences, and he never rested until he had satisfied himself with his own. "It ain't such a bad lot," he said; "I chew every day, get a big swag of booze once in a while, and when I 'm travelin' with Slim [his protector] I have a purty excitin' time." The boy found his man in Canal Street, just as he had expected.

Buffalo did not interest me. There was nothing new in the tramp line. I counted sixty-seven roadsters, and found that there was plenty to eat and drink and a little money also, if looked for very diligently

ASLEEP IN A FREIGHT-CAR.

in the main streets and offices; but there was nothing unique. My journey, when I arrived in Buffalo, had extended over three hundred miles (from Albany). I had had three meals every day, excepting the loss of a dinner while traveling from Rochester to Buffalo, and I had met three hundred tramps, who had probably had their meals just as frequently as I had had mine. This number does not include, of course, those who may have been traveling behind or before me, so that, not counting men who were certainly on the road, but out of my sight, here was a voluntary vagrant for every mile of the road between Albany and Buffalo. Further, I did not see a train going west on the Central Railroad that was not carrying at least one tramp, and I often saw a car passing by which appeared simply alive with dead-beats. The reader must remember withal that New York State is by no means such good tramp territory as certain other States. Pennsylvania supports three times as many vagrants as New York will tolerate.

Two extenuating statements ought to be made. In the first place, the Central Railroad is a very easy one to beat, and probably half of the tramps that I met were "residents" of other States. Secondly, a great many tramps loaf around the hop-country in the vicinity of Syracuse and Utica during the early autumn, in order to drink at the expense of the too light-hearted hop-pickers. The nationality of these men, so far as I could judge from pronunciation, some of their own statements, and their professional names, was almost entirely American. I met one German loafer called "Dutchy," and he was the only recognized foreigner that I found. The others may have had parents born in other countries, but they themselves were certainly Americanized. A good test of a tramp's nationality is his professional name. For every genuine hobo couples the name of his birthplace with whatever other name he chooses, and the reader will find, if he will visit watering-tanks or other available stationary railway property in his vicinity, like section-houses, shanties, etc., where tramps "sign," that the names registered there indicate, in the great majority of cases, a birthplace in the United States.

My return journey to New York is worthy of comment only because its quick performance may possibly interest the reader. I was desirous of learning how quickly a tramp can make a journey if he desires; and it being to my interest to be in New York at an early date, I decided to forego any specific study of tramp life on the Erie Railroad and simply to hurry over its tracks, if haste should prove possible. I left Buffalo for New York on the night of the 16th, and arrived on the morning of the 19th, although I took a very circuitous route. I traveled from Buffalo to Corry, Pennsylvania, over the W. N. Y. & P. R. R., and from Corry I rode to Binghamton over the Erie road. From this place I made a detour to Voorheesville, and then down the West Shore route to Weehawken, in order to confirm certain rumors that I had heard of its hostility to tramps. The entire trip was very tiresome and difficult, because, in order to travel rapidly, I was compelled to ride on top and on the bumpers of freight-trains, and on the trucks of passenger-trains. My companion, Pennsylvania Whitey, and I rode after the latter fashion from Elmira to Binghamton. It was a terrible ride. We made the mistake of getting on the trucks of the rear car—a Pullman sleeper—instead of a baggage-car. In doing this we suffered almost beyond description. The gravel and dust flew about our faces until the exasperation and pain were fearful. When I arrived in Binghamton my eyes were filled with dust, and I suffered with them for days after I arrived in New York. There are tramps, principally in the West, who are much more skilful truck-riders than I can claim to be. But then they have to excel in this mode of traveling, or they could not get over the country. In the far West the brakemen have no scruples about throwing tramps off freight-trains. In the East more civilized customs prevail, and the tramp is politely asked to "jump off after the train has stopped." Because railroad civilization is so backward in the West, the tramps have invented a seat which greatly aids their truck-riding. They call it a "ticket," but it is simply a small piece of board, with two cleats nailed on one side, which fit over a rod and keep the seat firm. Some of these tickets are quite elaborate, and are made to fold into a coat pocket.

The journey from Voorheesville to Weehawken proved interesting. My friend Whitey and I left Voorheesville for Coeyman's Junction on a local freight-train. We were on a flat-car, and entirely open to view, but were not once molested. During the ride I got a cinder in my eye, which my companion could not find. The pain was intense, and when we stopped next at a small station we jumped off in order that Whitey might inspect it more conveniently. He was still unsuccessful, and the station-master, standing by, beckoned me toward him and offered to take the cinder out, which he did very skilfully. The train was just ready to start when he called out, "Boys, don't miss your train." We followed his advice.

From the Junction down to Weehawken we underwent many trials. We left Coeyman's with fifteen other tramps on a through freight-train. All of us were huddled together on a flat-car, and of course the brakeman saw us. After finding out that none of us had any money to give him in aid of his collection for a "pint" (of whisky), he said: "You lads want to look out at Kingston. It 's all right until Catskill, but you 'll get collared at Kingston unless you 're careful." The minute the train slackened its speed at the hostile town, the roadsters jumped off *en masse*. Whitey suggested that we separate from the crowd, run around to the other end of the railroad yards, and catch the train again when it came out. We arrived there just in the nick of time, and rode away again triumphant. The next stop was Newburg, and just before we arrived the brakeman again warned us. "Look out here," he said, from the top of a car; "if you get pinched here, you 're sure for the Albany pen." We left the train again, and manœuvered in the same way as at Kingston. Again we traveled on without fear until nearing Haverstraw, and then came that same warning from the top of a car:

"Look out, you lads down there on the bumpers; Haverstraw is a hostile town." This was sickening. I had not complained before, but now I told Whitey that if ever I arrived in Weehawken safely I should forever forbid myself to tramp near the Hudson River. We were eventually successful in passing Haverstraw, and then the brakeman assured us that there was a safe route into Weehawken. His words proved true, and we arrived there at three o'clock in the morning. The puzzling question that I put to Whitey now was how to get over to New York without a cent of money. He told me not to worry, and that he would "work it all right." He spoke the truth, for we slipped into the ferry-house from the West Shore Railroad yards, and so eluded the sleepy gate-keeper. When we were on the ferry-boat I noticed four more tramps that I had met in Syracuse, and of course there was a general laugh.

On landing at Jay Street, Whitey asked me where I was going. I told him that I was afraid we must part company, and that I should have to walk up to Harlem. "I hate to see you do that," he said, "for it 's ag'in' the tramp natur' to like to hear of drilling [walking]. If you 'll wait for me up here on Broadway, I 'll go over to the post-office and hustle your car-fare." I thanked him, and waited on a corner for about five minutes, when, true enough, he returned with sufficient money for car-fare and slight refreshments over in the Bowery together. "Whitey, so long," I said; "be good to yourself." "So long, Cigarette; hope I 'll see you again." I left him standing in front of the Old Tree House, our ways henceforth forever separate, but as kindly sentiments inhabiting our bosoms as ever fell to the lot of knights of the road.

For every voluntary vagrant there is a voluntary taxpayer, and in the persons of these three hundred tramps I met three hundred voluntarily taxed citizens of the State of New York.

V

THE TRAMP AND THE RAILROADS

FIVE years had elapsed since my last journey with the hoboes—indeed, since I had so much as seen them. Study and recreation took me to Europe in the autumn of 1893, and I did not return to this country till the spring of 1898. Newspaper clippings containing accounts of the movements of the hoboes, and stories about their life, occasionally reached me, and once there came an invitation to be present at an Anti-Tramp Congress, but beyond this I heard very little about my old companions of the road. I always thought of them, however, when I saw the European vagabond trudging along on the public turnpikes, and wondered whether they were still permitted to travel on the railroads in their "side-door Pullmans" (box-cars) as they had done, and as they taught me to do when I was among them. In eastern Prussia I once stopped to talk with a foot-sore old wanderer on the *Chaussée*, and told him of the way the American tramp travels. "Ach, how beautiful that must be!" he exclaimed. "And to think that they would probably hang us poor fellows here in the Fatherland if we should try to ride in that fashion! In truth, son, a republic is the only place for the poor and outcast."

There had been rumors, while I was still on the road, that a day of reckoning was coming between the railroad companies and the tramps, and that when it arrived, the hobo, like the *Chausséegrabentapezirer*, would take to the turnpikes. Life in Hoboland is so precarious that it comes natural to the inhabitants to be on the watch for impending catastrophes, and I remember that I also believed that the railroad companies would eventually stop free riding as the tramp practised it. It did not seem natural that a class of people with so little influence as the tramps should be allowed to enjoy such a privilege long; and although I learned to ride in freight-cars with as much peace of mind and often more comfort than in passenger-coaches, there was always something strange to me in the fact that I never bought a ticket. During my first trip in Hoboland, which lasted eight continuous months, I must easily have traveled over twenty thousand miles, and there were not more than ten occasions during the entire experience when any payment was demanded of me, and on those occasions the "medium of exchange" consisted of such things as pipes, neckties, tobacco, and knives. Once I had to trade shoes with a brakeman merely to get across the Missouri River, a trip which ordinarily would have cost me but ten cents; but as that was the very sum of which I was short, and the brakeman wanted my shoes, the only thing to do was to trade.

Had any one told me, as I was leaving Europe, that a week after my arrival in this country I should be "hitting the road" again, I should not have believed him. Civilization had become very dear to me in the interval that had elapsed since my last tramp trip, and it seemed to me that my vagabond days were over.

Once a vagabond, however, like the reserve Prussian soldier, a man can always be called on for duty; and it was my fate, a few days after setting foot in my native land again, to be asked by the general manager of one of our railroads to make a report to him on the tramp situation on the lines under his control. For three years he had been hard at work organizing a railroad police force which was to rid the lines under his control of the tramp nuisance, and he believed that he was gradually succeeding in his task; but he wanted me to go over his property and give an independent opinion of what had been done. He had read some of my papers in the "Century" on tramp life, and while reading them it had occurred to him that I might be able to gather information for him which he could turn to good account, and he sent for me.

"On assuming management of these lines," he said to me in the conversation we had in his office, "I found that our trains were carrying thousands of trespassers, and that our freight-cars were frequently being robbed. I considered it a part of my business as a general manager to do my utmost to relieve the company of this expense, and I felt that the company owed it to the public to refuse to harbor this criminal class of people. In a way a railroad may be called the chief citizen of a State, and in this tramp matter it seemed to me that it had a duty as a citizen to discharge to the State.

"There are three conspicuous reasons that have deterred railroad people from attacking the tramp problem. First, it has been thought that it would entail a very great expense. Our experience on these lines has shown that this fear was not warranted. Second, it has been thought that no support would be given the movement by the local magistrates and police authorities. Our experience shows that in a great majority of cases we have the active support of the local police authorities and that the magistrates have done their full duty. Third, it was feared that there might be some retaliation by the tramps. Up to date we have but very little to complain of on that score. From the reports that I get from my men, I am led to believe that we are gradually ridding not only the railroad property, but much of the territory in which it is situated, of the tramp nuisance; but I should like a statement from you in regard to the situation, and I want to know whether you are willing to make a tramp trip and find out for us all that you can."

It was a cold, bleak day in March when we had this conversation, and there was every inducement to postpone a journey such as the general manager suggested; but I was so impressed with his seriousness in the matter, and so thoroughly interested in what he had done, that I agreed to begin the investigation at once. It seemed to me that a man who had written so much about the tramp problem ought to be willing to do what he could to help the community solve it, especially when he was to be reimbursed for his work

RIDING ON THE BUMPERS.

as liberally as I was to be; and although I suffered more on this particular journey than on any other that I have made, I shall never regret having undertaken it.

Before starting out on my travels a contract was drawn up between the general manager and myself. It secured to me a most satisfactory daily wage, and to the general manager weekly reports as long as I was out on the road, with a final statement when the investigation should be finished.

On no previous journey in Hoboland have I been such an object of curiosity to the tramps as on this one when writing my weekly reports. I was dressed so badly that I could write them only in lodging-houses where vagabonds sojourn, and it usually took me a full half-hour to finish one. It availed nothing to pick out a quiet corner, for the men gathered about me the minute they thought I had written enough, and they thought this before I was half through. If they had been able to decipher my handwriting I should probably have received pretty harsh treatment, but as they were not, they amused themselves with funny remarks. "Give 'er my love," they said. "Writin' yer will, are ye, Cigarette?" "Break the news gently." And they made other similar remarks which, if I had not been forced to write, would have smothered any literary aspirations that a lodging-house is capable of arousing. As it was, I managed to send in my reports more or less regularly, and faulty though they must have been, they served their purpose.

They told the story of the tramp situation on about

two thousand miles of railroad property, situated in five different States. The reports of the first month of the investigation pertained to tramps on lines in the neighborhood of the property I was investigating. I had not been an hour on my travels when it was made very plain to me that my employer's police force was so vigilant that it behooved me not to be caught riding trains unauthorized on his lines. Every tramp I met warned me against this particular road, and although a clause in my contract secured me the payment by the company of all fines that might be imposed upon me as a trespasser, as well as my salary during imprisonment, in case I should find it useful for my purposes to go to jail, I found it more convenient for the first month to wander about on railroads which I knew tramps could get over. I reasoned that the experience was going to be hard enough anyhow, without having to dodge a railroad police officer every time I boarded a train, and I knew that the trespassers on neighboring lines would be able to tell me what was the general opinion in regard to my employer's road as a tramp thoroughfare. All whom I interviewed spoke of it as the hardest railroad in the United States for a tramp to beat, and I could not have learned more of the tramps' opinion of it had I remained exclusively on the property. The roads that I went over crossed and recrossed my employer's road at a number of places, and I was frequently able to see for myself that it is a closed line for trespassers.

It may interest the reader to know how I lived during the time I traveled as a tramp. Except on one occasion, when my funds gave out, I paid my way regularly so far as food was concerned. A friend sent me a postal order for a few dollars nearly every week, and I managed to live rather comfortably at lodging-house restaurants. Occasionally I would meet a pal of former years, and if he had money, or found that I had, nothing would do but we should celebrate meeting each other again, and at such times my friend in the East got word that my remittance must be hurried up somewhat; but, as a general thing, I dined fairly well on two dollars a week. For sleeping-quarters I had bunks in lodging-houses, benches in police stations, and "newspaper beds" in railroad sand-houses. I chose one of these places as circumstances suggested. If there was nothing to be gained in the way of information by going to a sand-house or a police station, I took in a lodging-house, if one was handy. Once I slept in the tramp ward of a poorhouse, and never had I spent a more disagreeable night. A crowd of tramps to which I had attached myself had used up their welcome in a town where there were three police stations, and it had been arranged that on the night in question we should all meet at the tramp ward of the poorhouse. A negro was the first one to get there, and a more frightened human being than he was when the rest of us put in an appearance it would be hard to imagine. We found him in a cold cellar, absolutely without light and furnished with nothing but an immense bench, about four feet wide, four feet high, and ten feet long. In Siberia itself I have never seen a gloomier hole for men to pass a night in.

"I turned up here 'bout five o'clock," the negro said,

"'n' they sent me to the smokin'-room, where them luny blokes was smokin' their pipes. I never knew before that they sent luny people to poorhouses, 'n' I could n't understan' it. I told one of 'em what I was there for, 'n' he told me that this cellar down here has ghosts in it. Well, o' course, I ain't 'feard o' ghosts in most places, but, by jiminy, when the keeper came 'n' put me down here 'n' left me in the cold 'n' dark, somehow or other I got to thinkin' o' that luny bloke's stories, 'n' I jus' had to holler. W'y, I never felt so queer before in my life. Suppose I 'd gone crazy; w'y, I could 'a' sued the county for damages, could n't I? Don't you ever soogest any more poorhouses to me; I don't wonder people goes crazy in 'em." When the crowd first saw the negro he was shouting at the top of his voice: "Spirits! spirits! There 's spooks down here!"

We all spent a most miserable night in the cellar, and I doubt whether any one of us would willingly seek shelter there again.

Indeed, when the first month of my investigation was over, and war had been declared with Spain, it seemed to me that I had gone through so much and was so hardened that I could go to Cuba and worry through all kinds of trouble. I have since regretted that I did not go, but, at the time, I had become so interested in the work that, when I returned to my employer for further orders, and he said to me, "Well, now that you have satisfied me in regard to the attitude of the tramp toward the company's property, suppose you satisfy yourself concerning the attitude of the company toward the tramp," I readily fell in with the suggestion. To make my final report complete it was obvious that I ought to get an insight into the workings of my employer's police force, and for the second month he gave me permission to travel on freight-trains, engines, and passenger-trains, and a letter introducing me to the different employees of the company with whom I was likely to come in contact. With these credentials I was able to circulate freely over the property, to inquire minutely into the work of the police department, to meet the local magistrates, and particularly the jail- and workhouse-keepers. It was also possible for me to make an actual count of the trespassers who were daring enough to attempt to travel on this closed road.

This work was not so tedious and dangerous as that of the first month, and there were more comforts to be enjoyed; but I had to be up at all hours of the night, and the bulk of my time was spent in train-riding. After thirty days of almost constant travel I was convinced, first, that the tramps had told the truth about the road, and that it is exceedingly difficult to trespass on it with impunity; second, that although the police force is not perfect (none is), it was doing exceptionally good work in freeing the community of tramps and beggars. It differs from ordinary railroad police forces in that it is systematically organized and governed. In dealing with tramps and trespassers the plan is to keep up a continuous surveillance of them, and they are taken off trains one by one, day after day, rather than in squads of fifty and sixty, with no more effort in this direction for weeks and sometimes months, as is the prevailing custom on most railroads. There is consequently very little crowding of magistrates' courts and jails, and the taxpayers are not forced to board and lodge a great collection of vagabonds. I was also impressed with the fact that the force is on friendly relations with municipal and village police organizations along the road, and has the respect of communities formerly at the mercy of a constantly increasing army of hoboes.

So much for my personal experience and finding in this latest investigation in "trampology"; it was as interesting a tramp trip as I have ever made, and I learned more about the best methods to employ in attacking the tramp problem in this country than on any previous journey. It is now my firm belief that, if the tramps can be kept off the railroads, their organization will become so unattractive that it will never again appeal to men as it has done in the past. No other country in the world transports its beggars from place to place free of charge, and there is no reason why this country should do so.

The custom has grown up in the United States during the last thirty years. Before the Civil War there were comparatively few tramps in America, and practically no railroad tramps. After the war there suddenly appeared on the scene a large class of men who had become so enamoured of camp life that they found it impossible to return to quiet living, and they took to wandering about the country. Occasionally they worked a little to keep themselves in "pin-money," but by 1870 hundreds of them had given up all intention of working, and had founded the organization known to-day as the "Hobo-Push." By that year, also, they had discovered that our turnpikes, particularly in the West, were very poor roads to travel on, and they began to walk on the railroad-track.

If, at this time, the railroad companies had had laws passed, such as are in force to-day in Great Britain and on the Continent, forbidding everybody but an employee to walk on railroad property, except at public crossings, we should have learned, ere this, to obey them, and the railroad tramp would not have been developed. These laws not being enacted, however, it was not long before it became very clear to the tramp that it would be much more comfortable to sit in a box-car and ride, than to "drill" (walk) over the ties. An appreciation of this character is acted upon very soon in Hoboland, and by 1875 the majority of the professional vagrants were taking lessons in jumping on and off moving freight-trains. The trainmen, partly because they thought that many of these trespassers were deserving but penniless out-of-works, and partly on account of the inborn willingness of every American to help a man in unfortunate circumstances, made practically no serious effort to keep the tramp off their trains, and by 1880 the latter was accepted by railroad companies as an unavoidable nuisance on railroad property.

To-day it is the boast of the hoboes that they can travel in every State of the Union for a mill per mile, while in a number of States they pay nothing at all. On lines where brakemen demand money of them, ten cents is usually sufficient to settle for a journey of a hundred miles, and twenty cents often secures a night's ride. They have different methods of riding, among which the favorite is to steal into an empty box-car on a freight-train. At night this is comparatively easy to do; on many roads it is possible to travel this way, undisturbed, till morning. If the train has no "empties," they must ride on top of the car, between the "bumpers," on one of the car ladders, or on the rods. On passenger-trains they ride on top, on the "blind baggage," and on the trucks.

Taking this country by and large, it is no exaggeration to say that every night in the year ten thousand free passengers of the tramp genus travel on the different railroads in the ways mentioned, and that ten thousand more are waiting at watering-tanks and in railroad yards for opportunities to get on the trains. I estimate the professional tramp population at about sixty thousand, a third of whom are generally on the move.

In summer the entire tramp fraternity may be said to be "in transit." The average number of miles traveled daily by each man at this season of the year is about fifty, which, if paid for at regular rates, would cost, say, a dollar. Of course one should not ordinarily pay so much to ride in a box-car as in a passenger-coach, but the ordinary tramp is about as comfortable in one as in the other, and, on the dollar-a-trip basis, he and his 59,999 companions succeed in getting out of the railroad companies sixty thousand dollars' worth of free transportation every day that they all travel. Multiply this figure by a hundred, which is about the number of days in a year when all trampdom "flits," and you have an approximate idea of how much they gain.

A BRAKEMAN OF A FREIGHT-TRAIN COLLECTING FARES.

Another serious loss to the railroads is that involved in the disappearance of goods undergoing transportation, and in claims for personal injuries. Some tramps steal, and some do not, but every year considerable thefts are made from freight-cars, and tramps, or men posing as such, are generally the guilty parties. Professional thieves frequently become tramps for a time, both to minimize their guilt and to elude capture, and the probability is that the majority of the greater thefts are committed by them. Tramps proper are discouraged thieves, and I have seldom known them to steal anything more valuable than fruit from freight-cars and metal from idle engines. In a year's time, however, including all the thefts committed by both tramps and professional thieves, a very appreciable loss results to the railroads, and I can recall, out of my observation, robberies which have amounted to several thousand dollars.

That railroad companies should have to reimburse trespassers for the loss of a hand or foot while riding unauthorized on trains will strike every one as a very unjust tax on their resources, but such claims are constantly made. Let us say, for example, that a young boy who has been stealing his way on a freight-train loses a leg. There is a type of lawyer who at once takes up a case of this sort, going to the boy's parents or relatives and suggesting to them the advisability of claiming damages, asserting his readiness to serve them in the matter. "All right," says the father; "get what you can." In court the lawyer draws a horrible picture of these engines of death, the railroads, showing how they are constantly killing people.

If the boy's father is poor, this fact is also brought graphically to the attention of the jury, and the wealth of the corporation is described as something enormous. If the lawyer manages his case cleverly, making out that the boy was enticed on to the freight-train by the trainmen, or that he fell under the wheels through their carelessness, there are but few juries that will refuse to give the father at least enough damages to pay the lawyer's fee and the doctor's bill, and then there is a celebration over having "squeezed" another railroad company. For a private person to be compelled by a court to pay damages to the father of a boy who fell from an apple-tree in the private person's orchard, where the lad was an obvious trespasser and thief, would be considered an outrage.

I bring out these facts about the losses to the railroads in some detail because the public is really the railroad company, and consequently the sufferer.

To tell all that the country at large suffers from the free railroad transportation of tramps would take me beyond the limits of this chapter, but there are a few points which must be noted. In the first place, the railroads spread the tramp nuisance over a much greater stretch of territory than would be the case if the tramps were limited to the turnpikes. There are districts in the United States which are so difficult to reach by the highroad, on account of unprofitable intermediate territory, that the hobo would never attempt to go near them if it were not easy for him to get over the disagreeable parts of the journey in a box-car. Take the trip from Denver to San Francisco, for instance. There is not a vagabond in the country who would undertake to walk across the American Desert merely to reach "'Frisco," and if walking were the only way to get to that city it would be left largely to "coast beggars." As matters now stand, however, you may see a beggar one day in Fifth Avenue in New York city, and a fortnight later he will accost you in Market Street in San Francisco. Many tramps can travel as rapidly as the man who pays his way, and I have known those who could even "hold down" the Chicago Limited from Jersey City to Chicago without a break.

All this contributes to the difficulty of locating and capturing the dangerous characters of tramp life; and, as I have said, many professional criminals, who have nothing to do with beggars in other quarters, mix with them in freight-cars.

A remark, in this connection, of Mr. Allen Pinkerton is popular in Hoboland. He is reported by the hoboes to have once said, in a conversation about the capture of criminals, that he thought he could catch, in time, almost any kind of criminal except the tramp, and him he could not catch because it was so difficult to locate him. "One day he is in a barn, the next in a haystack, and the next Heaven only knows where he is, for he has probably got on to the railroad, and there you might as well look for a lost pin."

The railroads also help to keep the tramp element in our large cities. It very seldom settles in the country, and not for any length of time in provincial towns. New York, Chicago, Philadelphia, Boston, San Francisco, Buffalo, Baltimore, New Orleans, and other like places are its main strongholds. The more the criminal element of a country fastens itself upon its cities, the harder it is to break up, and in the United States this is what is taking place. Chicago, for instance, is as much a center in the criminal as in the business world, and almost every freight-train entering it brings a contribution to its criminal population. Even without railroads the tendency of crime to predominate in towns would exist; evil-doers feel more at home in city streets and haunts than in the country; but their present strength in our cities is largely due to the free transportation they get from the railroads.

Another striking fact is that out-of-works who beat their way on freight-trains very easily degenerate into professional vagabonds. I have traveled with men who, in six months' time, had become voluntary vagrants merely because their first stolen rides, while in search of work, had demonstrated to them how easy it is to manage without working and paying their way. The average unemployed man in the United States goes from one large city to another, rather than, as is the custom in Europe, taking in the intermediate towns and villages, where there is no such likelihood of the labor-market becoming congested. In a few weeks, unless he is a man of very strong character, he learns to travel merely for travel's sake, and develops into a "stake-man," who only works long enough to get a "stake" and then go off on a trip again. Among the so-called unemployed in this country there are thousands of this type, and they are the result of this love of side-door Pullman excursions.

A TRAMPS' DEPOT

There is one more fact which cannot be overlooked —the temptation which the railroads have for a romantic and adventuresome boy. A child possessed of *Wanderlust* generally wanders for a while, anyhow, but the chance he now has to jump on a freight-train and "get into the world quick," as I have heard lads of this temperament remark, has a great deal to do in tempting him to run away from home. Hoboland is overrun with youngsters who have got there on the railroads, and very few of them ever wander back to their parents. Once started "railroading," they go on and on, and its attractions seem to increase as the years go by. Walking has no such charms for them, and if it were their only method of seeing the world, the majority of those who now keep on seeing it, until death ends their roaming, would grow tired. The railroad, however, makes it possible for them to keep shifting the scenes they enjoy, and, in time, change and variety become so essential that they are unable to settle down anywhere. They are victims of what tramps call the "railroad fever," a malady for which a remedy has yet to be prescribed.

Can the tramps be driven off the railroads? It was to satisfy my own curiosity in regard to this question, and to find out how successful my employer, the general manager, had been in his attempt to answer it in the affirmative, that I undertook the investigation which I have described. Previous to his efforts to keep tramps off railroads, it had been thought, as he has stated, that it was cheaper to put up with them than to pay the bills which a crusade against them would occasion. It has at last been demonstrated, however, that they can be refused free transportation, with a saving of expense to the company, and with great benefit to the community; and the time has come when the public should demand that all railroads take a similar stand in regard to this evil.

If all the companies would take concerted action, in a few years very few tramps, if any, would try to beat their way on trains; an appreciable number would give up tramping entirely, because their railroad privileges are to many the main attraction of the life; a few would try to become professional criminals again, partly out of revenge and partly because tramping on the turnpikes would be too disagreeable; and a large number would take to the highways, where some at least might be made to do farm-work. The reader may take exception to the third possibility, and think that great harm would come of an increase in the professional criminal class; but, as I have said, tramps are really discouraged criminals, and a return to the old life, of which they had made a failure, would only land them in the penitentiary.

It is probably impossible ever entirely to eliminate the vagrant element in a nation's life, and no such hope is held out in connection with the reform advocated in this article; but this much is certain: had all the railroads been as closed to tramps, during my first excursions into Hoboland, as one of them has recently become, one man, at least, would not have attempted any free riding, and would not have found so many tramps to study.

PART III

SKETCHES

PART III

SKETCHES

PART III — SKETCHES

I

OLD BOSTON MARY

ON the southern outskirts of the city of Boston, hidden away in a field, and reached by streets that gradually degenerated into straggling lanes, stood until a few years ago an old shanty, noted for nothing but loneliness and spooks. No one in the neighborhood knew to whom it belonged or what was its history. It was almost too forlorn to be interesting, and few went near it. The children in the district claimed that queer noises were heard in the shanty at night, and their mothers threatened them with its sheltered ghosts when they were especially naughty. But this was the extent of the shanty's reputation in its own parish.

Its history, or at any rate so much of it as is known, is anything but romantic. When first built, it belonged to a "Paddy" on the railroad; and after various generations of this proprietary family had passed on to the better quarters that Boston provides for its ambitious Irish citizens, it became so dilapidated and forlorn that it was turned over to some cows pastured near by, as shelter for stormy days. It was still used for this purpose, I am told, when Old Mary rented it. How she discovered it, and why it attracted her, are questions which even her best friends found difficult to solve. But there was something about it which appealed to her, and for several months she lived her queer life in this uninteresting old building. Her neighbors knew almost nothing about her, except that she was an eccentric old woman, and that she harbored a strange class of friends who might with greater propriety have lodged in the city almshouse. But otherwise she was a foreigner in her own province, and no one could tell what she did or how she lived. Strange, too; for in some respects this old creature was a most notorious character, and had perhaps as many acquaintances and friends as any citizen of Boston. Almost every evening, after dark, had there been curious eyes on watch, stragglers of many sizes and conditions might have been seen wending their way, stealthily and catlike, to her shanty, and ears alert might have heard a queer password tapped on the wooden door, which, as of its own free will, swung back on noiseless leather hinges, and, closing, hid the strangers from view. This went on night after night, and no resident of the neighborhood knew or cared much about it. Whatever was done in the shanty passed off so quietly and unobtrusively that public curiosity was not awakened.

My first knowledge of the place was on this wise: One afternoon, while studying tramp life in New York, I dropped in for a moment at a popular resort of vagabonds in the Bowery. I had already had several months' experience in their company, and was casting about for some new feature or phase of the life; naturally enough, I turned to the saloon to hear of something which would put me on a fresh track. As luck would have it, I chanced to overhear two Eastern beggars discussing the customs and institutions of Boston. Their conversation interested me, and I drew nearer. During their talk, reference was made to Old Mary's place, which I had never heard of elsewhere, and I determined to see it.

It was not long before I had found a companion and persuaded him to accompany me to Boston. He also had heard of the place, and was fairly well acquainted with its mistress, who, he declared, had been a well-known hobo out West some years before. Her history, as he recollected it, and which I know now to be quite true, was something like this:

About forty years ago, a Gipsy girl in England, who had wandered about with her tribe through France as well as Britain, came to America, hoping to find her Rom friends here strong enough to afford her society and protection. But for some reason she failed to meet with the welcome she had expected, and as there was nothing else in the New World more akin to her old life than the tramp's peripatetic existence, she joined the brotherhood, and for over thirty years was recognized as a full-fledged member. Her specialty, the hobo said, was "ridin' the trucks"; and in this dangerous business she became an expert, and was probably the only woman in the world who ever made a practice of it. It may surprise some that a woman reared in Gipsy society, and accustomed to the rigorous social divisions which obtain there, should ever have entered trampdom, composed almost entirely of men. It must be remembered, however, that there are women in all classes of society who are men's women, not women's women, and at the same time none the worse for their peculiarity. There is a certain comradeship in their relations with men which even a stunted sense of honor will not abuse, and which adds piquancy to their friendship.

The Gipsy girl was one of these, and had her friends as well as her lovers. The lovers failed as she grew older, but this strong-souled companionship stood her in good stead, and held the friends she made. She who had been so poorly cared for all her life long had developed somehow a genius for taking care of others, and so, after thirty years of hard riding and hard faring of all sorts, her head not quite clear about a good many things that human justice calls crime, she set up a poor, miserable home for the brotherhood of tramps. It was a crazy idea, perhaps, but the woman herself was pretty well "crippled under the hat," my friend declared, and was known from Maine to California, in true tramp dialect, as "Bughouse Mary," or, as politer folk would say, "Crazy Mary."

She settled herself at first in a tumble-down old tenement-house in the very heart of Boston, and her place soon became known—too well known, in fact—to certain officious and official personages who had on more than one occasion found dangerous characters sheltered there. After some weeks she thought it necessary to move on, and pitched her tent on the spot already described. It was here that my companion and I first tested her sisterly welcome. A town tramp put us on the right road, and gave us explicit directions. He advised us not to go by daylight, and asked, "Does you blokes know the rules out at Mary's? I guess she 'd take you in anyhow, but mos' the blokes, when they goes out there, takes along a handful o' terbakker an' a chunk o' beef or somethin' else ter chew. She allus 'xpects her half, too. It 's a sort o' law out there, 'n' p'r'aps you lads 'u'd better do as I tells ye."

We followed his advice, and I looked for some beefsteak, while my companion found the tobacco and bread. About nine o'clock we started, and spent fully an hour in finding the place. At the door, as we knew of no especial knock, I whispered through one of the cracks the word "Hobo," knowing that this was the usual tramp call. We soon heard a queer voice asking our names.

"Cigarette," I replied.

"What Cigarette?" asked the voice.

I assured her that it was the Chicago brand.

This was sufficient, and the door opened far enough to allow us to squeeze through, and we were in the famous Boston hang-out.

The first attraction, of course, was Mary herself, and she was well worth a longer pilgrimage. I shall never forget the picture she made, as she stood in the middle of the floor surrounded by her pals, and welcomed us to her shanty. Her figure, although naturally strong and straight, looked cramped and bent, and had certainly suffered from long exposure and the hardships of truck-riding. Her dress, although picturesque in some particulars, looked just as tattered and worn out as did her poor old body. The original cloth and color of the skirt, if indeed it had ever had any, were disguised by fully a dozen different patches sewed on with coarse, straggling, Gipsy-like stitches. In place of a waist she wore an old coat and vest, given to her, as I afterward learned, by a clergyman. The coat was soldier's blue, and the vest as red as a robin's breast. A strange costume, it is true; but as I looked at her, it seemed, after all, a fitting one for such a unique being. The head that topped the costume was most interesting of all: a certain pose in moments of enthusiasm, and a certain toss at the climax of some story relating her early triumphs, gave it an air of wild nobility such as one sees in high-bred animals; and when, in the consciousness of her weakened powers, it dropped sadly on her breast, with the ragged gray locks streaming out in all directions, one could nót escape the sense of fallen greatness in the gaunt bowed figure and the tortured face.

Naturally she looked crazy, but I wished at the time that if crazy people must really exist, they might look like her. Her eyes were her most intelligent feature, and even they at times would become glazed and almost uncanny. They were the most motherly, and also the wickedest, I have ever seen on the road. This sounds paradoxical, I know, but as I have heard other men describe them in the same way, I think I must be right. And when she looked at me I felt that she was piercing my character and history in every possible corner. I have no doubt that she intended to impress me in this way. It is a Gipsy trick, and she evidently had not forgotten it.

But queer and crazy as Old Mary appeared, she was

nevertheless quite in harmony with her environment; for of all the odd hang-outs I have visited, hers was certainly the oddest. The shanty itself was in many respects just as the cows had left it, and the only furniture it contained was a stove, a few old benches, a greasy lamp, a supply of blankets, and a cupboard containing one or two frying-pans and some polished and renovated tomato-cans. These were all that the old Gipsy had been able to gather together, and it had cost her many days of fortune-telling to collect even these. But, fortunately, it was not for such things that the beggars visited her. What they wanted was simply a place where they could be away from the police, and in the company of Old Mary, whom they looked upon as a sort of guardian angel. On the night in question she had as guests men who represented nearly every kind of vagabondage. The "blanket-stiff," the "gay-cat," the "shiny," the "Frenchy," and the "ex-prushun" were all there. Some were lying on the floor wrapped in their blankets; some were mending their coats and darning their socks; while others were sitting around the stove playing a quiet game of poker, using as an "ante" pieces of bread which they had begged. In a corner there were still others who were taking off their "jiggers," reminding one of that famous *cour des miracles* which Victor Hugo has described in "Notre Dame"; for the jiggers were nothing but bandages wound around the legs and arms to excite the sympathy of credulous and charitable people.

Mary was exceedingly kind in her welcome to both my comrade and myself; but on learning that I was really the Chicago Cigarette she was a little partial to me, I think, and made me sit down on a bench, where we talked of various things and people, but especially of a St. Louis beggar called "Bud," who had spoken to her of a Cigarette with whom he once traveled. Learning that I was the very same, and that we had at one time made a long journey in the West, she wanted to know just when I had seen him last, how he looked, and what he was doing. I could easily see, from the passionate way she spoke of him and her eagerness for late news concerning his whereabouts, that he had once been a pal of hers, and I had to tell her as gently as I could that the poor fellow had been starved to death in a box-car in Texas. Some one had locked him in, and when the car was shunted on to an unused side-track, far away from any house or station, his fate was settled. Try as one will to get out of such a predicament, there is no hope unless one has a large knife and strength enough to cut through the walls. Poor Bud was without both, and he died alone and forsaken. I had heard of the accident from a man who was in the neighborhood where it happened; and thinking that the best thing I could tell Old Mary would be the truth, I stammered it out in a most awkward fashion.

I knew well enough that she would cry, but I hardly expected to see the sorrow that my story occasioned. It was almost indescribable. She wept and moaned, and swayed her old body back and forth in an agony of grief, but not once did she speak. I tried my best to comfort her, but it was of no use. She had to suffer, and no one could help her. I felt so bad that

I almost started to leave, but one of the men told me that she would be all right pretty soon, and I waited. True, she did become calmer, and in about an hour was enough herself to talk about other matters; but there was a grief still in her eyes that was most pitiful to see. And I shall always remember her strange and inarticulate agony. It showed, not a comrade's bereavement, nor yet the heart-wound of a motherly nature merely, but a phase of emotion belonging to younger hearts as well. I think also that there was a Gipsy strain in her suffering which I could not comprehend at all.

When fairly aroused from her sadness, she asked for our bundles of food, and made the men playing cards on the stove move away, that she might light a fire and cook our meal. While she attended to these things, I passed around among the tramps. The place hardly coincided with my expectations. I had looked forward to a rough hang-out, where there would be more fighting and cursing than anything else, but I found nothing of the kind. The men conducted themselves very respectably, at least while Mary was looking on. There were a few harsh words heard, of course, but there was none of that vulgarity that one would naturally expect, for the hostess forbade it. Not that she was a woman who had never heard bad words or seen vulgar sights, but there was something about her which certainly quieted and softened the reckless people she gathered together. What this was I cannot say, but I think it was her kindness. For if there is anything which a tramp respects, although he may forget it when it is out of his sight, it is gentleness, and it was this trait in Old Mary's character which won for her the distinction and privileges usually accorded the mistress of the house. She did everything she could to make her shanty comfortable and her guests happy. For example, one man had a sore foot, and while the meat was frying she bandaged it most tenderly, making her patient lie down on a blanket which she took from a cupboard. Others wanted string or tobacco, and she invariably supplied them. She gave each one the impression that she was really interested in him; and to know this is exactly as pleasant to a tramp as it is to any other human being.

When our supper was ready, Mary handed me a little pail, and said: "Cig, you 'd better run out 'n' hustle some beer. You kin find it 'bout half a mile up the road, ef you give the bloke a good story. But don't let the bulls catch ye. I don't wan' cher ter git sloughed up."

I took the pail and went in search of the beer, which I found at the place she spoke of. On my return she had the meat and bread placed on a shingle, and my companion and I, together with the hostess, sat down on a bench and had a most satisfying meal. During the repast Mary talked a good deal on numerous subjects, and commented on tramp life in various communities. She gave but little evidence of being crazy, but her mind would wander once in a while, and she would say in a dreamy sort of way, "Oh, Cig, this sort o' bummin' hain't like the old times. Them was the days fer beggars."

Those old days, I suppose, were when she first came

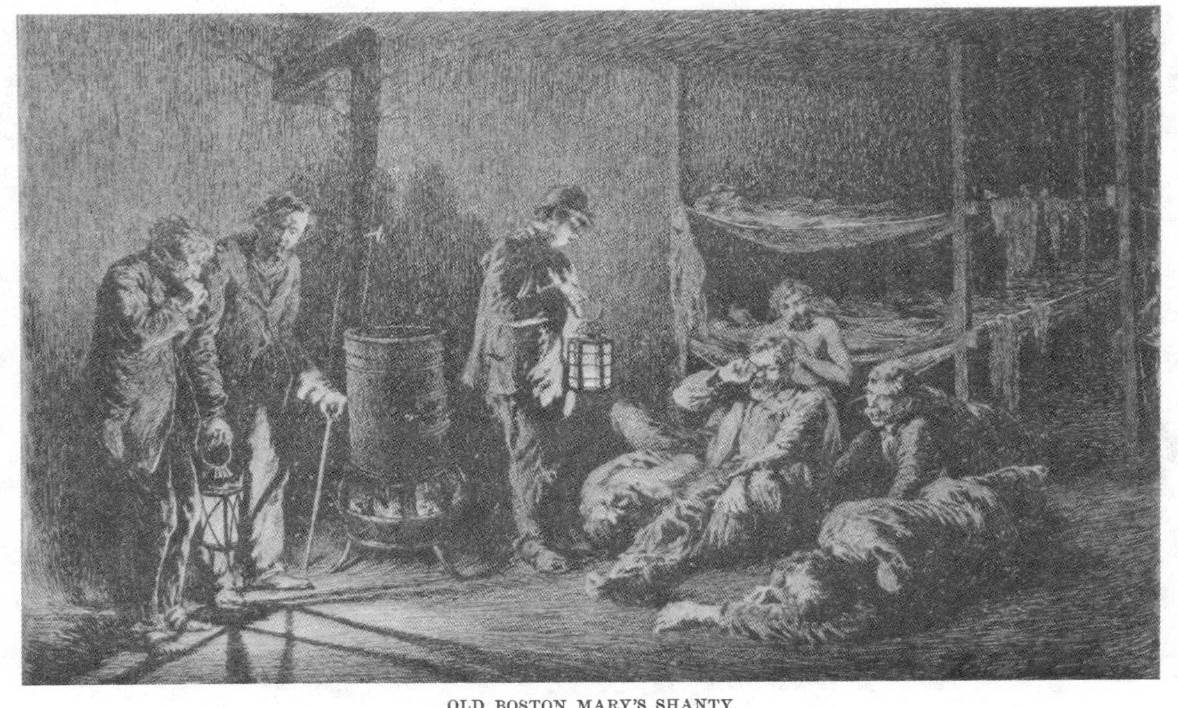

OLD BOSTON MARY'S SHANTY.

to this country; and I have been told that a beggar's life in that period was, if not more profitable, at any rate more comfortable. I also heard her mumbling and calling herself "bughouse," and with the word her old head would fall humbly on her breast. But her kindness was so sound and steadfast that this occasional lapse into her inane mumbling did not much impress me. She kept asking if I were having enough to eat, and offered to cook more meat if I were not. When we had finished, she handed me a new clay pipe, gave me some tobacco which was of a better brand than that which my companion had begged, and then told me to smoke my "vittals stiddy." We sat there for nearly an hour, not saying much, and yet knowing fairly well what each one was thinking. There is something in tramp nature which makes these silent conversations easy and natural.

At twelve o'clock we prepared for sleep. Mary was now at her best, and the way she assigned each man his place was worthy of a general. As we had to turn out about half-past four in the morning, so that all would be quiet before people were astir, I was glad enough to have a rest. The most of the men took off their coats and shoes, making of the former a blanket and of the latter a pillow, said, "Pound yer ear well," to their nearest neighbors, and then the candle was put out. Mary had a corner entirely to herself.

I had been asleep for about three hours, I think, when I was awakened by a light shining in my face, and a hand passing over a tattoo mark on my right arm. I started up, and saw Mary kneeling beside me and inspecting the "piece" very closely. Noticing that I was awake, she whispered: "Come out o' the shanty with me fer a minnit. I wants ter ask ye somethin'."

I rose and followed her quietly out of the building to a small hollow not far away.

"Now, Cig," she said, "tell me the truth. Did Bud croak down in Texas, dead sartain?"

I assured her that I had told her the truth.

"Well," she replied, "then the whole game is up. Ye see, Bud was a Rom, too, 'n' we use' ter be great pals. Fer nigh onter a tenner we bummed this kentry together 'n' never had a fight. But one day Bud got jagged, 'n' swore I had n' be'n square to 'im. So we had a reg'lar out-'n'-outer, 'n' I hain't seen 'im sence. I 's sorry that 'e 's croaked, fer 'e was a good bloke; yes, 'e was—yes, 'e was—" Here the poor creature seemed to forget herself, and I could hear her saying, "Bughouse—bughouse." I recalled her to consciousness, and said that I must leave, as it was nearly time for her to close up shop. She wanted me to promise to meet her on the Common in the afternoon, where she did most of her begging, and handed me a quarter to "keep me a-goin'" till then. I returned it, and told her that I had to leave Boston that morning, but would gladly visit her again some day. And I certainly intended to do so. But the natural course of events took me out of vagabondage soon, and it was not until quite recently that I heard any more of Bughouse Mary.

A short time ago, while seeking some special and late information regarding tramp life in the large cities, I chanced upon an old friend of Mary's, whom I plied with questions concerning her whereabouts and fate. It was a long time before he would give me anything I could call a straight story, but at last, finding I had been, years before, one of the brotherhood, with hesitation and real sorrow he told me what follows:

"I wuz drillin' one day, 'bout two months 'go, on the Boston 'n' Albany road, 'n' hed jes got into a jerk town [a village], where I battered [begged] fer some dinner. It begun to rain arter I 'd chewed, so I mooched down to the track 'n' found a box-car where I stopped fer a while. I wuz waitin' fer the 'xpress, too, so the wettin' wa'n't much uv a bother. Waal, I 'd be'n in the car a few minnits, when I got all-fired sleepy, 'n' ter save me gizzard I c'u'd n't keep me eyes open. So I jes lay down 'n' pounded me ear [slept]. I 'd be'n a-poundin' it, I guess, fer 'bout two hours—fer 't wuz 'bout five 'clock when I begun, 'n' 't wuz dead dark when I got me peepers open—when I heerd somebody pushin' away at the car door to beat the divil, 'n' o' course looked out; an' there on the groun' wuz one o' the funniest bums y' ever see—long, flyin' hair, big gray eyes, coat 'n' vest, 'n', ez sure 's I 'm a moocher, a skirt too, but no hat. Course I was int'rested, 'n' I jumps down 'n' gives the critter a big stare plump in the face, fer I had the feelin' I 'd seen it afore somewheres. See? An' it sort o' answered, fer it seed I wuz koorios. 'I say, blokey, kin yer tell me when the flyin' mail passes through these yere parts? I wants ter make it, ef it do.' Then I knew who 't wuz, fer ye kin tell Old Mary ev'ry time when she begins to chew the rag. I tole her that the mail come through 'bout twelve 'clock, 'n' then asked her where her hat wuz.

"'Waal, blokey,' she said, 'I hain't a-wearin' them air t'ings any more. I say, air yer right k'rect that the flyin' mail comes through these yere parts?' I guv it to her dead straight, 'n' tole 'er I wuz sartain. Then I asked, 'Mary, ain' cher recognizin' common peoples any more? Don't chu know old Tom?' Ye sh'u'd 'a' seen 'er look! She put 'er old bony han's on me shoulders, 'n' stuck 'er old phiz clos't ter mine, 'n' said, 'Who be ye, anyhow? I 's gettin' sort o' old-like 'n' bughouse, 'n' I can't call yer name. Who be ye? 'n' kin ye tell me ef I kin make the flyin' mail?' I tole 'er who I wuz, 'n' ye sh'u'd 'a' seen 'er! Ye see, I 's summat younger than 'er, 'n' she jes treated me like me old woman. It made me feel sort o' queer-like, I tell ye, for I use' ter like the old gal in great style.

"Waal, we had a good talk, as ye kin well 'xpect, but she kept askin' 'bout that blasted flyin' mail. I did n' wan' ter ride it that night, 'cause she wuz purty bughouse, 'n' I felt she 'd get ditched ef we tried it. So I jes argeyed with 'er, 'n' did me best ter make 'er stay where we wuz; but I might jes 's well 'a' tried to batter a dollar in the place. She was simply stuck on pullin' out that night. I asked 'er why she did n't go back to Boston, 'n' she said, 'Boston! W'y, I 's got the mooch out o' Boston. Ye see, Tom, I got ter tellin' fortunes, 'n' the bulls snared me, 'n' his Honor tole me to crawl. I did n' go at first, but arter a bit it got too hot fer me out at the shanty, 'n' I had ter mooch. So here I be, 'n' I guess I 'm a' right; but

I 's bughouse—yes, bughouse'; 'n' she kept a-squealin' that word till I wuz sick. But she wuz bughouse, dead sure. An' I guess that 's why she wuz on the road, fer when I use' ter know 'er she wuz too cute ter let any bull get roun' her; anyhow, no Boston bull c'u'd 'a' done it. P'r'aps a Chicago one might, but he 's all eyes anyhow.

"Waal, ez I wuz sayin', I tried ter keep 'er from ridin' the mail, but 't wa'n't no use. So I made up me mind that I 'd go with 'er 'n' help 'er along. An' when the train whistled roun' the curve, I got 'er over to the tank, 'n' made 'er lay low till the train wuz ready. Waal, the train had come, 'n' I looked it over to find a blind baggage, but I c'u'd n't. So I says to Mary, 'We 've got to truck it.' She got horstile 's the divil when I tole 'er that. 'Truck it!' she said. 'Course we 'll truck it. What else d' ye 'xpect us to do? I use' ter ride out West as well as any o' ye, but I 's gittin' old 'n' sort o' bughouse—yes, I is.' The train wuz mos' ready to pull out, 'n' the con wuz swingin' his lantern, so I took 'er hand 'n' got 'er into the baggage-car trucks. 'Get in carefully,' I said, ''n' be sartain ter hang on to the right rod.' She clumb in 'tween the wheels, 'n' fixed 'erself with 'er back to the engine. It would 'a' made ye cry to hear 'er beggin' me to look out fer 'er. 'Don't leave the old gal, will yer, blokey?' I tole 'er I w'u'd n't, 'n' got in alongside her jes ez the whistle blew; 'n' away we went, ridin', fer all either on us c'u'd tell, to the divil. 'T wa'n't no time to think 'bout that, though, fer I had to remember the old gal. I did n't dast ter hold 'er, fer I 'd 'a' fallen meself, so I jes had to holler at 'er, 'n' be sure that she hollered back. I kept a-bellerin', 'Hang on, Mary, hang on!' 'n' she kept sayin', 'I will, blokey, I will!' She meant, o' course, that she 'd do her best, but arter a few minnits I see clear 'nough she 'd never pull through. The way the wind 'n' the gravel 'n' the dirt flew round our faces, 'n' the cramps that took us, settin' so crooked-like, wuz 'nough to make bigger blokes 'n she give up, 'n' don' cher forget it. An' to make things worse, her hair blew all over me face, 'n' matted down me eyes so I c'u'd hardly see. I das' n't brush it away, fer I 'd tumbled sure. The gravel cut me face, too, 'n' onc't a good-sized stone hit me lips such a rap that I c'u'd feel the blood tricklin' on me chin. But worse than all, Old Mary got to screamin', 'n' I c'u'd n't see her fer her hair. She screamed 'n' screamed, 'The flyin' mail—oh, I say—the flyin' mail,' an' 'er shriekin' 'n' the rattlin' o' the wheels made me nigh bughouse, too. I called out ev'ry few minnits to keep 'er down to bizness, 'n' I got one more answer sayin' she was doin' 'er best. An' then some o' her hair flew in me mouth, 'n' try me best I c'u'd n't get it out, 'n' I did n't dast ter take me hands off the rod. So I c'u'd n't see 'er or speak to 'er any more. See? I heard 'er screamin' agen, 'Oh, I say—the flyin' mail—flyin'—bughouse,' an' then nothin' more. I c'u'd n't say nothin', so I jes made a big noise in me throat to let 'er know I wuz there. By 'n' by I heerd it agen,—'Bughouse—flyin' mail—blokey,'—an' agen I lost 'er. I wuz nearly bughouse meself. Ef that train hed only hauled up! Ef I hed only kept 'er from ever gettin' on to it! I c'u'd n' hold 'er, I c'u'd n' speak to 'er, I c'u'd n' see 'er, an' all the divils wuz dead agen' us. An' she wuz gettin' wilder ev'ry minnit. I shook me head up 'n' down, back'urd 'n' for'ard—'t wuz all I c'u'd do. Once agen she begun her screamin', 'Oh, I say, the flyin' mail—flyin'—flyin',' an' then I said the biggest thankee I ever said in me life fer bein' blinded in me eyes; fer when her old hair hed swished away, 'n' me eyes wuz free agen, I wuz hangin' on alone, 'n' the wheels hed carried me far away from where the old gal wuz lyin'. I c'u'd n't help it, Cig—no, I c'u'd n't; 'n' you mus' tell the other blokes that I done my best, but 't wa'n't no use—I done my best."

The tremor of the tone, the terror lest I should think he had not been faithful to his awful trust, told better than words that his tale was true, and that he had done his best to save the poor wrecked life so confidingly placed in his care.

But the end was not unfitting. The "flyin' mail," the cramped and painful ride, the pelting storm of dust and gravel, the homeless goal—what could be more symbolic of Old Mary's career? And on the wings of steam and wind her Gipsy spirit went flying —flying.

II

JAMIE THE KID

IT was my last night in San Francisco, and I could not leave without saying good-by to Old Slim. His place was almost empty when I strolled in, and he was standing behind his greasy bar counting the day's winnings. The *adios* was soon said, and I started for the street again. I had hardly left the bar when the door suddenly squeaked on its rickety hinges, and a one-armed man came in with a handsome kid. He was evidently dying of consumption, and as he shuffled clumsily across the floor, with the boy following solemnly at his heels, I fancied that he wanted Slim to help him into a hospital. He called for his drinks, and asked Slim if he knew of any one "bound East" the next day.

"W'y, yes," Slim replied; "that young feller right back o' ye leaves ter-morrer: ain't that right, Cigarette?"

The man turned and looked at me. Grabbing my hand, he exclaimed:

"Well, I 'll be jiggered! Where d' y'u come from? Don't remember me, eh? W'y, you little beggar, have you forgotten the time we nearly croaked in that box-car jus' out of Austin—have you forgotten that?" and he pinched my fingers as if to punish me.

I scrutinized him closely, trying to trace in his withered and sickened face the familiar countenance of my old friend Denver Red.

"Yes, that 's right, guy me!" he retorted nervously. "I 've changed a little, I know. But look at this arm,"—pushing back his sleeve from the emaciated hand,—"that crucifix ain't changed, is it? Now d' you know me?"

There was no longer any reason for doubt, for down in Texas I had seen New Orleans Fatty put that same piece on his lonely arm. But how changed he was! The last time we met he was one of the healthiest hoboes on the "Santa Fé," and now he could just barely move about.

"Why, Red," I asked, "how did this happen? You 're nearly dead."

"Sleepin' out done it, I guess," he answered hoarsely. "Anyhow, the crocus[1] says so, 'n' I s'pose he knows. Can't get well, neither. Be'n all over—Hot Springs, Yellarstone, Yosem'ty, 'n' jus' the other day come up from Mex'co. Cough like a horse jus' the same. But say, Cig, drink out, 'n' we 'll go up to Jake's—'s too public here. I 've got a lot to tell you, 'n' a big job fer you, too; 'll you come? A' right. So long, Slim; I 'll be in agen ter-morrer."

We were soon seated in a back room at Jake's. The boy stretched himself on a bench, and in a moment was asleep.

[1] Doctor.

"Purty kid, ain't he?" Red said, looking proudly at the little fellow.

"An' he 's a perfect bank, too, 'f you train 'im right. You oughter seen 'im over in Sac[1] the other day. He drove some o' them Eastern stiffs nearly wild with the way he throws his feet. Give 'im good weather an' a lot o' women, 'n' he 'll batter his tenner ev'ry day. They get sort o' stuck on 'im somehow, 'n' 'fore they know it they 're shellin' out. Quarters ev'ry time, too. He don't take no nickels—seems to hate 'em. A Los Angeles woman tried 'im once, 'n' what d' you think he did? Told 'er to put it in an orphan 'sylum. Oh, he 's cute, bet cher life. But, Cig,"—and his voice dropped to a lower pitch,—"he 's homesick. Think of it, will you, a hobo kid homesick! Bawls like the devil sometimes. Wants to see his ma—he 's only twelve 'n' a half, see? If 'e was a homely kid, I 'd kick 'im. If there 's en'thing I can't stand, it 's homely bawlin' kids. They make me sick. But you can't kick *him*—he 's too purty; ain't he?" and he glanced at the slumberer.

"You pull out at seven, do you?" he asked, after a pause.

"Well, Cig, I 'm mighty glad it 's you I found at Slim's. I was hopin' I 'd meet some bloke I knew, but I feared I would n't. They 're mos' all dead, I guess. Bummin' does seem to kill us lads, don't it? Ev'ry day I hear o' some stiff croakin' or gettin' ditched. It 's a holy fright. Yer bound fer York, ain't you, Cig? Well, now, see here; I 've got an errand fer you. What d' you think 't is? Give it up, I s'pose? Well, you see

[1] Sacramento.

that kid over there; purty, ain't he?" and he walked over to the bench and looked into the lad's face.

"Pounds his ear [sleeps] like a baby, don't he?" and he passed his hand delicately over the boy's brow.

"Now, Cig," he continued, returning to his seat, "I want—you—to—take—this—kid—back—to—the—Horn. That 's where he lives. What d' you say?"

There was only one thing I could say. A few months more at the outside and Red would be gone, and it was probably the last favor I could do him in payment for the many kindnesses he had shown me in the early days.

"If en'thing happens to 'im, Cig, w'y, it 's got to happen, I s'pose; but he 's so dead stuck on seein' his ma that I guess he 'll be purty foxy. I 'd take 'im myself, but I 'm 'fraid I can't pull through. It 's a tough trip 'tween here 'n' Omaha, 'n' I guess he 'll be safer with you. I hate to let 'im go at all, but the devil of it is I ain't got the nerve to hang on to 'im. You see, I 'm goin' to croak 'fore long—oh, you don't need to snicker; 't 's a fact. A few more months 'n' there 'll be one less hobo lookin' fer set-downs. Yes, Cig, that 's straight. But that ain't the only reason I 'm sendin' the kid home. I oughter sent 'im home 'bout a year ago, 'n' I said I would, too, 'f I found 'im. I lied, did n't I? Ye-es, sir; 'bout twelve months ago I told his mother I 'd fetch 'im back 'f I collared 'im. How 's that fer a ghost-story, eh? Would n't the blokes laugh, though, if they 'd hear it? Denver Red takin' a kid home! Sounds funny, don't it? But that 's jus' what I said I 'd do, 'n' I was n't drunk, nuther. Fill up yer schooner, Cig, 'n' I 'll tell you 'bout it."

He braced himself against the wall, hugged his knees, and told me what follows.

"You know where the Horn is right 'nough, don't you? Well, 'bout a year 'n' a half ago I got ditched there one night in a little town not far from the main line. 'T was rainin' like the devil, 'n' I could n't find an empty anywheres. Then I tried the barns, but ev'ry one of 'em was locked tighter 'n a penitentiary. That made me horstile, 'n' I went into the main street 'n' tackled a bloke fer a quarter. He would n't give me none, but 'e told me 'f I wanted a lodgin' that a woman called College Jane 'u'd take me in. Says he: 'Go up this street till you strike the academy; then cross the field, 'n' purty soon you 'll find a little row o' brown houses, 'n' in No. 3 is where Jane lives. You can't miss the house, 'cause there 's a queer sign hangin' over the front door, with a ball o' yarn 'n' a big needle painted on it. She does mendin'. I guess she 'll take you in. She always does, anyhow.' Course I did n't know whether he was lyin' or not,—you can never trust them hoosiers,—but I went up jus' the same, 'n' purty soon, sure 'nough, I struck the house. I knocked, 'n' in a minnit I heerd some one sayin', 'Is that you, Jamie?' Course that was n't my name, but I thought like lightnin', 'n' made up my mind that 't was my name in the rain, anyhow. So I says, in a kid's voice, 'Yes, it 's Jamie.' The door opened, 'n' there was one o' the peartest little women y' ever see.

"'Oh, I thought you was n't Jamie,' she says. 'Come in—come in. You must be wet.'

"I felt sort o' sheepish, but went in, 'n' she set me down in the dinin'-room. Then I told 'er a story. One o' the best I ever told, I guess—made 'er eyes run, anyhow. An' she fed me with more pie 'n' cake than I ever had in my life. Reminded me o' the time we thought we was drunk on apple-pie in New England. Well, then she told me her story. 'T wa'n't much, but somehow I ain't forgotten it yet. You see, she come from the soil, 'n' her man was a carpenter. After they 'd be'n West 'bout six years he up 'n' died, leavin' her a little house 'n' a kid. She called 'im Jamie. Course she had to live somehow, 'n' purty soon she got a job mendin' fer the 'cademy lads, 'n' she boarded some of 'em. That 's the way she got her monikey[1]—see? Well, things went along purty well, 'n' she was 'spectin' to put the kid in the 'cademy 'fore long. H-e-e-e did n't like books very well—hung around the station mos' the time. Sort o' stuck on the trains, I s'pose. Lots o' kids like that, you know. Well, to wind up the business, one night when he was 'bout 'leven year old he sloped. Some bloke snared 'im, prob'ly, an' ever since she 's be'n waitin' 'n' waitin' fer 'im to come back. An' ev'ry night she fixes up his bed, 'n' 'f anybody knocks she always asks, 'Is that you, Jamie?' Funny, ain't it? Well, somehow the bums got on to 'er, 'n' ever since the kid mooched she 's be'n entertainin' 'em. Gives them his room ev'ry time. An' she always asks 'em 'f they know where he is. She asked me too, 'n' made me promise 'f I found 'im that I 'd send 'im home. Course I never 'spected to see 'im, but I had to say somethin'.

[1] Nickname.

"Well, sir, six months afterward I was sittin' in Sal's place in K. C.,[1] when who should come in but New York Slim. He called me out, 'n' says, 'Red, wanter buy a kid?' As it happened, I did want one, so I asked 'im how much 'e wanted. He took me over to a joint 'n' showed me that kid over there on that bench. 'Give you a sinker [a dollar],' I said. He was satisfied, 'n' I took the kid.

"Well, sir, as luck would have it, 'bout a week later the kid got so stuck on me that he told me his story. I did n't know what to do. He did n't wanter go home, 'n' I did n't want 'im to. Course I did n't tell 'im nothin' 'bout seein' his ma—that 'u'd 'a' spoiled ev'ry-thing. Well, I did n't say nothin' more 'bout it, 'n' we come out here. I 've had 'im now fer 'bout a year, 'n' I 've trained 'im dead fine. W'y, Cig, he 's the best kid on the coast—yes, he is. But, as I 've be'n tellin' you, he 's homesick, 'n' I 've got to get 'im back to the Horn. I 'm 'fraid he won't stay there—he 's seen too much o' the road; but I 'll croak jus' a little bit easier from knowin' that I sent 'im back. I 'd like it 'f he 'd stay, too; 'cause, to 'fess up, Cig, I ain't very proud o' this bummin', 'n' 'f 'e keeps at it 'e 'll be jus' like me 'fore long. So when 'e wakes up I 'm goin' to lecture 'im, 'n' I don't want you to laugh. May help, you know; can't tell."

Two hours later we were in the railroad yards waiting for my train to be made up. There were still about fifteen minutes left, and Red was lecturing the kid.

"See here, kid," I heard him saying; "what 's you learnt since I 've had you—en'thing?"

[1] Kansas City.

BEATING A PASSENGER-TRAIN.

"Bet cher life I has!" the little fellow returned, with an assumed dignity that made even Red smile.

"Well, how much? Rattle it off now, quick!"

The boy began to count on his fingers:

"Batterin', one; sloppin' up, two; three-card trick, three; an'—an'—that song 'n' dance, four—four; an' —an' enhalin' cig'rettes, five—five—" Here he stopped and asked if he should take the next hand.

"Yes, go on; let 's have the hull of it."

"Well, then, I knows that cuss-word you taught me —that long one, you know; that 's six, ain't it? Oh, yes, 'n' I knows that other cuss-word that that parson told us was never forgiven—remember, don't you? Well, that 's seven—seven. I guess that 's about all —jus' an even seven."

"You sure that 's all, kid?"

"Well, darn it, Red, ain't that enough fer a prushun? You don't know much more yerself—no, you don't, 'n' you 's three times old 's I am"; and he began to pout.

"Now, kid, d' you know what I wants you to do?"

"Bet cher life I do! Ain' cher be'n tellin' me fer the las' year? You wants me to be a blowed-in-the-glass stiff. Ain't them the words?"

"No, kid. I 've changed my mind. Yer goin' home now, ain' cher?"

"Jus' fer a little while. I 'm comin' back to you, ain't I?"

"No, you ain't, kid. Yer goin' home fer good. Cigarette 's goin' to take you, 'n' you must n't come back. Listenin'?"

"Say, Red, has you gone bughouse? I never heerd you talk like that in my life."

"See here, kid,"—and there was a firmer tone in his voice,—"we ain't foolin' now—understan'? An' in about five minnits you 'll be gone. Now, I wants you to promise that ye 'll ferget ev'ry darn thing I 've taught you. Listenin'?"

The kid was gazing down the track.

"Listenin'?" Red cried again.

The kid turned and looked at him. "Can't I enhale cig'rettes any more? Has I got to ferget them, too?"

"Well, kid, you *kin* tell yer mother that I says you kin do that—but that 's all. Now, 'll you promise?"

"Gosh, Red, it 'll be hard work!"

"Can't help it—*you got to do it.* You don't wanter be like me. You wanter be somethin' dead fine—'spectable."

"Ain't you somethin' dead fine? I heerd 'Frisco Shorty say onc't you was the fliest bloke in yer line west o' Denver."

"You don't understan', kid"; and he stamped his foot. "I mean like yer mother. Listenin'? Well, 'll you promise?"

The kid nodded his head, but there was a surprise in his eyes which he could not conceal.

The train was at last ready, and we had to be quick.

"Well, Cig, so long; take care o' yerself. Be good to the kid."

Then he turned to the boy. It was the tenderest good-by I have ever seen between a prushun and his jocker. A kiss, a gentle stroke on his shoulder, and he helped him climb into the box-car.

The last we saw of Red, as we stood at the door

while the engine puffed slowly out of the yards, he was standing on a pile of ties waving his hat. Six months afterward I was told in the Bowery that he was dead.

The journey to the Horn was full of incident. For six long days and nights we railroaded and railroaded, sometimes on the trucks and the blind baggage, and again lying flat on top, dodging the cinders as they whizzed about our heads, and the brakeman as he came skipping over the cars to tax us for the ride. It was hard work, and dangerous, too, at times, but the kid never whimpered. Once he wanted to, I thought, when a conductor kicked him off the caboose; but he faked a professional little laugh in place of it. And he also looked rather frightened one night when he nearly lost his grip climbing up the ladder of a cattle-car, but he was afterward so ashamed that it was almost pitiful. He was the "nerviest" child I ever traveled with. Even on the trucks, where old natives sometimes feel squeamish, he disguised his fear. But he was at his best at meal-time. Regularly he would plant himself before me in waiter fashion, and say:

"Well, Cig'rette, what 's it to be? Beefsteak 'n' 'taters 'n' a little pie—'ll that do?"

Or if he thought I was not having enough variety he would suggest a more delicate dish.

"How 'll a piece o' chicken taste, eh?" And the least eagerness on my part sent him off to find it.

It was not, however, an entirely one-sided affair, for I was in his service also. I had to protect him from all the hoboes we met, and sometimes it was not so easy as one might think. He was so handsome and clever that it was a temptation to any tramp to snare him if he could, and several wanted to buy him outright.

"I 'll give you five balls fer 'im," one old fellow told me, and others offered smaller sums. A Southern roadster tried to get him free of cost, and the tales he told him, and the way he told them, would have done honor to a professional story-teller. Luckily for me, the kid was considerably smarter than the average boy on the road, and he had also had much experience.

"They 's got to tell better short stories than them 'fore they get me!" he exclaimed proudly, after several men had tried their influence on him. "I 'm jus' as cute as they is, ain't I? I know what they wants—they think I 'm a purty good moocher, 'n' they 'll make sinkers out o' me. Ain't that it?"

None the less I almost lost him one night, but it was not his fault. We were nearing Salt Lake City at the time, and a big, burly negro was riding in our car. We were both sleepy, and although I realized that it was dangerous to close my eyes with the stranger so near, I could not help it, and before long the kid and I were dozing. The next thing I knew the train was slowing up, and the kid was screaming wildly, and struggling in the arms of the negro as he jumped to the ground. I followed, and had hardly reached the track when I was greeted with these words: "Shut up, or I 'll t'row de kid under de wheels."

The man looked mean enough to do it; but I saw that the kid had grabbed him savagely around the neck, and, feeling sure that he would not dare to risk his own life, I closed with him. It was a fierce tussle, and the trainmen, as they looked down from the cars and flashed their lanterns over the scene, cheered and jeered.

"Sick 'em!" I heard them crying. "Go it, kid—go it!"

Our train had almost passed us, and the conductor was standing on the caboose, taking a last look at the fight. Suddenly he bawled out:

"Look out, lads! The express 's comin'!"

We were standing on the track, and the negro jumped to the ditch. I snatched the kid from the ground and ran for the caboose. As we tumbled on to the steps the "con" laughed.

"Did n't I do that well?" he said.

I looked up the track, and, lo and behold! there was no express to be seen. It was one of the kind deeds which railroad men are continually doing for knights of the road.

As we approached the Horn the kid became rather serious. The first symptom I noticed was early one morning while he was practising his beloved "song 'n' dance." He had been shaking his feet for some time, and at last broke out lustily into a song I had often heard sung by jolly crowds at the hang-out:

> Oh, we are three bums,
> Three jolly old bums,
> We live like royal Turks.
> We have good luck
> In bummin' our chuck.
> To hell with the man that works!

After each effort, if perchance there had been one "big sound" at all like Red's, he chuckled to himself:

"Oh, I 'm a-gettin' it, bet cher life! Gosh! I wish Red was here!" And then he would try again. This went on for about half an hour, and he at last struck a note that pleased him immensely. He was just going to repeat it, and had his little mouth perked accordingly, when something stopped him, and he stared at the floor as if he had lost a dime. He stood there silently, and I wondered what the matter could be. I was on the point of speaking to him, when he walked over to the door and looked out at the telegraph-poles. Pretty soon he returned to the corner where I was reading, and settled down seriously at my side. In a few moments he was again at the door. He had been standing in a musing way for some time, when I saw him reach into his inside coat pocket and bring out the tattered bits of pasteboard with which he did his three-card trick. Unfolding the packet, he threw the paper on the track, and then fingered over each card separately. Four times he pawed them over, going reluctantly from one to the other. Then, and before I could fancy what he was up to, he tossed them lightly into the air, and followed them with his eye as the wind sent them flying against the cars. When he turned around, his hands were shaking and his face was pale. I cruelly pretended not to notice, and asked him carelessly what was the matter. He took another look at the world outside, as if to see where the cards had gone, and then came over to the corner again. Putting his hands in his trousers pockets, and taking a long draw at his cigarette, he said, the smoke pouring out of his nostrils, "I 'm tryin' to reform."

He looked so solemn that I did not dare to laugh, but it was all I could do to keep from it.

"D' you think I 'll make it go?" he asked, after a pause, during which his feet had tried to tempt him from his good resolution, and had almost led him into the forbidden dance. Almost every hour from that time on he asked that same question, and sometimes the childish pathos that he threw into his voice and manner would have unmanned an old stager.

The last day of our journey we had a long talk. He was still trying to reform, but he had come to certain conclusions, and one of them was that he could not go to school any more; or, what was more to the point, that he did not see the need of it.

"Course I don't know ev'rything," he explained, "but I knows a lot. W'y, I kin beat Red figgerin' a'ready, an' I kin read things he can't, too. Lots o' words he don't know 't I does; an' when he 's drunk he can't read at all, but I kin. You oughter seen us in Cheyenne, Cig"; and the reminiscence made him chuckle. "We was both jagged, 'n' the copper served a paper on us, *'n' I had to read it to Red.* Ain't that purty good? Red said 't was, anyhow, 'n' he oughter know, ought n't he? No, I don't think I need much schoolin'. I don't wanter be President of the country: 'f I did, p'r'aps I oughter know some more words; but seein' 's I don't, I can't see the use o' diggin' in readers all the while. I wish Red had given me a letter 'bout that, 'cause ma 'n' I 'll get to fightin' 'bout it, dead sure. You see, she 's stuck on puttin' me tru the 'cademy, 'n' I 'm stuck on keepin' out of it, 'n' 'f we get to scrappin' agen I 'm afraid I won't reform.

She 'll kick 'bout my smokin', too; but I 've got her there, ain't I? Red said I could smoke, did n't 'e—h'm? Tell you what I guess I 'll do, Cig. Jus' after I 've kissed 'er I 'll tell 'er right on the spot jus' what I kin do. Won't that be a good scheme? Then, you see, she can't jaw 'bout my not bein' square, can she? Yes, sir; that 's jus' what I 'll do"; and he rubbed his tattooed hands as if he had made a good bargain.

The next morning, just as the sun was rising over the prairie-line, our train switched off the main road, and we were at last rolling along over the Horn. The kid stood by the door and pointed out the landmarks that he remembered. Ere long he espied the open belfry of the academy.

"See that cup'la, Cig?" he cried. "Dad helped to build that, but 'e croaked doin' it. Some people says that 'e was jagged, 'cause 'e tumbled. Ma says the sun struck 'im."

A few minutes later the train stopped at the watering-tank, and my errand was done. There was no need to jocker the boy any longer. His welfare depended upon his mother and his determination to reform. He kissed me good-by, and then marched manfully up the silent street toward the academy. I watched him till the train pulled out. Thus ended one of the hardest trips of my life in Hoboland.

ONE warm summer evening, about three years after leaving the Horn, I was sitting in a music-hall in the Bowery. I had long since given up my membership in the hobo fraternity, but I liked to stroll about now and then and visit the old resorts; and it was while on such an excursion that I drifted into the variety show. I watched the people as they came and went, hoping to recognize some old acquaintance. I had often had odd experiences and renewal of friendships under similar circumstances, and as I sat there I wondered who it would be that I should meet that night. The thought had hardly recorded itself when some one grabbed my shoulder in policeman style, and said, "Shake!" I looked around, and found one of the burliest rowdies in the room. He turned out to be a pal that I had known on the New York Central, and, as usual, I had to go over my remembrances. He also had yarns to spin, and he brought them so up to date that I learned he was just free of a Virginia jail. Then began a tirade against Southern prisons. As he was finishing it he happened to remember that he had met a friend of mine in the Virginian limbo. "Said 'e knew you well, Cig, but I could n't place 'im. Little feller; somethin' of a kid, I guess; up fer thirty days. One o' the blokes called 'im the Horn kid, 'n' said 'e use' ter be a fly prushun out in the coast country. Old Denver Red trained 'im, he said. Who is he? D' you know 'im? He was a nice little feller. W'y, what 's wrong, Cig? You look spiked [upset]."

I probably did. It was such a disappointment as I had hardly imagined. Poor kid! He probably did so well that his mother tried to put him into the academy, and then he "sloped" once more. I told the tramp the tale I have just finished. He was too obtuse to see the pathetic side of it, but one of his comments is worth repeating:

"You can't do nothin' with them kids, Cig. After they 's turfed it a bit they 're gone. Better let 'em alone."

But I cannot believe that that kind-hearted little fellow is really gone. Whoever meets him now, policeman or philanthropist, pray send him back to the Horn again.

III

ONE NIGHT ON THE "Q"

IF there is any one thing that the hobo prizes more than another it is his privilege to ride on the railroads free of charge. He is as proud of it as the American is of his country, and brags about it from morning to night. Even the blanket-stiff in the far West, who almost never sees the inside of a railroad-car, will wax patriotic when on this subject. And well he may, for no other country in the world provides such means of travel for its vagabonds. From Maine to "'Frisco" the railroads are at the tramp's disposal, if he knows how to use them, and seldom does he take to the turnpike from any necessity.

There are, however, some difficulties and trials even in his railroad life. When he rides a "passenger," for instance, either on top or between the wheels, he encounters numerous dangers and hardships, and it is months before he knows how to meet them heroically. Even on freight trains his task is not so easy as some people think. A man must train for such work, just as a pugilist trains for a fight, and it is only when he is a real artist that he can enjoy it. The main difficulty in riding freight-trains is with the brakeman. No matter where the hobo goes, he runs the risk of meeting this ubiquitous official. If he is on the "bumpers," the brakeman is usually "guying" him from the top of a car; and if he goes "inside," so too does the brakeman. Even at night the "brakey" and his free passenger are continually running up against each other. Sometimes they become fast friends. The tramp will help put on the brakes, and the brakeman will help conceal the tramp. But there are other times when things are different. The brakeman tries to "ditch" the tramp, and the latter tries to "beat" the brakeman. On such occasions something happens. Usually the brakeman "gets left." The hobo is too clever, and beats him at his own game. But now and then even the hobo falls into a trap. Of course he gets out sooner or later, but while in it he is an interesting study. When free again, he usually tells his cronies all about it, and they pity or applaud him, as the case may be. But once in a long while the trap he falls into turns out such a joke that he says nothing about it, out of respect for the profession. He hates to be laughed at just as much as other people, and no matter how good the joke is, he keeps it to himself if it will tell against him.

I happen to know of just such a joke. It has been kept quiet now for a number of years, but I think that it can do no harm to tell it, since I was one of the sufferers.

One night I chanced to be in Galesburg, Illinois, situated on the Chicago, Burlington, and Quincy Railroad. I was with a hobo called "Elmira Fatty," and we were on our way to "Chi," or Chicago, as polite peo-

A RIDE ON A TRUCK.

ple call it. We had just come in from the West, where we had spent some time with the blanket-stiffs, and as far as Galesburg we had had no misfortune or bad luck to report. In fact, from Salt Lake City on everything had gone just as we had planned, and we were hoping that night that nothing might interfere to prevent us from arriving in "Chi" the next morning. We expected to travel on a freight-train that was due in Galesburg about nine o'clock. It was a mean night for traveling, for the rain came down in torrents and the wind blew most exasperatingly. Nevertheless, we wanted to push on if practicable, and about half-past eight went over to the railroad yards to wait for the freight. It came in on time, and Fatty and I immediately took different sections of it in search of an "empty." He looked over the forward part, and I inspected the cars near the caboose. We met again in a few minutes, and reported that "there was n't an empty in the whole line."

"W'y," said Fatty, "it 's nothin' but a —— ole steer-train! Ev'ry blasted car is full of 'em."

I suggested that we wait for another, but he would not listen to me.

"No, sir. If we break our necks, we 'll ride that train."

"But where are you going to ride?" I queried.

"On top, o' course."

I knew that it was useless to argue with him, and followed him up the ladder. We sat down on the top of a car, with the rain simply pouring down upon us. Pretty soon the whistle tooted and the train started. As we pulled out of the yards the brakeman came over the train, and espied me instantly.

"Hello, Shorty!" he said, in a jovial way. "Where you goin'?"

"Oh, just up the road a bit. No objections, have you?"

"No, I guess I ain't got no objections. But say, you lads are big fools."

"Here, here!" said Fatty, angrily. "Who you callin' fools?"

"I 'm callin' you fools, 'n' y' are, too."

"See here," continued Fatty; "if you call me a fool agen I 'll put yer face in—I will, by gosh!" and he stood up to make good his threat.

"Don't get 'uffy; don't get 'uffy," said the brakey, soothingly. "Lemme tell you somethin'. See them hay-boxes over there on the corner o' the car?"

"Hay-boxes!" exclaimed Fatty, and he looked at me in surprise.

"Come over 'n' look at 'em."

We followed him to the end of the car, and there, true enough, after he had lifted the lid, was a most comfortable hay-box, nearly full of nice soft hay.

Fatty was almost wild with delight, and patting me on the back, said:

"W'y, Cig, this is a perfect palace-car, ain't it? Gosh!"

The brakeman held his lantern while I got into the box. The opening was not very large, hardly more than a foot wide—plenty large enough for me, it is true, but I was much smaller than Fatty. When he tried to get in there was some trouble. His head and shoulders went through all right, but then he stopped, for his paunch was the broadest part of him, and he complained that "it pinched ter'bly." Exactly what to do was a poser, but finally he nerved himself for another squeeze. He twisted, slipped, and grunted, and at last had to beg me to hold his head and steer him, so helpless had his exertions made him. I guided him as best I could, and pretty soon he came "ka-plunk," as he called it, on the hay. The brakey closed the lid and left.

Fatty had hardly settled himself before he began to wonder how he would get out in the morning.

"By gosh!" he said, "p'r'aps I 'll jus' have to stay here, 'n' they 'll carry me right over to the stock-yards. Would n't I be a great steer, eh?"

But I was too tired to speculate, and in a few minutes was asleep. What Fatty did for the next fifty miles I can't say, but in about two hours he cruelly awakened me and asked for a match.

"Why, you 're not going to smoke here?" I said.

"Cert," he crisply replied. "Why not?"

"You 'll set the place afire, with all this loose hay about."

"Set yer gran'mother afire! Gimme a lucifer."

I told him I had none, and then he wanted me to get out and ask the brakey for one. I did not want to do it, but I felt sure that he would trouble me all night unless I did, so I consented to go. But, lo and behold! when I tried to lift the lid it would not lift.

"Fatty," I said, "we 're ditched."

"Ditched yer gran'mother! What 's the matter?"

"This lid won't move."

"Lemme get at it."

Fatty weighed two hundred and fifty pounds,—"punds," he called them,—and he put every one against that lid. It squeaked a little, but still would not lift.

"Fatty," I repeated, "we 're ditched."

But he was determined not to give in, and lay on his back to kick the lid. He reasoned that that ought to mean fifty pounds more, and if three hundred "punds' could n't budge the thing, then something was going to happen. He kicked and kicked. The lid squeaked a good deal, but was as stubborn as ever. Then you should have heard Fatty scold. He scolded everybody, from the president of the road down to the humblest switchman, and then, as if he had not done enough, said:

"By gosh, Cig, we 'll prosecute 'em! This is simply scandalous! Tramps can't ride this way, and they ought to know it. Yes, sir, we 'll prosecute 'em."

Then he began to swear, and never in my life have I heard such maledictions hurled at poor erring railroad officials. Soon even cursing tired him, and he tumbled back on the hay exhausted. After he had rested a bit, a new phase of the situation presented itself to him, and he felt around in the box to see how much hay there was between us and the steers.

"There ain't much, Cig," he whined; "—— little; an here we are locked in! By the hoky-poky, I 'd like to git hold o' that brakey's throat! I 'd squeeze it, take my tip for that. An', by gosh, if them steers kill us, he 'll croak for it, an' don' cher forget it!"

"Steers!" I exclaimed. "What do you mean, Fatty?"

"W'y, don' cher know them steers is right under us?"

"Well, what of that?"

"W'y, they 've got horns—big ones, too."

"Well, what of that, Fatty?"

"W'y, you fool, we ain't got any."

"But, Fatty, what does that matter?"

"Matter! Matter! Ain' cher got no sense? Don' cher know nothin'? Ain' cher never heard o' steers hookin' a bloke before? You must be a tenderfoot."

Then I grasped the situation. We were at the mercy of those Texas steers! Soon I heard Fatty saying, in a most pitiful voice:

"Cig, I guess we 'd better say our little prayers right now, 'cause if we get to sleep we 'll forget all about it. So you begin, 'n' while yer chewin' the rag I 'll watch the hay."

He wanted me to pray, and actually thought that that was the only thing that would save us. He always was a religious fellow in great emergencies, and his scheme did not much surprise me; but as I knew of no prayer fitted for such an occasion, I told him so, and added that even if I did know one I should prefer to leave it unsaid, considering the circumstances.

"We had no business letting the brakey lock us in here, and you know it, too. So we 'll have to get out the best way we can."

This bravery was a little faked, but I thought it best to keep as cool as possible, for Fatty was continually fuming and scolding. And every few minutes he would feel around in the hay, and then say, most forlornly:

"Cig, them pokers is gettin' nearer. Prepare to die."

Once I thought he was joking, and told him to stop if he thought he was scaring me.

"I ain't tryin' to scare you," he whined; "I 'm simply tellin' you the truth."

This was certainly alarming, and I almost confessed my fear. But I managed to control myself, and persevered in my artificial boldness.

"Well, Fatty, let 's die game, anyhow. If the horns come up here we can kick at them, and perhaps the steers will be frightened. Can't tell, you know."

"No, that won't work," he replied hopelessly, and he measured the hay once more. This time his hand struck the thin and widely separated slats, the only barriers between us and the steers. We both knew that if the horns ever came through them, we would be done for.

"We 're gone, Cig," Fatty continued; "no doubt of it. But, jus' the samey, I 'm goin' to pound my ear, anyhow. I 'd rather die asleep than awake. So, so long, Cig; if you croak first, I 'll pray for you."

Then, much to my surprise and indignation, he curled into a big ball and "pounded his ear." I remained awake for a while longer, listening to the steers chewing away at the hay. But, in spite of the nearing danger, I became sleepy, too, and was soon lying beside Fatty. In the morning, about half-past five, we awoke simultaneously. I felt around in the box, and the hay seemed almost gone.

"I wish that I 'd died in the night," said Fatty, angrily. "Now I 've got to go when I 'm awake."

The train began to slow up—perhaps we were to be

saved, after all. It came to a full stop, and we could hear footsteps. Some one was walking along the path near the track.

"Shall I holler?" asked Fatty.

"Perhaps it 's a policeman," I returned, "and that means thirty days in the Bridewell. Would n't you rather die?"

"But p'r'aps 't ain't!" And he called through one of the cracks, "Hobo! Hobo!"

Luckily it was a hobo.

"Come up here," cried Fatty, "'n' unjail us, for heavin's sake. We 're locked in the hay-boxes; climb on top 'n' loose the cover."

We heard him quickly obeying the call. He climbed up the ladder, loosened the latch, and seemed to wonder at our eagerness to leave such a nest of comfort. Fatty was helped out immediately, although we were still six miles from "Chi"; but I made him wait while I looked to see just what danger we had escaped. There is so much compensating consolation in a view of perils safely passed. There was still a fair amount of hay in the box. I rooted down to the slats for a last look at our tormentors, and there, right before me, stood those awful beasts, wild and fresh from the fields of the Lone Star State. There were nearly twenty of them, I should say, but not a single one had a horn!

Fatty sneaked off to the watering-tank, and I waved adieu to him from the top of the car. His face wore the grimmest of grins, and his last words were, "If you ever tell this joke at the hang-out, Cig—" And I never have.

IV

A PULQUE DREAM

THE freight had just pulled out of Querétaro, and Barcas and I were lying on the floor of the car near one of the side doors, commenting on the landscape. We were on our way to the city of Mexico, and it was my first visit. Barcas had been there before, three times, he said, and as the train drew nearer the town he fell to telling me of what I should see and how I should act. I was still quite a tenderfoot in Hoboland, and needed Barcas's instruction.

He had just finished a very comprehensive explanation of the Spanish language and its uncalled-for differences, as he thought, from his mother-tongue, and was beginning to describe certain hang-outs that he was sure I would like, when the train stopped again for a moment at a little station. Some half-breed Indians were standing on the platform, sharing the contents of a green bottle. It was being passed around for another "draw" when Barcas happened to notice it.

"See that, Cig?" he said, tapping me quickly on the shoulder. "That 's pulky [pulque]. I mus' tell you 'bout that, too."

The train started just then, and he waited until it

was well under way. It was rolling along at a lively pace, and the brakes were rattling as they only can over a Mexican railroad. Barcas had to use the very top of his voice, but he chattered on, just the same.

"Yes, Cig, that 's the most important thing this side the line. Course the langwich 's important, too, 'n' y'u got to learn it, but y'u mus' understan' pulky first. If I 'd understood it when I was down here in '78, I 'd never got into trouble at all. Shorty 'n' Slim was with me, 'n' a lot o' other blokes that I don't rek'lect. But we was sixteen altogether. I 'd never been here before, could n't even say *adios*, so I thought I 'd jus' look roun' a bit. An' for nigh on to a month we had a rip-snortin' time—drunk ev'ry day, 'n' so much to chew that I actually had to let my belt out a couple o' notches. An' we learned the langwich, too; by gosh! I could say ev'rythin' I wanted to. Course I did n't wanter say very much, I was so jagged, but I said enough, anyhow—see?

"Well, this went on for pretty nigh a month, as I said, 'n' we was sloppin' up ev'ry day—but not on whisky. We went on the principle, do in Rome as the Dagoes does; so we drunk what them Indians was drinkin', pulky—mighty fine drink, too. Ain't had such dreams in a tenner as I had then. It jus' makes you feel 'appy all over, 'n' I use' to dream the whole twenty-four hours. Once I thought I was the pres'-dent o' the New York Central—hope to die 'f I did n't. An' my pal he woke me up one night 'bout twelve o'clock 'n' told me that he was the Emp'rer o' the North Pole. An' the rest of 'em was jus' about as bad. We all thought we was kings 'n' queens 'n' royal flushes. Even tried to play poker with oursel's, 'n' I was the jack-pot for a while.

"Well, one afternoon we was specially stuck on oursel's, 'n' went paradin' roun' the hang-out as if we was the high-monkey-monks of ev'rythin'. An' pretty soon a bloke called Curly soogested that we go over 'n' steal some more pulky at a Mexy's shanty clos't by. We was jus' drunk 'nough to do it, 'n' piled over there 'n' drunk ev'ry drop we could find. An' when we was through there was n't en'thin' too good for us. We all thought we was royal families, an' a bloke called Red thought he was the chief of all. He was a big fella, 'n' that prob'ly swelled his head—see? Well, Red swaggered about for a while, 'n' then all of a sudden he swung his arms up Indian fashion, 'n says, 'Blokes, let 's take the town.' He meant the' city o' Mexico, the place we 're goin' to see. Well, somehow or other it jus' struck us as a grand idee, 'n' we whooped 'n' hollered 'n' swore we 'd foller 'im. Pretty soon we started. I was so jagged I could hardly keep on me pins, but that did n't matter; I was goin' to help take the city or break my neck.

"It took us nearly four hours to reach the town, though it was only a mile away. We 'd go a few steps, y'u know, 'n' then sprawl all over oursel's. I have to laugh now when I think of it. An' once we locked arms, thinkin' we could go it more steady-like. 'Fore we 'd taken ten steps we tumbled ka-plunk, jus' like dominoes when y'u set 'em up in a row 'n' then knock the firs' one down. Well, that 's the way we went, 'n' y'u should 'a' seen us when we struck the town. We looked 's if we 'd drilled two thousand miles, 'n' was blowin' 'n' a-puffin' like an injin in a snow-bank. So o' course we had to rest a bit, 'n' while we was a-doin' it Red gave us instructions.

"'Now, blokes,' says he, 'you want to do yer best. 'Member yer all 'Mericans, 'n' that yer fightin' Mexies. If we lick 'em it 'll go up in history, dead sure. An' I 'll bet a sinker it 'll beat that Bally Klavvy bizness if we do it well. So put in yer best licks, 'n' keep yer eyes on me.' Then he told us who was of'sers 'n' who was n't. I was nothin' but a sojer, a private, but he made my pal, the Emp'rer o' the North Pole, he made him firs' leftenant, so I did n't mind much s' long 's he was somethin'.

"Well, 'bout half-pas' seven in the evenin' we was ready 'n' still pretty jagged, too. But Red said we oughter begin, so we started single file for the insides o' the town. The only weapons we had was a few ole razors 'n' our fists, but we was so bughouse we cal'lated they oughter do the biz. Red said the Mexies was cowards, anyhow, 'n' that we could do 'em easy enough; but he told a big whoppin' lie, 'n' we foun' it out, too, 'fore we 'd been scrappin' twenty minnits. The firs' street we struck where there was many people we begun fightin', 'n' for a few minnits we did well. We knocked down ev'rybody we saw, 'n' was so stuck on oursel's that Red said, 'Now, let 's go to the prison 'n' free the priz'ners.' That fired us,—a big scheme,—'n' we piped off for the jail. But we had n't gone more 'n two blocks when we was all sewed up. Seemed 's if ev'ry jay in the town was against us, 'n' I could n't see en'thin' but heads 'n' heads. Looked 's if the whole world was there—see? Red would n't give in, though, 'n' knocked a policeman into a cocked hat. That started the rest of us. We slashed right 'n' left with our razors, 'n' I put my fist into more Mexies' faces than y'u can figger up. It reminded me o' the time I got into that scrap with the bulls [policemen] in Chi [Chicago]. An' all the while Red was gettin' fiercer.

"'Come on, blokes,' I heard him hollerin'; 'we 'll make history 'fore we 're done. Come on; knock 'em down, 'n' keep yer eyes on me.' Then he waded into that crowd for all he was worth, 'n' he did it well, too. But they was too many for us; as soon as one would tumble down another would step into his shoes, 'n' o' course that beat us.

"Well, in a few minnits there was only five of us left, 'n' Red saw 't wa'n't no use to keep on, so he bellered out, 'Make a break, anyhow, 'n' perhaps we 'll give 'em the slip.' You should 'a' seen 'im then! He started right plump for the crowd, wavin' his knife 'n' swearin' like the devil. How he ever got through I can't tell, but he did, 'n' they ain't caught 'im yet. The rest of us was so played out that we had to s'render uncondish'nully on the spot. We thought, o' course, that they 'd treat us like priz'ners o' war, else we 'd kept on scrappin' till we croaked. But them hoosiers could n't see the thing in that way, 'n' actually wanted to lynch us. But some cool-headed bloke got 'em out o' doin' it, 'n' made 'em take us to the jail, where we stayed jus' one year. You see, the judge gave us ten months apiece, 'n' we had to wait two months for trial.

"That 's the way we captured the city o' Mexico, 'n' lemme tell y'u, Cig, if you 'n' pulky fall in love down here, don't you try any funny work, 'cause it 's jus' like a woman, pulky is. It tempts you 'n' then leaves you in the soup."

He had no time for further comment, for the engineer was already blowing his whistle, and the lights in the yards could be seen. But Barcas did not postpone action long. At the first joint we visited he illustrated the effects of pulque in a manner even more vivid than his story. The next morning I had to make a heavy draft on my small exchequer to free him from limbo.

V

A HOBO PRECEDENT

THE trouble began in this way: Ohio Slim had made up his mind to reform and go home. He was lying in jail in western Pennsylvania at the time, in company with Chicago Bud and several other cronies. Bud was his chum, and Slim told him of his decision. This was his first mistake. When a tramp wants to reform he should say nothing about it to anybody, but scamper from the road as fast as his legs will carry him. Slim knew this perfectly well, but he was so tickled to find that he had nerve enough to make the resolution that he was obliged to tell his pal. Bud did not exactly see the point of it all, but he patted him on the back just the same and wished him good luck. Then Slim made friends with the Galway (the Catholic priest) who visited the jail on Sundays, and asked him to write a letter to his parents, explaining his yearning for home and stating that he needed five dollars to get there respectably. The good man did all this, and in due time the money came. Slim cautiously asked the Galway to keep it for him until he was free.

The day of release arrived at last, and the men

marched out of their cells pale but hopeful. Slim, of course, looked up the Galway immediately. He got his money, and then returned to the park where the men were waiting to bid him good-by. Just before separating from them, he called Bud aside and had a few last words with him.

"I 'd like to give you more, Bud," he said, as he handed him a fifty-cent piece, "but I 've only got enough for my ticket and a dinner on the way—understan', don't cher?"

Bud did not want to take the money, but Slim pressed it upon him, and then they parted, Slim starting for the railway-station, and Bud, with a few pals, for a saloon. They never expected to meet again.

But the best-laid plans of mice and men go wrong just as easily in Hoboland as anywhere else. Poor Slim simply could not get to the station. He stopped at every saloon on the way, and by the time the train was ready to leave, his money was half gone and he was don't-care drunk. I got a glimpse of him in the afternoon as he stood, or rather staggered, in front of a billiard-hall. He was singing some verses of the song "Gwine Home." His voice was all in his nose, and he wheezed out the words like a tired-out barrel-organ. But he was clever enough not to be too uproarious, and later in the afternoon laid himself away in a brick-yard. The next morning he was sober.

Meanwhile Bud and a pal, called "Rochester Curly," had also got drunk. They invested the fifty cents in whisky well called "rot-gut," and it unhinged their brains. At night they were so bad that when a little policeman tried to arrest them they both took it as an insult, and drew their razors. The officer called for assistance, and after a severe tussle, in which Bud had his head badly bruised, they were landed at the police station. The next morning the magistrate gave them ninety days apiece.

How Bud ever learned of Slim's conduct remains a mystery to this day. The Galway did not tell him, I did not, the other men had left town, and neither he nor Curly saw Slim in the streets, but he got wind of it just the same. Possibly a city tramp told him. "If I ever meet that fella again," he said to some friends who visited him in the jail the following day, "I 'll break his head into sixty-seven pieces. W'y, I would n't have treated a dog that way. I don't care if he did want to reform; he had no right to change his mind without divvyin' that boodle. Fifty cents! H'm! He wanted all the good booze himself, that 's what was botherin' him. But he 'll suffer fer it, take my tip fer that. He knew well enough that Curly an' me would drink rot-gut if we could n't get anythin' else, 'n' he was jus' mean enough to let us do it. Oh, I 'll teach him such a lesson when I find him that that thing won't happen again in this country. If he 'd been square, Curly 'n' me would n't be where we is now."

Everybody knew that Bud was a man of his word, but fancied, none the less, that his wrath was more the result of his bruises than of any deep-seated hatred of his old comrade. Slim had in the meantime looked up the Galway again and confessed his behavior. He was so sincerely penitent that the good man bought him a ticket out of his own pocket, and sent him home.

He stayed there for just three months. Some days he did very well, hardly swore, and then, without the slightest notice, he would break through all restraints and go on a terrible tear. He had been too long on the road; he could not conquer the wild habits that he had formed; they had become an everlasting part of him; and, one day, when his people thought he was doing better than ever, he stole away and wandered back to his old haunts. They never saw him again.

This, I believe, is a straightforward account of the quarrel, and both Bud's friends and Slim's tell the same story. It is what happened after this that divides them into parties. I did not see the fight myself, but I have heard it described so often that I believe I can do it justice.

It took place one cold autumn night, nearly two years after the quarrel, in a barn not far from Newark, New Jersey. Some twenty hoboes had gathered there for the night, and Bud was among them. His friends say that he was in a most peaceable mood and with no thought of Slim in his mind, but they do admit that he had been looking for him ever since the separation. It was almost time to blow out the candle, and several of the men had already selected their nooks in the hay. Suddenly the door squeaked on its rusty hinges, and three newcomers walked in. The tallest one was Slim. He recognized Bud immediately, walked up to him as to an old pal, and said, "Well, Bud, old socks, how are you? S'pose you did n't expect to see me again? I could n't make it go, Bud; liquor would n't leave me alone. But shake, anyhow," and he held out his hand.

It was certainly a friendly greeting, but Bud returned it with a blow in the face which knocked Slim off his feet. He was so stunned that all he could do was to lie there and exclaim against the surprise Bud had been keeping for him. "W'y, Bud, have you gone bughouse? Don't cher know that I 'm Slim? What cher knockin' me about that way for?"

"Get up out o' that, you long-legged devil, you!" cried Bud, in a sudden rage. "Mean to tell me that you 's forgotten how you did me 'n' Curly with yer rotten fifty cents? Well, you 'll 'member it 'fore you get out o' here. Stand up till I put cher face in fer you!"

Slim was not a coward, and got up and squared for the row. Then Bud decided that he preferred to fight with razors, and drew one from under his shirt-bosom. This was serious, and the crowd gathered around and asked for explanations. Both men gave their separate accounts of the trouble. All agreed that Slim had been greedy, even he himself, and he offered to beg Bud's pardon; but the majority claimed that the offense could not be settled that way, and the fight must consequently go on. Nevertheless, several tried to stop it, and argued earnestly with both men. Slim was willing enough not to quarrel further, but Bud would hear of nothing but satisfaction.

"I said I 'd do that fella," he cried to those trying to pacify him, "and I will. Jus' let me alone; if you don't, you 'll get the worst of it."

It was no use to argue with him while in such a mood, and he threw off his coat. Slim did likewise, and a friend lent him a razor. A Canadian was chosen for referee.

"Is this thing for a finish?" he asked, as he examined their razors.

"'T is 'f I can make it so," said Bud, doggedly.

"And you, Slim?" queried the Canadian, further.

"Well," Slim replied, in his slow and measured way, "I guess I 'll do my share; but before the show begins I jus' want to ask you a question, Bud. Ain't got any objections, have you?"

"No; but be spry about it," snarled Bud.

"Well, now, Bud, d' you 'member the time when I took thirty days fer you down in Alabama so that you could go off 'n' cure yer diseases? 'Member how we worked it, don't cher—how I walked in to see you to let you walk out in my togs? Guess y' ain't forgotten that, have you?"

"What 's that got to do with this circus?" Bud sneeringly returned.

Slim looked at him steadily, and his friends say that Bud winced; but that was all it amounted to, for in a minute the referee was calling them to action.

"Get ready," he commanded, handing them their razors.

They pushed the blades back against the handles and held them tightly with their fingers, leaving the edges bare.

"Y' all right?" asked the Canadian.

"I am," Bud answered.

"Here, too," drawled Slim.

"Then drive away," the referee shouted, stepping back at the same time out of harm's reach; and the crowd followed his example.

Both men were trained "cutters," and it is said that

there has not been another such exhibition of skill of this sort in Hoboland in the last ten years. There were three rounds. The first was merely preliminary. Each studied the tactics of the other and noted his weak points. It is reported that Slim was not in the best of form, and that even the referee, on seeing him parry, advised him to demand a fight with fists; but it was too late. He had warmed to the work, and, handicapped or not, he intended to see it through. Slash, slash, slash, went the razors, but all that one heard was the tiptoeing backward and forward of the fighters, as they charged or defended. A half-minute rest, and the third round began. Both Bud and Slim were badly cut, and their faces showed it, but Slim's pals claim that Bud was getting the worst of it. They say that he was misjudging his reach more and more, and that a wound over his right eye damaged his sight. This may be true; at any rate, one of Bud's cronies, who was holding the candle, suddenly dropped it. Whether Bud sprang quickly for Slim's neck or was lively enough to make a pass at him while he was unguarded, I cannot say, but when the candle was lighted again Slim lay on the floor, mortally wounded. He died that same night in a Newark hospital.

Bud carries to-day a useless right arm and a blind eye. He is the proprietor of an outcasts' saloon in St. Louis, and sometimes when in his cups he brags of the deed done in the barn. But no one has ever heard him tell that incident of the story which, if not accident as well, made a dark deed forever darker.

PART IV

THE TRAMP'S JARGON

PART IV—THE TRAMP'S JARGON

❦

ALMOST the first thing that one remarks on getting acquainted with tramps is their peculiar language. In every country where they live they have dialects of their own choosing and making, and the stranger who goes among them must learn to speak these before he can associate with them on terms of intimacy. Indeed, the "tenderfoot" in tramp life, the beginner, is recognized by his ignorance of the "lingo." The way he carries himself, shakes hands, and begs are also signs by which the "professional" determines the newcomer's standing in the brotherhood; but they are not so unmistakable as his use of the tramp dialect, and it is seldom necessary to talk with him for more than a few minutes to discover how long he has been on the road.

On starting out on my first trip among the hoboes, I thought that I had provided myself with a sufficient number of words and phrases to converse with them more or less as one of their own kind; but I soon discovered how little I knew of their language. My stock of slang consisted of expressions taken from dictionaries and acquired in association with gamins of the street, and I was naïve enough to think that it would suffice for companionship with the regular tramps. It is true that the hoboes make use of a great deal of slang that is popular in the streets and not unknown to "respectable" people, but for social intercourse they rely mainly on their own jargon. In Germany, where the police collect tramp and criminal slang into dictionaries, in order that they may be able to understand the conversations of the *Chausséegrabentapezirer* and *Gauner*, it is less difficult for one to pick up the local tramp lingo; but in the United States there is no dictionary sufficiently up to date to give the beginner much assistance. Martin Luther was one of the first in Germany to take an interest in collecting the vagabond's "cant" phrases. He published in Latin a small volume, called "The Book of Vagabonds," which includes all the tramp slang he could pick up; and ever since the publication of this interesting little work, which is now very rare, German philologists and policemen have printed, from time to time, supplementary dictionaries and glossaries.

In all Continental countries the Hebrew and Gipsy languages have been levied upon by the tramps for contributions to their dialects, and even in England the tramp jargon contains a number of words which have been imported from Germany, Bohemia, Russia, and France. In this country, on the other hand, the tramps have relied largely on their own ingenuity for cant phrases, and they often claim that expressions thus invented are much more forcible and succinct than any that they might have borrowed from foreign languages. They think that a good word is as much the result of inspiration as is a successful begging trick; and they believe, furthermore, that America is entitled to a cant language of its own.

It is easy to see how this dialect originated. It came into existence primarily as a means of talking in public without being understood by others than those intimately connected with the life. It is also true that some of the words have sprung from those necessities of expression which ignorance and lack of education could not supply. In the United States, as a general rule, thanks to reformatories and prison libraries the majority of tramps are fairly well read, and can speak English with considerable correctness; but it often happens that they have thoughts and feelings which their faulty vocabularies cannot make clear, and they are obliged to invent their own words and phrases.

Take the word "bughouse," for example. As it is now used it means actually crazy, and when first used it signified a state of mind bordering on insanity; but it was not invented for purposes of secrecy. Old Boston Mary was the originator of it. Sitting in her little shanty one day, and talking with some tramps seated about her, she exclaimed suddenly: "Blokes, I 'm bughouse." Asked what she meant, she said: "I 'm losin' me brain." It hit off exactly her poor, failing condition, and the word went like a flash all over America. To-day it is the most popular word in the lingo for the ordinary word "insane." "Crippled under the hat" is also heard, but "bughouse" supplants this expression on all occasions when men talk to their fellows, and not to the public. It is most interesting to ferret out the origin of these words.

Many of them are so old that no one remembers exactly how they came into popularity, and even about words more or less modern there are different explanations; but I have succeeded in a number of cases in getting fairly trustworthy stories.

In Chicago I met, one day, the man who, according to report, was the first to use the tramp word for a Catholic priest, "Galway." He was nearly eighty years old when I saw him, but remembered very distinctly how he came by it.

"I was batterin'," he said, "one moon [night] on the Dope [Baltimore and Ohio Railroad], an' a stiff 'e says: 'Blokey, squeal at that house over there—it 's a priest; he 'll scoff ye.' I goes over 'n' toots the ringer [bell]. The baldy [old man] 'e comes himself, 'n' asted what I wanted. 'I 'm starvin', father,' I yapped, 'n' begun to flicker. 'Go 'way, you lazy man,' 'e said; 'I 've fed ten like you since noon.' I was horstile. I dunno how the word come to me, but I yapped it in his phiz: 'Y' ole Galway, you, yer an ole hypocrite'; 'n' then I mooched. Lots o' words comes to me that way when I 'm horstile."

"Punk" is another interesting word. Some say that it comes from the French word *pain*, and immigrated to the United States from Canada, where the hoboes had heard their Canadian *confrères* use it; and this may be the case. Certainly it is as near the French pronunciation as the average vagabond can come. But a more natural explanation is that punk being dry, and bread, particularly that given to tramps, being also often dry, the resemblance of the two impressed itself on some sensitive tramp's mind. The disgust with which beggars frequently speak the word helps to substantiate this theory.

"Flicker," meaning to faint, comes from the flickering of a light, "battering" (begging) from knocking at back doors, and "bull" (policeman) from the plunging, bullying attitude of these officers when dealing with rowdies.

A number of words used by tramps are also in vogue among criminals, who are even more in need of a secret language than are vagabonds. It must be remembered, however, that in America at least, and to some extent in other countries as well, a great many tramps are merely discouraged criminals, and it is not unnatural that they should cling to expressions which they found valuable when they were more intimately connected with criminal life. Even as tramps they are continually making the acquaintance of criminals, and it is one of their main delights to be seen in the company of notorious thieves and burglars; they enjoy such companionship as much as certain "middle-class" people enjoy the society of "aristocrats."

The word "elbow," meaning detective, is one of the slang terms common among both hoboes and criminals. It comes from the detective's habit of elbowing his way through a crowd, and it is the gloomiest word, as I heard a hobo once say, that the outcast ever hears by way of warning. Be he beggar or thief, a shiver invariably runs down his spinal column if a pal whispers or shouts "Elbow" to him while he is "at work" in a public thoroughfare. The word "finger," which is synonymous with "bull," has very nearly, but not quite, the same effect, because the finger is in uniform, whereas the elbow prowls about in citizen's clothes. "Finger" comes from the policeman's supposed love of grabbing offenders. "They like to finger us," a hobo said to me, one night, in a Western town where we were both doing our best to dodge the local police force. "Some people calls 'em the eye o' the law, but that ain't what they is; they 're the finger o' the law."

"Revolver," or "repeater," is both a tramp and a criminal term for the professional offender, the man who is continually being brought up for trial. "Lighthouse" is one of the most picturesque words in the lingo. It means a man who knows every detective of a town by sight, and can "tip them off" to visiting hoboes and criminals. As mariners at sea look for the beacon light which is to guide them safely into harbor, so tramps and criminals look for their "lighthouse." He is one of the most valuable acquaintances in the outcast world, and more advice is taken from him than from any other inhabitant. Such expressions as a "yellow one" for a gold watch, a "white one" for a silver watch, a "leather" for a pocket-book, and a "spark" for a diamond, explain themselves, and I have heard them used by others than those in criminal life; but they are distinctly lingo terms.

"Flagged" is a word which is not so clear, although it has been taken from the railroader's parlance. It is used a great deal by pickpockets, and means that they have allowed a certain person whom they intended to victimize to pass on unmolested. It comes from the flagging of a train, which can be either stopped or made to go on by the waving of a flag. The person "flagged" seldom knows what has taken place, and every day in city streets people are thus favored by gracious "dips," or pickpockets. The dip's companion, the one who bumps up against the victim or otherwise diverts his attention while the dip robs him, is called the "stall."

"Just broken out" and "squared it" are phrases which very few would understand on hearing them spoken by tramps and criminals in public. The man who has "just broken out" is not, as I thought when I first heard the words, one who has escaped from limbo, but rather one who has newly joined the fraternity. The term is used in the sense in which it might be applied to an epidemic. *Wanderlust* (love of tramping, thieving, drunkenness) is the disease with which the newcomer in outcast life is supposed to be afflicted, and on allying himself with the brotherhood, the malady is "officially" recognized as having appeared, or broken out. "Squared it" I took to mean that a bargain or a quarrel had been settled, but I was again mistaken. It signifies that a tramp or criminal has reformed and become respectable. One who leaves the "road" for this reason is said to have "squared it," because he has settled his account with the brotherhood—he has finished with it.

The word "dead" is practically synonymous with "squared it." In using it the tramp does not mean that the pal of whom he is speaking has departed this life; "croaked" is the term for that. "Dead" means that he has left the fraternity and is trying to live respectably. On one of my tramp trips I was entertained at supper by a carpenter in Detroit, and during the meal he confessed that he used to belong to my "push," the tramp brotherhood.

"I 've be'n dead now about ten years," he said. "I learned my trade in the pen, 'n' when I got out I decided to square it. I was petered out."

On leaving his house he cautioned me not to say anything to the "'boes" (hoboes) about his being my "meal-ticket." This is a tramp term for a person who is "good" for a meal, and the carpenter did not care to have this reputation.

When a man denounces to the police a beggar who has accosted him in the street, the latter, in relating the experience at the "hang-out," says that the "bloke beefed" on him (gave him away). In Cincinnati, one day, I met an old tramp acquaintance who had been given away by a pal. He had just come out of prison when I saw him, and looked so poorly, even for a recently discharged convict, that I asked him for an explanation.

"Oh, it was a soaker [a sickening experience], Cig," he said. "Mike, my pal, he beefed [turned state's evidence], 'n' the screws [prison officers] they did me dirt from the start. Got the cooler [dark cell] ev'ry time I did en'thin'. Had fifteen days there twice. It was that killed me. But wait till I catch that gun Mike. It 'll be his last beef if I ever find him."

"Gun" means practically what "bloke," "stiff," and "plug" do—a fellow; but there is a shade of difference. It comes from the verb "to gun," to do "crooked work." Consequently a "gun" is more of a professional thief than is the "bloke." "Mug," on the contrary, is the exact equivalent of "bloke," but the verb "to mug" implies photography. In some cities suspicious characters are arrested on general principles and immediately photographed by the police authorities. Such towns are called "muggin' joints," and the police authorities "muggin' fiends."

Some tramp words are popular for only a few years, and are then supplanted by others which seem to make the thing in question more vivid and "feelable." Not so very long ago, "timber" was the favorite word to describe the clubbing given to tramps in certain "horstile" towns. A hobo has recently written me that this word is gradually giving way to "saps," because the sticks or clubs used in the fracas come from saplings cut down for the purpose.

On account of this continual change it is difficult to keep up with the growth of the language, and in my case it has been particularly so because I am not regularly in the life. If one, however, is always in the way of hearing the latest expressions, and can remember them, there is not much else in the language that is hard. The main rule of the grammar is that the sentence must be as short as possible, and the verb omitted whenever convenient. As a general thing the hoboes say in two words as much as ordinary people do in four, and prefer, not only for purposes of secrecy, but also for general intercourse, if in a hurry, to use their own lingo.

How many words this lingo contains it is impossible to say absolutely, but it is my opinion that during the last twenty years at least three thousand separate and distinct expressions have been in vogue, at one time or another, among the tramps and criminals in the United States. The tramp who wrote to me concerning the word "timber" added the information that for practically everything with which the hobo comes in contact he has a word of his own choosing, and if this is true, then my estimate of the number of words that he has used during the last two decades would seem to be too small; but I am inclined to think that my correspondent gives the hobo's inventive powers more credit than is due them. It is not to be denied that he has a talent for coining words, but he has also a talent for letting other people do work which he is too lazy to do, and my finding is that, although he has a full-fledged lingo, he is continually supplementing it with well-known English words which he is too lazy to supplant with words of his own manufacture. When detectives and policemen surround him, and it is necessary to keep them from understanding what is being discussed, he manages to say a great deal without having recourse to English; but it is a strain on both his temper and lingo to have to do this, and he gladly makes use of our articles, conjunctions, and prepositions again when out of ear-shot of the eavesdropping officers.

So far as I know he has not yet attempted to write anything exclusively in his jargon which can be termed tramp literature; but he knows a number of songs which are made up largely of tramp words, and his stories at hang-outs are almost invariably told in the lingo, or, at any rate, with so little English interspersed that a stranger would fail to appreciate the most interesting points.

Nevertheless, it is one of the regrets of the hobo that his dialect is losing much of its privacy. Ten years ago it was understood by a much smaller number of people than at present, and ten years hence it will be known to far more than it is now. There are hundreds of "stake-men" and "gay-cats" on the road to-day where there were dozens a decade ago, and they are continually going and coming between civilization and Hoboland. The hobo dislikes them, and, when he can, refuses to associate with them; but they pick up his jargon whether he will or no, and on leaving the road temporarily in order to get a "stake," they tell the world at large of what they have seen and heard. In this way the secrets of Hoboland are becoming common property, and the hobo is being deprived of a picturesque isolation which formerly few disturbed.

At present he likens himself to the Indian. "They can never kill us off the way they have the Injuns," a hobo once said to me, "but they 're doin' us dirt in ev'ry other way they can. They 're stealin' our lingo, breakin' up our camps, timberin' us, 'n' generally hemmin' us in, 'n' that 's what they 're doin' to the Injuns. But they can never croak us all, anyhow. We 're too strong for that, thank God!"

No, Hoboland can never be completely depopulated. It will change with the years, as all things change, but it is impossible to wipe it off the map. As long as there are lazy people, discouraged criminals, drunkards, and boys possessed of *Wanderlust*, Hoboland will have its place in our social geography, and a jargon more or less exclusively its own.

GLOSSARY

The following collection of tramp words and phrases is not intended to be at all exhaustive. I have merely explained the slang used in the text, and added certain other words which I thought might interest the reader.

BALDY: an old man.

BALL: a dollar.

BATTER: to beg.

BEEFER: one who "squeals" on, or gives away, a tramp or criminal.

BLANKET-STIFF: a Western tramp; he generally carries a blanket with him on his travels.

BLIND-BAGGAGE: the front end of a baggage-car having no door.

BLOKE: a fellow; synonymous with "plug," "mug," and "stiff."

BLOWED-IN-THE-GLASS STIFF: a trustworthy "pal"; a professional.

'BO: a hobo.

BRAKEY: a brakeman.

BUGHOUSE: crazy.

BULL: a policeman.

BUNDLE: plunder from a robbery.

CHEW: to eat or "feed."

CHEW THE RAG: to talk.

CHI (pronounced "Shi"): Chicago.

CINCIE: Cincinnati.

CON: a conductor.

COOLER: a dark cell.

COP: a policeman. To be "copped" is to get arrested. A "fly-cop" is a detective.

CRIB: a saloon or gambling-place; more or less synonymous with "joint" and "hang-out."

CROAK: to die, or to kill.

CROCUS: a doctor.

CROOK: a professional criminal. "Crooked work" means thieving.

DEAD: reformed. A "dead" criminal is either discouraged or reformed.

DICER: a hat.

DIP: a pickpocket.

DITCH, or BE DITCHED: to get into trouble, or to fail at what one has undertaken. To be "ditched" when riding on trains means to be put off, or to get locked into a car.

DOPE, THE: the Baltimore and Ohio Railroad.

DOSS: *noun*, sleep; *verb*, to sleep.

DOSS-HOUSE: a lodging-house.

DUMP: a lodging-house or restaurant; synonymous with "hang-out."

ELBOW: a detective.

FAWNY MAN: a peddler of bogus jewelry.

FENCE: a receiver of stolen goods.

FINGER: }
FLATTY: } a policeman; synonymous with "bull."

FLAGGED: when a man is said by criminals or tramps to be "flagged," it means that he is permitted to go unmolested.

FLICKER: *noun*, a faint; *verb*, to faint or pretend to faint.

GAG: any begging trick.

GALWAY: a Catholic priest.

GAY-CAT: an amateur tramp who works when his begging courage fails him.

GHOST-STORY: any statement or report that is not true. When told to young boys it means a "faked" story of tramp life.

GRAFT: a line of business; synonymous with "spiel."

GRAFTER: a pickpocket.

GUN: a fellow; more or less synonymous with "bloke," "stiff," "mug," and "plug."

GUY: a fellow.

HAND-OUT: a bundle of food handed out to a beggar at the back door.

HANG-OUT: the hobo's home.

HIT THE ROAD: to go tramping.

HOBO: a tramp. Derivation obscure. Farmer's "Americanisms" gives: "HO-BOY, or HAUT-BOY: a New York night-scavenger."

HOISTER, or HYSTER: a shoplifter.

HOOSIER: a "farmer." Everybody who does not know the world as the hobo knows it is to him a "farmer," "hoosier," or outsider.

HORN, THE: a triangular extension of the Chicago, Burlington and Quincy Railroad, running from Red Oak, Iowa, southwest some twenty miles, and then northwest to Pacific Junction on the main line.

HORSTILE: angry, unfriendly, hostile.

JIGGER: a sore, artificially made, to excite sympathy.

JIGGERED: "done," beaten. When used as an exclamation, as in "I 'll be jiggered," it means "I 'll be damned," or words to that effect.

JOCKER: a tramp who travels with a boy and "jockers" him—trains him as a beggar and protects him from persecution by others.

JOINT: practically, any place where tramps congregate, drink, and feel at home.

KIP-HOUSE: a lodging-house.

KIP TOWN: a good lodging-house town.

LEATHER: a pocket-book. "To reef a leather" means that the pickpocket pulls out the lining of a pocket containing the "leather"; this is frequently the best way of capturing a pocket-book.

LIGHTHOUSE: one who knows every detective by sight, and can "tip him off" to his comrades.

MAIN GUY: the leader.

MARK: a person or house "good" for food, clothes, or money.

MEAL-TICKET: a person "good" for a meal.

MONIKEY: the tramp's nickname, as "New Orleans Blackie," "Mississippi Red," etc.

MOOCH: to beg; also, to "light out," "clear out."

MOOCHER: a beggar. This word is the generic term for tramps in England.

MUG: *noun*, a fellow; *verb*, to photograph.

MUSH-FAKIR: an umbrella-mender. The umbrellas which he collects are frequently not returned.

OFFICE: to "give the office" is to give a signal to a confederate. It is usually done by raising the hat.

ON THE HOG: on the tramp; also, "busted," "dead broke."

P. A.: Pennsylvania.

PAPER: stocks and bonds.

PEN: a penitentiary.

PENNSYLVANIA SALVE: apple-butter.

PENNYWEIGHTERS: jewelry thieves.

PETER: a safe thief. "Knock-out drops" are also "peter."

PHILLIE: Philadelphia.

PLUG: a fellow; synonymous with "bloke" and "stiff."

POKE-OUT: a lunch; synonymous with "hand-out."

POUND THE EAR: to sleep.

PRUSHUN: a tramp boy. An "ex-prushun" is one who has served his apprenticeship as a "kid" and is "looking for revenge," *i. e.*, for a lad that he can "snare" and "jocker," as he himself was "snared" and "jockered."

PUNK AND PLASTER: bread and butter.

PUSH: a gang.

Q.: the Chicago, Burlington and Quincy Railroad, popularly known as the C., B. & Q.

QUEER, THE: counterfeit money.

REPEATER, or REVOLVER: an old-timer; a professional criminal and a "blowed-in-the-glass" tramp.

RINGER: a bell.

RUBE: a "hoosier," or "farmer."

SAPS: a clubbing with weapons made from saplings; synonymous with "timber." (See below.)

SCOFF: *noun*, food, "nourishment"; *verb*, to "feed," to "gorge."

SCRAPPER: a victim of either tramps or criminals who "puts up a fight."

SCREW: a prison turnkey.

SET-DOWN: a square meal.

SETTLED: in prison.

SHACK: a brakeman.

SHATIN' ON ME UPPERS: to be "shatin'" on one's "uppers" is to be "dead broke."

SHOVE: a gang.

SHOVER: a man who passes counterfeit money.

SIDE-DOOR PULLMAN: a box-car.

SINKER: a dollar; synonymous with "ball."

SLOPE: to run away.

SLOPPING-UP: a big drunk.

SNARE: to entice a boy into tramp life.

SNEAKS: flat or house thieves. A bank sneak is a bank thief.

SNIPE: cigar-butts—the favorite tobacco among hoboes.

SONG AND DANCE: a begging story or trick.

SPARK: a diamond.

SPIEL: something to peddle. Hoboes often carry needles, pins, court-plaster, and the like. On meeting one another, they ask: "What's your spiel?" ("What are you hawking?") (See "graft.")

SPIKED: upset, chagrined, disappointed, disgusted.

SQUEALER: one who gives away the gang.

STAKE-MAN: a fellow who holds a position only long enough to get a "stake"—enough money to keep him in "booze" and tobacco while he is on the road. The tramps call him a "gay-cat."

STALL: the pickpocket's companion.

STIFF: a fellow; synonymous with "bloke" and "plug."

SUCKER: a victim of both tramps and criminals.

THROW THE FEET: to beg, "hustle," or do anything that involves much action.

TIMBER: a clubbing at the hands of the toughs of a town unfriendly to tramps. (See "Saps.")

TOMATO-CAN VAG: the outcast of Hoboland; a tramp of the lowest order, who drains the dregs of a beer-barrel into an empty tomato-can and drinks them; he generally lives on the refuse that he finds in scavenger barrels.

TOOT THE RINGER: ring the bell.

TURF: the road, or low life in general.

TURF IT: to be on the road.

YAP: *noun*, a farmer or "hoosier"; *verb*, to say or to tell.

YORK: New York city.

INDEX

INDEX

Patterson Smith Reprint Series in
Criminology, Law Enforcement, and Social Problems

1. Lewis: *The Development of American Prisons and Prison Customs, 1776-1845*
2. Carpenter: *Reformatory Prison Discipline*
3. Brace: *The Dangerous Classes of New York*
4. Dix: *Remarks on Prisons and Prison Discipline in the United States*
5. Bruce *et al: The Workings of the Indeterminate-Sentence Law and the Parole System in Illinois*
6. Wickersham Commission: *Complete Reports, Including the Mooney-Billings Report.* 14 Vols.
7. Livingston: *Complete Works on Criminal Jurisprudence.* 2 Vols.
8. Cleveland Foundation: *Criminal Justice in Cleveland*
9. Illinois Association for Criminal Justice: *The Illinois Crime Survey*
10. Missouri Association for Criminal Justice: *The Missouri Crime Survey*
11. Aschaffenburg: *Crime and Its Repression*
12. Garofalo: *Criminology*
13. Gross: *Criminal Psychology*
14. Lombroso: *Crime, Its Causes and Remedies*
15. Saleilles: *The Individualization of Punishment*
16. Tarde: *Penal Philosophy*
17. McKelvey: *American Prisons*
18. Sanders: *Negro Child Welfare in North Carolina*
19. Pike: *A History of Crime in England.* 2 Vols.
20. Herring: *Welfare Work in Mill Villages*
21. Barnes: *The Evolution of Penology in Pennsylvania*
22. Puckett: *Folk Beliefs of the Southern Negro*
23. Fernald *et al: A Study of Women Delinquents in New York State*
24. Wines: *The State of the Prisons and of Child-Saving Institutions*
25. Raper: *The Tragedy of Lynching*
26. Thomas: *The Unadjusted Girl*
27. Jorns: *The Quakers as Pioneers in Social Work*
28. Owings: *Women Police*
29. Woolston: *Prostitution in the United States*
30. Flexner: *Prostitution in Europe*
31. Kelso: *The History of Public Poor Relief in Massachusetts: 1820-1920*
32. Spivak: *Georgia Nigger*
33. Earle: *Curious Punishments of Bygone Days*
34. Bonger: *Race and Crime*
35. Fishman: *Crucibles of Crime*
36. Brearley: *Homicide in the United States*
37. Graper: *American Police Administration*
38. Hichborn: *"The System"*
39. Steiner & Brown: *The North Carolina Chain Gang*
40. Cherrington: *The Evolution of Prohibition in the United States of America*
41. Colquhoun: *A Treatise on the Commerce and Police of the River Thames*
42. Colquhoun: *A Treatise on the Police of the Metropolis*
43. Abrahamsen: *Crime and the Human Mind*
44. Schneider: *The History of Public Welfare in New York State: 1609-1866*
45. Schneider & Deutsch: *The History of Public Welfare in New York State: 1867-1940*
46. Crapsey: *The Nether Side of New York*
47. Young: *Social Treatment in Probation and Delinquency*
48. Quinn: *Gambling and Gambling Devices*
49. McCord & McCord: *Origins of Crime*
50. Worthington & Topping: *Specialized Courts Dealing with Sex Delinquency*

PATTERSON SMITH REPRINT SERIES IN
CRIMINOLOGY, LAW ENFORCEMENT, AND SOCIAL PROBLEMS

51. Asbury: *Sucker's Progress*
52. Kneeland: *Commercialized Prostitution in New York City*
53. Fosdick: *American Police Systems*
54. Fosdick: *European Police Systems*
55. Shay: *Judge Lynch: His First Hundred Years*
56. Barnes: *The Repression of Crime*
57. Cable: *The Silent South*
58. Kammerer: *The Unmarried Mother*
59. Doshay: *The Boy Sex Offender and His Later Career*
60. Spaulding: *An Experimental Study of Psychopathic Delinquent Women*
61. Brockway: *Fifty Years of Prison Service*
62. Lawes: *Man's Judgment of Death*
63. Healy & Healy: *Pathological Lying, Accusation, and Swindling*
64. Smith: *The State Police*
65. Adams: *Interracial Marriage in Hawaii*
66. Halpern: *A Decade of Probation*
67. Tappan: *Delinquent Girls in Court*
68. Alexander & Healy: *Roots of Crime*
69. Healy & Bronner: *Delinquents and Criminals*
70. Cutler: *Lynch-Law*
71. Gillin: *Taming the Criminal*
72. Osborne: *Within Prison Walls*
73. Ashton: *The History of Gambling in England*
74. Whitlock: *On the Enforcement of Law in Cities*
75. Goldberg: *Child Offenders*
76. Cressey: *The Taxi-Dance Hall*
77. Riis: *The Battle with the Slum*
78. Larson *et al: Lying and Its Detection*
79. Comstock: *Frauds Exposed*
80. Carpenter: *Our Convicts.* 2 Vols. in 1
81. Horn: *Invisible Empire: The Story of the Ku Klux Klan, 1866-1871*
82. Faris *et al: Intelligent Philanthropy*
83. Robinson: *History and Organization of Criminal Statistics in the United States*
84. Reckless: *Vice in Chicago*
85. Healy: *The Individual Delinquent*
86. Bogen: *Jewish Philanthropy*
87. Clinard: *The Black Market: A Study of White Collar Crime*
88. Healy: *Mental Conflicts and Misconduct*
89. Citizens' Police Committee: *Chicago Police Problems*
90. Clay: *The Prison Chaplain*
91. Peirce: *A Half Century with Juvenile Delinquents*
92. Richmond: *Friendly Visiting Among the Poor*
93. Brasol: *Elements of Crime*
94. Strong: *Public Welfare Administration in Canada*
95. Beard: *Juvenile Probation*
96. Steinmetz: *The Gaming Table.* 2 Vols.
97. Crawford: *Report on the Pentitentiaries of the United States*
98. Kuhlman: *A Guide to Material on Crime and Criminal Justice*
99. Culver: *Bibliography of Crime and Criminal Justice: 1927-1931*
100. Culver: *Bibliography of Crime and Criminal Justice: 1932-1937*

Patterson Smith Reprint Series in
Criminology, Law Enforcement, and Social Problems

101. Tompkins: *Administration of Criminal Justice, 1938-1948*
102. Tompkins: *Administration of Criminal Justice, 1949-1956*
103. Cumming: *Bibliography Dealing with Crime and Cognate Subjects*
104. Addams *et al: Philanthropy and Social Progress*
105. Powell: *The American Siberia*
106. Carpenter: *Reformatory Schools*
107. Carpenter: *Juvenile Delinquents*
108. Montague: *Sixty Years in Waifdom*
109. Mannheim: *Juvenile Delinquency in an English Middletown*
110. Semmes: *Crime and Punishment in Early Maryland*
111. National Conference of Charities and Correction: *History of Child Saving in the United States*
112. Barnes: *The Story of Punishment*. 2d ed.
113. Phillipson: *Three Criminal Law Reformers*
114. Drähms: *The Criminal*
115. Terry & Pellens: *The Opium Problem*
116. Ewing: *The Morality of Punishment*
117. Mannheim: *Group Problems in Crime and Punishment*
118. Michael & Adler: *Crime, Law and Social Science*
119. Lee: *A History of Police in England*
120. Schafer: *Compensation and Restitution to Victims of Crime*. 2d ed.
121. Mannheim: *Pioneers in Criminology*. 2d ed.
122. Goebel & Naughton: *Law Enforcement in Colonial New York*
123. Savage: *Police Records and Recollections*
124. Ives: *A History of Penal Methods*
125. Bernard (Ed.): *The Americanization Studies*
    - Thompson: *The Schooling of the Immigrant*
    - Daniels: *America via the Neighborhood*
    - Thomas *et al: Old World Traits Transplanted*
    - Speek: *A Stake in the Land*
    - Davis: *Immigrant Health and the Community*
    - Breckinridge: *New Homes for Old*
    - Park: *The Immigrant Press and Its Control*
    - Gavit: *Americans by Choice*
    - Claghorn: *The Immigrant's Day in Court*
    - Leiserson: *Adjusting Immigrant and Industry*
126. Dai: *Opium Addiction in Chicago*
127. Costello: *Our Police Protectors*
128. Wade: *A Treatise on the Police and Crimes of the Metropolis*
129. Robison: *Can Delinquency Be Measured?*
130. Augustus: *A Report of the Labors of John Augustus*
131. Vollmer: *The Police and Modern Society*
132. Jessel: *A Bibliography of Works in English on Playing Cards and Gaming*. Enlarged
133. Walling: *Recollections of a New York Chief of Police*
134. Lombroso: *Criminal Man*
135. Howard: *Prisons and Lazarettos*. 2 vols.
136. Fitzgerald: *Chronicles of Bow Street Police-Office*. 2 vols. in 1
137. Goring: *The English Convict*
138. Ribton-Turner: *A History of Vagrants and Vagrancy*
139. Smith: *Justice and the Poor*
140. Willard: *Tramping with Tramps*